Mastering C++

A Step by Step Guide for the Beginner and Advanced User, Including 26 Quizzes and 120+ Questions

Table of Contents

Introduction **11**

Chapter 1: Setting up your Environment **12**

  Setting up your Environment **13**

    Windows 14

    Mac OS 16

    Linux 18

Chapter 2: Beginner's Guide **22**

  The Basics of C++ **22**

  C++ Comments **26**

  Quiz 1 .... **30**

  User Interaction and Variables **31**

    Declaring Variables 32

    Using Variables 32

    Shorthand Method of Adding or Subtracting One: 36

    Using (And Misusing) Variables 39

    Case Sensitivity 40

    Naming Variables 41

    Storing Strings 41

  Quiz 2 .... **48**

  If Statements **50**

  Expressions **52**

    The Bool Type 54

    Else statements 55

    Else-if 56

    String Comparisons 57

Boolean NOT 59

Boolean AND 60

Short-Circuiting Checks 60

Boolean OR 61

Combining Expressions 62

Order Of Evaluation 63

Quiz 3 ....**65**

Loops **66**

While Loops 66

For Loops 69

Do-while Loops 71

Loop Control Flow 73

Nested Loops 76

Choosing the Right Loop 78

Quiz 4 ....**81**

Functions.. **82**

Function Syntax 82

Local and Global Variables **84**

Definitions and Declarations..91

Function Naming and Overloading 94

Quiz 5.. **96**

Switch Case and Enums **97**

Using Enums to Create Simple Data Types..................**102**

Quiz 6 .... **106**

Randomizing Your Programs **107**

Random Numbers In C++ 108

Quiz 7 .... **113**

Chapter 3: Intermediate Guide **115**

Arrays..**115**

    Using Arrays With For Loops 118

    Passing Arrays to Functions 120

    Sorting Arrays..124

Quiz 8 ....**133**

Structures..**135**

    Passing Structures 139

Quiz 9 ....**144**

Introduction to Pointers **146**

    Variables Vs. Addresses 148

    Memory Layout 149

    Invalid Pointers 151

Memory and Arrays **152**

Quiz 10..**154**

Getting to Grips with Pointers **156**

    Declaring a Pointer...156

    Using a Pointer 158

    Uninitialized Pointers and NULL...................................163

    Pointers And Functions 164

    References 166

    References vs. Pointers...168

Quiz 11 ....**170**

Dynamic Memory Allocation...........................**172**

    Pointers and Arrays 173

    Multidimensional Arrays..177

    Pointer Arithmetic..178

    Two-Dimensional Arrays..179

    Pointers-to-Pointers 181

    Two-Dimensional Arrays and Pointers-to-Pointers...................183

Quiz 12 ....**186**

Introduction to Data Structures and Linked Lists **188**

    Pointers and Structures 191

    Creating Linked Lists 193

Traversing Linked Lists **197**

    Arrays vs. Linked Lists 198

Quiz 13 .... **203**

Recursion **205**

    How to Think of Recursion.. 205

    Recursion And Data Structures 209

Loops And Recursion **213**

    The Stack 216

    Downsides to Recursion 220

    Debugging Stack Overflows 221

Quiz 14 ....**226**

Binary Trees **228**

    Implementing a Binary Tree 231

    Real-World Uses for Binary Trees............................... 252

Quiz 15 ....**254**

The Standard Template Library **256**

    Vectors 257

    Other Vector Features 260

    Maps 261

    Iterators 262

Quiz 16 ....**269**

Let's Talk Strings **271**

    Reading Strings In 271

    String Length and Individual Elements 274

    Searching and Substrings 275

Passing by Reference 277

Const Propagation 280

Const and the STL 282

Quiz 17 ....**285**

Debugging with Code::Blocks.. **286**

Breaking into the Program 289

Debugging Crashes 291

Breaking into Hung Programs...295

Modifying Variables 299

Chapter 4: Advanced Guide........................... 301

Writing Larger Programs **301**

Breaking Your Program Down 302

The C++ Build Process 302

Handling Multiple Source Files 315

Quiz 18 ....**317**

Introduction to Program Design **319**

Redundant Code 319

Design And Comments 324

Quiz 19 ....**327**

Hiding the Representation of Structured Data...........................**328**

Method Declaration and Call Syntax...331

Quiz 20 ....**335**

The Class...**337**

Hiding the Way Data is Stored 338

Declaring Class Instances..341

Quiz 21 ....**345**

The Life Cycle of a Class **347**

Object Destruction...356

Copying Classes 363

Preventing Copying 373

Quiz 22 .... **375**

Inheritance and Polymorphism **378**

Inheritance 380

More Uses (and Misuses) of Inheritance 386

Object Construction and Destruction........................... 387

Object Destruction and Polymorphism 391

The Slicing Problem 394

Code-Sharing with Subclasses 397

Class-Wide Data 399

Implementing Polymorphism 401

Quiz 23 .... **405**

Namespaces **408**

Quiz 24 .... **414**

File I/O **416**

Reading from Files 416

Writing Files 426

File Position 428

Accepting Command Line Arguments 435

Binary File I/O 439

Storing Classes in Files 446

Quiz 25 .... **456**

Templates in C++ **457**

Template Functions... 458

Duck Typing... 460

Templates and Header Files 468

Analyzing Template Error Messages............................. 469

Quiz 26 .... **476**

Conclusion **478**

Quiz Answers **479**

Introduction

Are you ready to start learning how to program? C++ is one of the most powerful programming languages in the world and will give you a decent grounding in the techniques for modern programming. Many of the C++ concepts are shared with other languages, when you learn one you've got a great head start for another one. And it's fair to say that you'll need to learn more than one—very few programmers work with single languages.

C++ has for a long time, and continues to be, the language of choice for high-performance applications that run fast and are continually being updated with new features. Dating back to 1979, C++ was developed by Bjarne Stroustrup and came about as a result of a Ph.D. thesis. From there, it has grown by leaps and bounds, becoming the strong object-oriented language it is today.

I have split this book into several parts. In the first part, you will be introduced to the language, learn how to get it on your computer and start writing programs with it. You won't be a C++ master but will have a decent understanding of it, along with the groundwork to learn some of the more advanced concepts. From there, we go on to working with large data amounts, file input and efficient data processing. You will learn some shortcuts too. I've also included quizzes, with the answers provided at the end of the book.

By the time you reach the end, you should have no problem reading C++ code and writing programs that are both interesting and useful. So, let's dive in and learn C++.

Chapter 1: Setting up your Environment

If you want to control your computer, you have to be able to speak to it. In order to do that, you need a programming language. All this language is, is a piece of text, much like a book, that has its own definitive structure. That structure is stricter than a standard language and has a much smaller, more defined vocabulary. C++ is one of the most popular programming languages.

What's The Difference Between C and C++?

C programing language was originally developed for the Unix operating system. It's a powerful language but doesn't include any of the more useful modern constructs. C++ is newer and is based on the C language. Added modern features make it far easier to use than C, allowing for more sophisticated programs to be written.

With C++, memory management is easier. There are more features available for object-oriented and generic programming—you'll see what this means later. For now, all you need to know is that C++ gives programmers an easier ride than C does.

Because C++ is a superset of the C language, you don't need to have prior knowledge or experience with C; if you do, then you'll just find C++ that much easier to grasp. And, contrary to what many people will tell you, no, you do not need to know math to become a programmer!

For the most part, computer programming is all about logical reasoning and design, not complex arithmetic, calculus and algebra. Where math and programming overlap is in the area of precise thinking and logical reasoning; the only time you need to have substantial math skills is if you intend to go into advanced 3D graphics engine processing statistical analysis or some other specialized numerical programming that is.

Terminology

Throughout this guide, you will see a lot of new terms. To start off, I'll give you two of the more basic concepts that you really need to know before beginning:

- **Programming** – the act of writing a set of instructions that a computer can read, understand and execute. These instructions are known as "source code" and that is what you will be writing if you follow this guide.
  - – this is the result of your programming—a file that can be executed. This means that your computer can run it. If you have a Windows system, for example, these instructions are known as EXE files. In order to create an executable file, you must have a compiler. This is a program that converts your source code into executable code. If you don't have one of these, all you can do with your source code is look at it.

Next, we will set up our environment so that we can write source code and execute it.

Setting up your Environment

What we will be doing is setting up a compiler and a text editor, the latter of which is where you create the source code in the correct format. You must write your code in plain text format; these files will have nothing more than the text you write. They won't have any information about fonts, text size, etc.

A text editor will also provide some extra features which are helpful, namely auto-indentation and syntax highlighting. With syntax highlighting, you get the benefit of colored coding. That makes it easy for you to tell the different parts of your program apart. With auto-indentation your code becomes easier to read.

For those on Mac or Windows systems, we'll be using something called an IDE— Integrated Development Editor. This is a combination of an editor and compiler.

Let's get set up so we can get down to work.

Windows

For this, we'll use Code::Blocks. This is a free C++ environment that is easy to download and to use:

Your first step is to download Code::Blocks. To do this, go to http://www.codeblocks.org/downloads. Click on the link that reads "Download Binary Release" and then go to the section for Windows.

Next, look through the files until you find one with mingw in the name— something like codeblocks-10.05mingw-setup.exe (the number might be different). Click it and save it onto your Windows desktop.

Now it's time to install it. Double-click on the installer from your desktop and then follow the instructions, hitting "Next" until you come to the Installation screen. Click on the "Select Type of Install" menu and choose the Full Installation option. Last, click on Launch Code::Blocks.

A compiler's auto-detection window will pop up; just click on "OK." If you get a message asking you to associate Code::Blocks as the default C++ file viewer, say "Yes."

Click the File menu and click on New -> Project.

Click on Console Application and click Go.

Click on Next and the Language Selection window will appear. Choose C++ as the language and click on Next. Now you need to decide where you want the console application saved. I recommend creating a separate folder and giving it a meaningful name. Click on Next.

Now you are going to be asked to set the compiler up. All you need to do is click on Finish to accept the default options.

On the left of the window, you should see a file called main.cpp. If you don't, look for the Sources folder and expand it. This file, with an extension of .cpp, can now be modified as you wish. Open it and you should see a simple Hello World application. Click on F9 or go to the Build menu and click on Build and Run. The file is now compiled and will run.

Now, go to the line on the code that reads

return 0;

and edit it so it reads

kreturn 0;

Hit F9 again and see what happens.

Compiler Errors

If you modify your code in any way that the compiler does not understand, you will get an error. To see why you got a particular error, look at the window entitled "Build Log" which shows you all the issues with the code and "Build Messages" which will show you the compiler error.

In our case, it should show you the file name, the number of the line where the compiler error is and a bit of text that tells you what the error is. For us, this is simple; the modification we made to 'kreturn 0;' isn't valid C++. Just change it back to how it was and press F9 again.

Whenever you're writing your programs, always keep an eye on this window—it will help you a lot to figure out what went wrong.

As we go through this guide, there are going to be a lot of code samples. To follow these, you have two choices: modify your existing source code or write a new console application for each sample. I recommend the latter for each new program. That way, you can change the sample code as you want and save it for review at a later time.

What is Code::Blocks?

Code::Blocks is an IDE that makes it incredibly easy for you to write your source code and compile it in one place. It isn't a compiler in itself but, when you download it, you also download a compiler with it. There's one called GCC from MinGW, which is a free Windows compiler. Code::Blocks does all the work to set this up and call it when needed.

Mac OS

OS X already has a Unix-based shell environment built into it, so most of the tools that are available to Linux users will also be accessible by you. However, bear in mind that XCode, which is Apple's proprietary development environment, is required to use any Linux tools.

It isn't a requirement that you use the XCode environment for C++ development, but it is needed for Mac UI development.

XCode

XCode is free with OS X but isn't installed by default. You have two options—find it and install it from your OS X program CD or download the latest version. The first option is best as downloading from the internet will give you a very large file, containing all the documentation.

Even basic compilers like g++ and gcc, usually installed in Linux by default, will not be installed on Mac systems. In order to obtain them you'll need to download the XCode developer tools.

If you haven't already done so, you'll need to register as a developer with Apple. Do this by going to http://developer.apple.com/programs/register/. You have a choice of a paid or free account; sign up for whichever one you want.

Once you've done that, head to http://developer.apple.com/technologies/xcode.html and click on the Login button. Click on the disk image file (it will have an extension of .dmg) and then click on the Xcode.mpkg file.

Accept the licensing agreement and you'll see that the next window lists all the different components that you can install. Go with the defaults and run the installer.

Running XCode

When it's installed, go to Developer -> Applications -> XCode and run it. There is a lot of documentation, so you might want to take some time to read through the tutorial on getting started with XCode, just to get a general idea of how it works.

Your First XCode C++ Program

When you start XCode, the main window will open. Click on the option to "Create a New XCode Project." From the left of the screen, click on Mac OS X -> Application and then click "Command Line Tool."

Change the project type to C++ stdc++ and then click on Choose. Decide where you will save the project and give it a name. Your project will be saved to a newly created directory in the place you choose; this will be named the same as your project. I'm using the name "Hello World" for this but you can use whatever you want—so long as you can identify it later on.

Click the Next button and a new screen will open. If you see that the box beside "Create Local git Repository for This Project" is checked, uncheck it. Git is a system of source control that lets you keep several versions of one project but we are not using it. Once you are done with this screen, click on "Create."

In the next window, you will see options for Source and Products on the right side of the screen. The source code will be listed under the new directory created for your project and the rest of the screen will show information about compiler configuration. We're not doing anything with this yet and can move on.

Click on Source and then click on the file called main.cpp on the left side of the screen. Single-clicking will bring up the source file in the main editor window and this is where you type. If you double-click, you'll get a moveable editor window.

XCode gives you a sample file to play with so what we'll do now is compile it and run it. Click on the toolbar button that says "Run." You will see the output in the main window. That is your very first XCode window.

From now on you can use this project that you just created or create new projects for the code in this guide. Either way, you will need to use the main.cpp file.

Compiler Errors

If your program doesn't compile there could be any number of reasons, but the main one is usually a typographical error. The compiler will show you messages in the source code itself, on the line where the error occurs. Once the error has been fixed, just press the Run button once more.

Linux

The last system is Linux and it's almost certain that a C++ compiler is already installed in it. This will be a compiler called g++ which is part of GCC—The GNU Compiler Collection.

First, check that the compiler is installed by opening a terminal window and typing g++. Press Enter and you should see

g++: no input files

on the screen.

If you instead see

command not found

then g++ needs to be installed. Which version you need depends on your Linux distribution's software for package management. For example, if you're using Ubuntu all you need to type at the command prompt is

aptitude install g++

To determine the steps for your specific distribution, read the documentation we mentioned earlier.

To run g++ is pretty easy, so let's go ahead and create a new program. Create a file that has a .cpp extension with the following text:

#include <iostream>

int main ()

{

   std::cout << "Hello, world" << std::endl;

}

Save it as hello.cpp and remember where you saved it to.

Now, go to the terminal window and switch to the directory where the program was saved.

Next, type the following:

g++ hello.cpp -o hello

Press the Enter key.

When you use the -o option, a name is provided for your output file; if you didn't use it, the default name assigned will be a.out.

Now we can run the program. At the prompt, type in

./hello

The output will appear on your screen as:

Hello, world

Compiler Errors

As with Windows and Mac, if there's an error in the code, a compiler error appears. Let's say that, for example, where it says 'cout' in the code, if you add an 'x' before it, you get errors like this:

gcc_ex2.cc: In function 'int main ()':

gcc_ex2.cc:5: error: 'xcout' is not a member of 'std'

Each of the errors provides a file name, the number of the line where the error is and the error details.

Setting up the Text Editor

Unlike other operating systems, Linux users will need to download an additional text editor. One of the easiest to learn is called nano. It's a simple editor but does have automatic indentation and syntax highlighting.

It might be installed in your system already. At the command prompt, just type

nano

to find out. If it starts automatically, all well and good. If you get a message like

command not found

you will need to install it. A quick Google search will bring up the latest version for your Linux distribution.

Configuration

To use some of the features in nano, you need a nano config file. This is called .nanorsc and lives in your home directory. Check that it is there and edit it as you require. If not, you need to create it and, again, the instructions to do so can be found with a quick Google search. I can't provide you will the instructions as there are so many different Linux distributions, each with different requirements.

Chapter 2: Beginner's Guide

The Basics of C++

Now that we have the development environment set up we can start getting to grips with the actual language. I'm going to introduce you to some concepts that you will see constantly throughout your programming experience: program structure, main function, compiler-provided standard functions, adding comments and a quick look at how to think the way a programmer does.

A Simple Program

The starting point is a program that does nothing. Here it is:

```
int main ()

{

}
```

Now let's see what it's all about.

The very first line, int main (), is informing the compiler that there's a function that we called main and which will return an integer. In most programming languages, C++ included, integer is shortened to "int." Functions are bits of code written by a programmer; sometimes they're very basic language, other times they use other functions. For now, our function isn't doing anything.

The main function is special because it's the only one that every C++ program must have and is where the program begins when it's run. The main function is always preceded by the return value type, in our case, int. When a value is returned by the function, the piece of code that calls it can access the value. Where the main function is concerned, the value is returned to the operating system.

The {} brackets in the code mark the start and end of the function. As there isn't anything in between those brackets, we know that the function doesn't do anything and therefore, when run, will not yield any output.

Let's take a look at a program that is slightly more interesting:

```
#include <iostream>

using namespace std;

int main ()

{

        cout << "Hey there, I'm alive! Oh, and Hello World!\n";

}
```

First, we actually have some code between the brackets this time and that means the program is going to do something.

The first line, #include <iostream>, is what we call an include statement. This tells the compiler that the code should be taken from the header file named "iostream" and put into the program before the executable file is created. The iostream file comes as part of the compiler and is what allows inputs and outputs to be performed. When you use the #include <iostream> statement, everything is taken out of the header and pasted to your program, thereby giving you access to many of the functions that the compiler provides.

Whenever you want to access any basic functions, you will need to include the relevant header file that provides those functions. Right now, most of what we want is in iostream, and you will see the #include statement at the top of virtually all your programs. Usually, you will have more include statements after this one.

The next line of our code, using namespace std;, is what we call boilerplate code and is in pretty much all C++ programs. For now, include it in all your programs underneath the include statements. What this does is make it easy to use shorter versions of some routines in the iostream file. Later, we'll talk more about this, but for now, just make sure you include it.

Note the semicolon at the end of the line. This is a vital part of the C++ syntax and tells the compiler that the statement is ended. Most statements end with the semicolon and omitting it is the most common newbie mistake. If your program won't work, that's the first thing to check.

The next part of the code is the main function and this is where the program begins.

Next, we have a << symbol followed by some text. What is happening here is that the cout (C out) object is being used by C++ to display the text. We specifically wanted the iostream header file in order to be able to access the cout. The << symbols are called insertion operators and indicate what the output should be. So, what cout << results in is a function call that has a function argument of some text. The function call will run whatever code goes with the function.

Usually, a function will take one or more arguments that the code uses. In our case, we have an argument of a text string. Functions will also take variables as their arguments and, in our case, the output is the provided argument. The quotation marks are used to let the computer know that the literal string should be output as it is except for specific sequences.

One of those sequences is the \n sequence and this is treated as one character that means "newline." Much the same as when you press the Enter key, the cursor on the screen is moved to the next line. Note that sometimes, you will see "endl" used instead of \n but it means exactly the same.

Lastly, that semicolon. As a function is being called, the semicolon is required.

The closing bracket ends the function. Compile and run this and see what happens. Type it into the compiler—when you copy and paste, you don't really learn very much.

Now, depending on your compiler and operating system, the program output might appear as a flash on the screen so quick that you don't see what it is. That shouldn't happen if you're using an environment recommended here, but if you use a different environment, just include the following line at the end of the program:

cin.get();

What this does is make the program wait until you've pressed a key before the results window is closed.

Basic C++ Program Structure

Now let's forget the details for a minute and examine what a basic program structure looks like.

[include statements]

using namespace std;

int main()

{

      [your code goes here];

}

Now, what if you were to omit one of these from your code? What would happen?

If you leave out the #include <iostream> or namespace std, your program simply will not compile. When your program doesn't compile it means that the compiler didn't understand something. This is usually incorrect syntax or a missing file. When you're starting to learn to program, these compiler failures aren't always easy to find, mostly because you don't really know what you're looking for. To help you, remember that a failure to compile will result in at last one compiler error. That error will tell you why it failed. An example message might look like this:

error: 'cout' was not declared in this scope

When you see an error message like this, always look to see that the #include <iostream> statement is there to bring the iostream header file in and that you have used using namespace std; at the start of the message.

Compiler error messages might not always be that straightforward though. If you omit semicolons, all kinds of errors will appear, and normally they will be on the line after the one that should have had the semicolon. If you see a lot of errors that you don't understand, always look at the line prior to the error and check that the semicolon is in place, if it is needed.

Don't worry; as time goes on and you gain more experience, you will add your semicolons without even thinking about them and will find compiler error messages much easier to interpret. In fact, getting these errors is the best way to learn!

C++ Comments

One of the most important things that you need to learn to use is a feature called "comments." This is the process of telling yourself what your code is doing and can help others who might read your code later on down the line. As we go through this guide, you will see that I have added many comments, for the sake of clarity .

Comments are ignored by the compiler, so long as they are done properly. Telling the compiler that a piece of text is a comment is simple:

Use // before the comment to tell the compiler that everything after it is a comment

Or use /* and */ to tell the compiler that everything in between is a comment.

Let's make that clearer:

// this is a single-line comment

This will be ignored by the compiler and will not be treated as a part of the code.

/ this is a multi-line comment*

And this line is also part of the same comment

*/

Some compilers will use syntax highlighting to show the comment in different-colored text. This tells you, at a glance, what is or isn't a comment.

When you start learning to program, if you comment certain parts of your code out, you can see what the effect on the output is. To comment out a section of code, simply enclose it in the comment markers you see above. Let's say, for example, that you want to see what will happen if you don't have the cout statement. Instead of omitting the statement altogether, you could just comment it out, like this:

#include <iostream>

using namespace std;

int main ()

```
{

//                cout << "Hey there, I'm alive! Oh, and Hello World\n";

}
```

Just be very careful that you don't comment out any really important stuff!

If you do, let's say, comment the header file out for example, the program won't compile as it should. If you find a section of code is giving you compilation trouble, try commenting out what you don't see as valid in the code. If it compiles properly, you've narrowed down where the error is.

Think Like a Programmer; Create Reusable Code

Just moving away from the syntax for a minute, let's talk about programming experience. Computers are incredibly literal. They will only do what they are told to do, nothing more, nothing less. Implicit intention is lost on them. Let's say that you take your car to a car wash; it will wash your car and automatically rinse it off, without being told to. With a computer not only do you have to tell it to wash the car, but you also have to tell it to rinse the car afterward, otherwise it will not do so.

To start with, the level of detail needed can be quite overwhelming because you have to think through every individual step to make sure you haven't missed anything. Fortunately, there is a nice way around this—reusable code. By writing down a series of steps or instructions that you know you will use over and again, and giving them a name, you can call on them and reuse them over and over, without having to continually rewrite the code. You will see how this works later on, when we get to the section on functions.

Congratulations, you now know what a basic program looks like and how to run it. Before we move on, as I will do regularly throughout this book, I've provided a quiz. Take it—it's a great way to learn! The answers are at the back of the book, but please don't cheat—you won't learn anything that way.

Quiz 1

Think about a program completing successfully—what would be the right value returned to the operating system?

    A. -1
    B. 1
    C. 0
    D. A program doesn't return a value

Name the single function that must be included in every C++ program:

    A. start()
    B. system()
    C. main()
    D. program()

What type of punctuation is used for starting and ending a code block?

    A. {}
    B. ->and <-
    C. BEGIN and END
    D. (and)

What punctuation mark is used for ending most C++ code lines?

    A. .
    B. ;
    C. :
    D. '

Which of these is written correctly as a comment?

A. */ Comments */
B. ** Comment **
C. /* Comment */
D. { Comment }

To access cout, which of the header files is needed?

A. stream
B. None, it's already there as a default
C. iostream
D. using namespace std;

User Interaction and Variables

Up to now, we have learned about simple programs that will display the information you input into the program. You also learned about comments. But what if we want to take things one step further and interact with users?

To do that, you need to be able to accept input, which is information that a user inputs into the program, and that means having somewhere to store the information. With computer programming, data and input are stored inside a variable. There are a few different types of variables and each stores a different type of information. When you declare a variable you have to tell the compiler what the data type is and the name of the variable.

The most common variables are char, double and int. The char variable type stores one single character; the int variable stores integers, which are the numbers without decimal places; and the double variable stores the numbers that have a decimal place. The name of the type is the keyword that you need to use for declaring the variable.

Declaring Variables

Before a variable can be used, the compiler needs to know about it. That's done by declaring it using the syntax

type;

Take a look at a couple of examples on how to declare a variable:

int whole_number;

char letter;

double number_with_decimals;

You can also declare several variables on one line, so long as they are all of the same type and separated by a comma.

int a, b, c, d;

Best practice would be to try and put them all on separate lines though, just for the sake of clarity.

Using Variables

Declaring variables is one thing; how do we use them?

To use a variable to accept input, "con" (pronounced "see in") is used, with an insertion operator following it (it must go in the other direction - >>), followed by the variable where you want the user value inserted.

Below is a program that shows you how to use a variable:

#include <iostream>

using namespace std;

int main ()

```
{
        int thisisyournumber;

        cout << "Please input a number: ";

        cin >> thisisyournumber;

        cout << "You input: " << thisisyournumber << "\n";
}
```

Let's break this down. The first part is familiar to you now, as we discussed it in the last chapter, so we'll start with the main function body.

On this line

int thisisyournumber;

we are declaring a variable called thisisyournumber which is an integer (int) type.

The next unfamiliar line is

cin>>thisisyournumber

cin >> is a function that stores the value the user inputs into thisisyournumber, but before the number can be read by the program, the Enter key has to be pressed.

But what if, when you run the program, it exits straight away? Earlier we looked at using cin.get() to stop a program from doing this, but the program above shut down right away when it was run, and it would do that even if you used cin.get(). In order to avoid this, add the following line before the cin.get() call:

cin.ignore();

That is another function, this time one that reads a character and discards it; in our case, it would be the Enter key press. That's because that key press is counted as part of the input, but we don't need that key press and can throw it away. Usually, you will only use the above function if you use cin.get() to make the program wait for a key press before closing. If you don't use it, cin.get() reads the newline character (\n) and the program closes down.

Another thing to note is that we declared the variable as an integer. However, if the user types a decimal number as the input, it will be truncated. That means the part after the decimal place is discarded and only the whole number is kept. So, for example, 2.354 will become 2, with the .354 discarded.

When you run the sample program, try typing in different numbers as the user input, including decimal place numbers and characters; the result will differ depending on what the input is. You may also notice errors when you do this—we'll discuss error handling later.

Let's continue breaking the program down.

cout << "You input: " << thisisyournumber << "\n";

That is the line that will print the user input back. Note that we don't use quotation marks when we print variables. If you added quotation marks around thisisyournumber, you would get an output of "You input: thisisyournumber." When you don't add quotation marks, the compiler can see that it's a variable, and the program needs to ensure the value is substituted in place of the variable name when the result is printed.

Did you spot two insertion operators on the same line? This is acceptable and all output from the line will still go to the same place. In fact, string literals, which are strings inside quotation marks, and variables should each have their own insertion operator to separate them. If you tried to display a string literal and variable together with just one insertion operator, you would get an error message:

cout << "You entered: " thisisyournumber;

Last, we have the semicolon at the end, as with any function call. Forget to add it and you will get a compiler error.

Changing, Using And Comparing Variables

It will soon get boring reading in variables and printing them back so let's look at how to modify them. When you modify a variable, you can change the way your program behaves, based on the variable value, and you'll be able to respond in different ways to user inputs.

Values can be assigned to variables by using the assignment operator (=):

int x;

x = 5;

This is saying that x is equal to 5. You could be forgiven for thinking that the = sign would compare the values on the left and right, but computer programming doesn't do that. C++ does provide an operator to do that; it's the ==, or quality operator. That operator will get used quite often in loops and statements and, in the next few sections, you will learn quite a bit more about the quality operator and other comparison operators as we look at how to go through a program differently depending on what the input is from the user.

a == 5   // This won't assign a with a value of 5. Instead, it looks to see if a is equal to 5.

Arithmetic operations can also be performed on variables:

* is used to multiply two values together

- is used to subtract one value from another

+ is used to add values together

/ is used to divide one value by another

Take a look at these examples:

a = 4 * 6; // (Note that we used a semicolon and comments) a is 24

a = a + 5; // a is equal to the original value of a with 5 added

Shorthand Method of Adding or Subtracting One:

It's common in C++ to add one to a variable:

int x = 0;

x = x + 1;

This is a pattern that you will see frequently in this guide as we begin to look at some C++ concepts such as loops. In fact, it's such a common pattern that it even has an operator all of its own: - ++. We could write the code from above like this:

int x = 0;

x++;

At the end, x would have a value of 1. The ++ operator is often called the increment operator and using it is called incrementing the variable. There is another operator that subtracts one from a variable—the decrement operator, which is --.

In fact, by now you should have guessed where C++'s name comes from. The original language was called C, and C++ is C plus One—a language based on C with some extras.

Back to the programming. You can use other shortcut operators for other math operations on variables:

x += 5; // This will add 5 to x

x -= 5; // This will subtract five from x

x *= 5; // This will multiply x by 5

x /= 5; // This will divide x 5 by five

Lastly, as well as using the increment or decrement operators after variables, you can also use them in front:

--x;

++y;

The difference between these two methods is the value that results from the expression. For instance, if you were to write:

int x = 0;

cout << x++;

The output would be 0.

Why? Because, although x has been modified, the x++ expression will return the original value. Because ++ is after the variable, you can see it as being executed after the variable value is obtained. On the other hand, if you do things the other way around:

int x = 0;

cout << ++x;

The output will be 1. First, 1 is added to x, and then the value of x is obtained.

Using these operations, it's possible to make a small calculator program:

```cpp
#include <iostream>
using namespace std;
int main()
{
    int first_argument;
    int second_argument;
    cout << "Enter the first argument: ";
    cin >> first_argument;
    cout << "Enter the second argument: ";
    cin >> second_argument;
    cout << first_argument << " * " << second_argument << " = " <<
first_argument * second_argument << endl;
    cout << first_argument << " + " << second_argument << " = " <<
first_argument + second_argument << endl;
    cout << first_argument << " / " << second_argument << " = " <<
first_argument / second_argument << endl;
    cout << first_argument << " - " << second_argument << " = " <<
first_argument - second_argument << endl;
}
```

Using (And Misusing) Variables

When you declare a variable, you're providing your program with something new to do. However, whenever you get your declaration wrong, it can cause some problems. Let's say you try to use variables that haven't been declared; the program will not compile and a compiler error will pop up telling you there is an undeclared variable. Usually, you will see an error like this:

error: 'x' was not declared in this scope

While you can use several variables of the same type, you can't have several variables with the same name. You could not, for example, have an int variable and a double variable both called my_val. When you declare more than one variable with the same name, you will get an error message that looks like one of the following:

error: conflicting declaration 'double my_val'

error: 'my_val' has a previous declaration as ìnt my_val'

error: declaration of `double my_val'

error: conflicts with previous declaration ìnt my_val'

Another error involves not putting the semicolon at the end of the code line, like this:

int x

An error like that can cause all sorts of different error messages, depending on what comes after the variable declaration. Usually, the error message will pinpoint the line that immediately follows the declaration, so always look to the line above to see if that all-important semicolon is there.

Not all errors happen at compile time; some wait until run time. When a variable is first declared, it's not initialized. All variables must be initialized before they can be used. To do that, they need a value assigned to them. If you don't, you'll see some odd behavior. One of the most common problems occurs when you do this:

int x;

int y;

y = 5;

x = x + y;

What has happened here is that y has been set to a value of 5 before y is used, but the initial x value is not known. Instead, it gets randomly chosen at run time and the value that results might be anything. Never assume that your variable will be initialized to convenient values, like 0!

Get into the habit of initializing your variables at the time you declare them. For example,

int x = 0;

is sufficient to show that the variable has that value when it gets created. Establishing this habit right from the start will save you many headaches later on.

Case Sensitivity

Now is a pretty good time to discuss another concept that can get your head in a spin— case sensitivity. It really does matter in C++ whether you use uppercase letters or lowercase. Two names that look identical, like Dog and dog, actually means two completely different things. Every keyword, variable name and function name is case sensitive in C++.

Using the incorrect case in declaration variables and in those places where variables are used could throw up an undeclared variable error, even though you declared it—or thought you did.

Naming Variables

When it comes to naming a variable, while you can name it almost anything, you should opt for names that mean something in terms of what the variable is. For example, you shouldn't do this:

*val1 = val2 * val3;*

What does that even mean? Nobody will know.

When you write a program, you may think that what you write is obvious—until you reread it the next day. Then, the chances are you won't have a clue what it all means. Using descriptive names for your variable names can help keep things in your code clear. Take a look at this example:

area = width * height;

That's a whole lot clearer, and all we did was change the name.

Storing Strings

So far, we have concentrated on using data types that hold simple values—one integer, one character, for example. While you can do a lot with that, C++ also provides other data types to work with. One of the more useful ones is the string data type. Strings can store several characters, which you've already seen examples of when text is displayed on the screen.

One of the most useful data types is the string. A string can hold multiple characters. You've already seen this data type used when displaying text on the screen:

cout << "Hey, you, I'm alive! Oh, and Hello World!\n";

The string class in C++ lets you do more; you can save strings, modify them and do other things that make them easier to work with.

Declaring a string is quite simple:

```
#include  <iostream>

using namespace std;

int main ()

{

        string my_string;

}
```

Note that the header file is required for using strings, not like other built-in types that don't require it. This is because that type is not built directly into the compiler like the integer type. Strings come from the standard library, which is a huge library full of C++ code that can be reused. And, like other basic C++ types, we can use cin to read in a user-supplied string:

```
#include  <iostream>

#include  <string>

using namespace std;

int main ()

{

        string user_name;

        cout << "Please input your name: ";

        cin >> user_name;

        cout << "Hello " << user_name << "\n";

}
```

What this program does is create a string variable, ask a user to input their name and then print that name out.

Like the other variables we looked at, the string can also be initialized using a value:

string user_name = " ";

You can also put two or more strings together. This is called "appending" and to do it, we use the + sign:

#include <iostream>

#include <string>

using namespace std;

int main ()

{

      string user_first_name;

      string user_last_name;

      cout << "Please input your first name: ";

      cin >> user_first_name;

      cout << "Please input your last name: ";

      cin >> user_last_name;

      string user_full_name = user_first_name + " " + user_last_name;

      cout << "Your name is: " << user_full_name << "\n";

}

The program will take the values from three individual strings—the first and last name of the user and a single space in between. All three areas are appended into one value.

When strings are read in, you might want to read one entire line in one go. C++ has a function for that, called getline. The function will automatically discard the new character at the end of the line.

Using getline is easy enough; the input source is passed in (cin, in our case), the string being read into is passed in and a character that the input is to be terminated on is also passed in. Have a look at the next example; this will read the first name of the user input:

getline(cin, user_first_name, '\n');

You might also find this function useful when you want to read the input from a user up to a specific character, such as a comma. Even so, the user will still need to press the Enter key before the data is accepted:

getline(cin, my_string, ',');

If the user types in

Hello, World

The value of "Hello" goes into my_string and the remaining text stays put inside the input buffer until it's read using another input statement.

What about all the other types though?

We're going to tread in advanced territory here for a minute, so please don't worry if it doesn't make sense yet. Later, you can come back to it and it will.

Why do we have so many basic variable types?

This requires a quick introduction to two of the basic building blocks for computers and computer gaming: the bit and the byte. The bit is the basic storage unit in a computer system and is nothing more than a switch that holds one of two values—0 or 1. Which value will depend on which way the switch goes.

A byte consists of eight bits. So, eight bits in a byte means that there are 256 potential configurations of 0 and 1. How do we come to that? There are eight positions and each one potentially has two values. One bit stores 0 or 1, which is two values. One more bit will give us twice that: 00, 01, 10, 11. Add another and we double that again by adding a 0 or 1 to any of those two-bit numbers. So each of the bits gives us double the number of values.

For n bits, we represent 2n values. One byte of eight bits potentially represents 28 configurations. Add another byte and you have 16 bits, representing 216 values.

Please don't worry if you didn't understand that yet. All I want you to take away from this for now is that the higher the number of bytes, the more data can be stored.

For example, chars are only able to store limited data ranges—256 different values. A char is just one byte, whereas an integer is usually four bytes, and that means it can store a potential four billion different values.

An example of two variables that are different only in how much space they require is the double type and float type. The float was originally the type used for storing decimal numbers; the name comes from the decimal that can float to different positions. In other words, you can have two digits before and four after, or four before and two after. In fact, there are no limits to how many digits can go before and after the decimal.

Again, if you didn't get that, don't worry. A floating point number is a number that has a decimal place. However, they have just four bytes of space whereas the double has eight, which means it can store twice as many values. Back in the days when computers had much smaller amounts of memory than they do today, this was very important and programmers would do whatever they could just to save a byte or two These days, the double is used more than the float, but where you are programming for space-critical devices, the float may be used instead.

The char is the smallest data type at just one byte and you could be forgiven for thinking that there is no need for a char anymore, now that space isn't too much of an issue. Well, the answer to that is that the char also has a special meaning—input and output isn't done in terms of numbers; it's characters instead. When values are read into char variables, the user can input a character. When the character is printed, cout will display the character that represents the variable value rather than the number that is in the variable.

What on earth does all that mean? It means that a character or letter is stored in a computer as a number representing that character. If you look up the ASCII table online, you'll see which numbers represent which characters.

Floating point numbers hide a bit of a secret. They sound great because they can hold huge ranges of values—a double can represent a maximum of 1.8×10^{308} and that equates to a number that has 308 zeroes at the end of it. However, doubles are only eight bytes, so doesn't that equate to 2^{32} values, not 308?

That's quite correct: the maximum number of values that double can represent is 18 quintillion. But that still isn't 308. A floating point number will allow you to represent a small number of the values in a range and this is done using a format that is much like a scientific notation.

In scientific notations, numbers are written in the format of $x \times 10^y$. The x stores the first couple of digits while the y, the exponent, stores the power that the number is raised to. What this does is allow a computer to store values that are very big just by placing the large number into the exponent. The non-exponent portion can't store 300 digits, only 15, so that's the precision you will get with a floating point number: just 15. If your values are quite small, the difference between the number and what the computer stores will be small, but when you talk in terms of huge numbers, that difference can also be enormous.

Most of the time, the fact that floating point numbers aren't exact will not get in your way, not unless you're doing scientific computing, and we're not at that stage just yet.

Integers also have a little secret of their own. Integers and floating points simply do not get along. Unlike the floating point, an integer will always store the exact integer value you put into it, but integers not like decimal numbers. When you do a math operation using an integer and don't get an integer as a result, that result will be truncated, as I mentioned earlier. The non-decimal part of the number will remain exact but the decimal part is discarded.

For example, if you were taking a math exam and you said the result of 5/2 was 2, you would get the question wrong. That, though, is exactly what the computer does. So, if you want an answer that has decimal places, you need to use a type that isn't an integer. When you write numbers into your computer program, it's assumed that they're integers, which is why 5/2 will evaluate to 2. If, however you place a decimal point in 5.0/2.0, you will get the answer you want—2.5—because the computer will assume the operation is a floating point operation and will treat it as such.

Quiz 2

To store a number like 3.1415, what variable type do you use?

    A. int
    B. char
    C. double
    D. string

To compare two variables, which of these is the right operator?

    A. :=
    B. =
    C. equal
    D. ==

How do you access the string data type?

    A. You don't have to because it's already built into the C++ language
    B. The iostream header file must be included because strings are used for IO
    C. include the string header file
    D. Strings are not supported in C++

Which of these isn't a correct variable type?

    A. double
    B. real
    C. int
    D. char

How do you read in a whole line from a user?

    A. use cin>>
    B. Use readline
    C. use getline

D. Not very easily!

Take this expression: cout<<1234/2000. What would you expect to see as the output?

   A. 0
   B. .617
   C. Approximately .617, but this could not be stored precisely in a floating point number.
   D. It all depends on what values are on the two equation sides.

If we already have integers, why is there a need for a char type in C++?

   A. Because they are two different data types—one is a letter, one is a number.
   B. To enable backward compatibility with C.
   C. Because it's far easier to read in and print out characters than it is numbers, even though the char gets stored as a number.
   D. For the purposes of internationalization support, to make it easier to handle languages that have many characters.

If Statements

Having looked at programs that go from one statement to the next without being able to vary what happens and only displaying the values that come from user input, the next logical step is to look at program control. With the if statement, you can decide whether the program goes into a given code section or not. To do that, we use conditions that can be true or false. For example, you could use an if statement to determine if the correct password was entered by a user: if yes (true), the user can access the program, but if not (false), the user is locked out.

The basic syntax for the if statement is:

if ( )

    This statement should be executed

Or

if ( )

{

    Everything in this block should be executed

}

The code that comes after the if statement is what gets conditionally executed and is known as the if statement body. Take a look at a silly example of the syntax in use:

if (5 < 10)

    cout << "Five is less than ten, who would have guessed it";

All we have done here is evaluated a statement of "is five less than ten" just to see whether it's true or not. Here's another example that uses multiple statements and brackets:

```
if ( 5 < 10 )

{

        cout << "Five is less than ten, who would have guessed it\n";

        cout << "I really hope this computer is working properly.\n";

}
```

If there's more than one code line following an if statement, the brackets are required to ensure that the whole block of code is executed if the statement evaluates true. As a best practice, get into the habit of putting the brackets around the statement body; that way you won't have to keep remembering to include them when you have more than one statement that needs to be executed. It also makes the statement body clearer.

One of the most common errors is adding another statement into the body without using brackets—this will cause the new statement to always execute, regardless of conditions.

```
if ( 5 < 10 )

        cout << "Five is less than ten, who would have guessed it\n";

        cout << "I really hope this computer is working properly.\n";
```

Indentation can make it hard to spot the errors, so stick with using the brackets; it's safer!

Let's take a look at a more complex if statement that will work with some user input:

```
#include  <iostream>
```

```
using namespace std;

int main ()

{

    int x;

    cout << "Input a number: ";

    cin >> x;

    if ( x < 10 )

    {

        cout << "You input a value that was less than 10" << '\n';

    }

}
```

This is different from the first example because it's reading a user-provided value rather than one that was hard-coded into the comparison.

Let's look at how flexible if statements can be.

Expressions

If statements are used for testing one expression. An expression is one or more statements that are linked, evaluating to one value. Wherever you can use constant or variable values in your code, you can also use expressions. In fact, constant and variable values really are no more than simple expressions, and math operations, like multiplication and addition, are just more complex expressions. When you use an expression in the context of comparisons, the result will be either true or false.

What Is Truth?

As far as the compiler is concerned, expressions are true if they evaluate to non-zero numbers and false if they evaluate to zero. So a statement like this

if (1)

is always going to make the statement body execute, but a statement like this

if (0)

is always going to ensure that the statement body is never executed.

In C++, there are two keywords that you can write straight into your code: true and false. If you display the integer value that goes with true, it will be 1, while the integer associated with false is 0.

When you use a relational operator for performing comparisons, the operator will either return true or false. For example

0 == 2

will evaluate false. Note the double equal signs (==) This is used for equality whereas the single equal sign is for assigning values to variables. Another check

2 == 2

will evaluate to true.

When relational operations are done in an if statement, the result doesn't need to be checked directly against true or false:

if (x == 2)

is exactly the same as

if ((x == 2) == true)

and it's clear that the first version is a lot easier to read.

When you're programming, more often than not you will be checking if a value that is stored in a variable is equal to, larger than or smaller than another value.

The following relational operators let you compare values:

> - greater than. For example, 6>5 is true

< - less than. For example, 5<6 is true

>= - greater than or equal to. For example, 5>=5 is true

<= - less than or equal to. For example, 5<=6 is true

== - equal to. For example, 6==6 is true

!= - not equal to. For example, 6!=4 is true

The Bool Type

In C++, there is a special type called the bool that is used for storing comparison operation results. It isn't all that different from an integer, but does have an advantage in that it's very clear there will only ever be two possible values in use: true or false. Using the true and false keywords with the bool type just makes things even clearer, and, you might like to know, all comparison operators will result in a Boolean.

int x;

cin >> x;

bool is_x_two = x == 2; // note that we used the double-equals for comparison

if (is_x_two)

```
{

        // do something now, x is two!

}
```

Else statements

Sometimes, you're going to be looking for your program to carry out a test. If the test is true, you'll have the program do one thing. If the test is false, you'll want the program to do something else. We use else statements to do the if-else comparisons—the code that follows an else statement, be it one line of code or a code block between brackets, will be executed only when the condition that the if statement checks evaluates as false.

Take a look at an example. Here we are testing whether a user gave us a negative number or not:

```
#include <iostream>

using namespace std;

int main()

{

        int num;

        cout << "Input a number: ";

        cin >> num;

        if ( num < 0 )

        {

                cout << "You input a negative number\n";

        }
```

```
        else

        {

                cout << "You input a non-negative number\n";

        }

}
```

Else-if

Another way of using the else statement is when you have several conditional statements, all of which have the potential to evaluate true, but you only want to execute the body of one if statement. Let's say, for example, that you want to change the code above to find three different cases: zero numbers, positive numbers and negative numbers. An else-if statement could be used after an if statement body; if the first statement evaluates true, the else-if statement gets ignored. If it evaluates false, on the other hand, the condition will be checked for the else-if statement.

If the if statement evaluates true, the else statement won't be checked against the condition. It is perfectly possible and acceptable to use several else-if statements in a series to ensure that just one code block is executed.

Using an else-if statement, the above code could be changed so it checks for zero:

```
#include <iostream>

using namespace std;

int main()

{

        int num;
```

```cpp
cout << "Input a number: ";

cin >> num;

if ( num < 0 )

{

        cout << "You input a negative number\n";

}

else if ( num == 0 )

{

        cout << "You input zero\n";

}

else

{

        cout << "You input a positive number\n";

}

}
```

String Comparisons

You can use all those comparisons with a string object in C++ and write a small program, comparing string objects, to determine if a user input the correct password:

```cpp
#include  <iostream>

#include  <string>
```

```cpp
using namespace std;

int main ()

{

    string password;

    cout << "Type in your password: " << "\n";

    getline( cin, password, '\n' );

    if ( password == "xyzzy" )

    {

        cout << "Access allowed" << "\n";

    }

    else

    {

        cout << "Incorrect password. Access denied!" << "\n";

        // this is a very convenient way of stopping the program,
        by returning

        return 0;

    }

    // continue on!

}
```

What we have here is a program that reads a user input and compares it with a password of xyzzy. If the user input doesn't match the password, the program will immediately return from main.

Other comparison operators can also be used on a string; for example, you could compare strings to see which is first alphabetically or use the != operator to check whether strings differ from one another.

Using Boolean Operators

So far, all we've done is check a single condition at a time. However, if you want to check two, for example the correct username and password, you need to come up with a strange if-else statement. Thankfully, with C++ we can use a Boolean operator to carry out multiple checks.

Boolean operators make it much easier to create slightly more complex conditional statements. For example, let's say you have a variable named age and want to check if it's greater than 10 and less than five at the same time. The Boolean AND operator could be used to ensure that both conditions, age>5 and age < 10, are true.

Boolean operators work in much the same way as a comparison operator; they will return true or false based on the resulting expression.

Boolean NOT

The Boolean NOT operator will accept a single input. If the input evaluates true, the result is false, and if the input evaluates false, the return is true. For example, not(false) would evaluate true and not(true) would evaluate false. And the expression of not(any number but zero) would also be false.

The NOT operator symbol is an exclamation mark (!)

Here's an example:

if (! 0)

```
{
    cout << "! 0 evaluates to true";
}
```

Boolean AND

The Boolean AND operator will return true if both of the inputs evaluate true. For example, true AND false evaluates false because one input is false—for it to evaluate true, both inputs must be true. So true AND true will evaluate trues and (any number but zero) AND false will evaluate false.

The symbol used for the AND operator is a pair of ampersands (&&). Do *not* make the mistake of thinking that the operator is checking for equality between the numbers; it only does this if both of the arguments evaluate true:

```
if ( 1 && 2 )
{
    cout << " 1 and 2 both evaluate to true";
}
```

Short-Circuiting Checks

If the first expression in a Boolean AND operation is false, the second one won't be checked. This is known as short-circuiting. This is quite useful because it's possible to write expressions where one condition should be checked only if the first one evaluates true. For example, this will guard against the dreaded division by zero problem.

Here's an example of an if statement checking if 10/x is less than 2:

```
if ( x != 0 && 10 / x < 2 )

{

        cout << "10 / x is less than 2";

}
```

Once the if statement has been evaluated, the program will first check whether x is 0. If it is, there's no need to check the following condition so it gets skipped over. What this means is that division by zero, which would make your program crash, is no longer a concern.

If we didn't have this short-circuiting, you would need to write your code like this:

```
if ( x != 0 )

{

        if ( 10 / x < 2 )

        {

                cout << "10 / x is less than 2";

        }

}
```

Short-circuiting lets us write code that is a great deal cleaner and easier to read.

Boolean OR

The Boolean OR operator will return true if one or both of the provided values is true. For example, true OR false will evaluate to true, whereas false OR false will evaluate to false.

The symbol used for the OR operator is a pair of pipe characters (||) and, like the Boolean AND operator, the OR operator will also short-circuit. If condition 1 is true, the second is ignored.

Combining Expressions

Using these basic Boolean operators, two conditions can be checked at once. But what if we want to make things even more powerful? Remember that you can make an expression from operators, variables and values, but you can also make them out of other expressions.

For example, you could combine a Boolean AND with the equality comparison operators to check if x is 3 and y is 4:

$x == 3$ && $y == 4$

Here's how we could use the Boolean AND to make a program that checks that a username and a password are correct:

```
#include <iostream>

#include <string>

using namespace std;

int main ()

{

        string username;

        string password;

        cout << "Input your username: " << "\n";

        getline( cin, username, '\n' );

        cout << "Input your password: " << "\n";
```

```
        getline( cin, password, '\n' );

        if ( username == "root" && password == "xyzzy" )

        {

                cout << "Access allowed" << "\n";

        }

        else

        {

                cout << "Incorrect username or password. Access denied!"
        << "\n";

                // this is a very convenient way of stopping the program,
        by returning

return 0;

        }

        // continue on!

}
```

When you run the program, only a user called root, who has the correct password, will be granted access. It would be easy enough to extend this for several users, each with their own password, and you would do this using the else-if statements.

Order Of Evaluation

In the last example, we had a few sub-expressions, such as:

username == "root"

and

password == "xyzzy"

Both expressions will be evaluated before the Boolean operator and this comes down to operator precedence; this determines which order the operators are evaluated in.

As far as the arithmetic operators go, the precedence matches that of standard math: division and multiplication first, followed by addition and subtraction. With the Boolean operators, NOT is evaluated first, and then the comparison operators. Then the Boolean AND followed by the Boolean OR.

Parentheses can be used for controlling the evaluation order of the arithmetic and the Boolean operators.

Our last example:

You can always use parentheses to control the order of evaluation for both Boolean operators and arithmetic operators such as addition and subtraction.

For example, take our previous example:

x == 3 && y == 4

If you want it to say "when the condition is NOT true," you should use the parentheses:

! (x == 3 && y == 4)

Quiz 3

Which of these is true?

    A. 1
    B. 66
    C. .1
    D. -1
    E. All of the above

Which of these is the Boolean "AND" operator?

    A. &
    B. &&
    C. |
    D. |&

Take the expression !(true && ! (false || true)). What does it evaluate to?

    A. true
    B. false

Which of these is the right syntax for an if statement?

    A. if expression
    B. if { expression
    C. if (expression)
    D. expression if

Loops

Although you now know how to make your program behave in a different way, depending on what the user input is, it still runs only once. Going back to the password checker in the last section, it will only ask for the password once and then exit. To make it keep on promoting the user when the password fails, you might have thought about adding a series of if statements that will keep on checking it.

What we want is a way of letting a user reenter their password until they get it right. That's what we use loops for. Loops will execute a code block over and again and are one of the most powerful concepts in C++. Basically, a loop will let a user write one simple statement and repeat it over and over to get a better result. Users can be prompted to input their passwords as often as they are prepared to keep trying!

In C++, we have three different kinds of loop, each slightly different than the last: while loops, for loops, and do-while loops. We'll look at each of them now.

While Loops

The while loop is the simplest and has a basic structure of

while ( ) { Code that will be executed while the condition evaluates true}

As you might have spotted, while loops are not that much different from an if statement. The difference is that the while loop body will be repeated but, like the if statement, we use a Boolean condition.

Take a look at an example of a while loop that has two conditions:

while (i == 2 || i == 3)

This is a very basic example:

```
while ( true )

{
        cout << "Let's get looping \n";

}
```

Just a quick warning: if you run the code above, the loop will never stop. This is known as an infinite loop and to get it to stop you would need to kill off your program by closing the window or pressing CTRL+C or CTRL+Break. Avoid getting into this situation by making sure your loop condition doesn't evaluate true all of the time.

One of the most common causes of infinite loops is only using one equal sign instead of two in the condition.

If you do this:

```
int i = 1;

while ( i = 1 )

{
        cin >> i;

}
```

the loop will carry on reading the user input until something other than 1 is entered. However, because the loop condition has been written as

```
i = 1
```

and not

```
i == 1
```

all it will do is assign the value of 1 to i. And, as it happens, assignment expressions act as though they return the assigned value and, here, this would be 1. You already know that 1 is not zero; it is true, and that means the loop will just continue on forever.

Here's a program where the while loop displays numbers from 0 to 9—and the loop works:

```cpp
#include <iostream>

using namespace std;

int main ()

{

        int i = 0;  // Don't forget your variables

        while ( i < 10 ) // While i is less than 10

        {

                cout << i << '\n';

                i++;        // Update i so that, at some point, the condition
        will be met

        }

}
```

An easy way to think of loops is this: when the program gets to the end of the body of the loop, it goes straight back to the start of the body; the condition is checked again and, depending on the result, the loop has to decide whether to do it again or move on to the statement that comes after the code block.

For Loops

For loops are incredibly versatile and convenient. The syntax for a for loop is

for (variable initialization; condition; variable update)

{

       // Code to be executed for as long as the condition evaluates true

}

There's quite a lot going on there. Let's see an example of one in action, this one acting much like the while loop from earlier:

for (int i = 0; i < 10; i++)

{

      cout << i << '\n';

}

So, what's going on here?

First the variable is initialized. Ours is int=0. This lets us declare and assign a value to a new variable or one that already exists. We declared a variable called i. When there is only one variable in the loop that needs to be checked, it often gets called a 'loop variable' and, in programming, you will commonly see loop variables called 'i' and 'j.' When a variable gets incremented every time the lop goes through, it's called a 'loop counter.'

Next comes the condition. This is what tells the program that the loop should repeat all the time the condition is true. We are checking to see if x is less than 10 and, like the while loop, the condition gets checked before the first loop execution—that way, if it immediately evaluates false, the loop will never run.

Lastly, the variable update. This is where we update the loop variables; if you wanted to, you could make a function call here (the function wouldn't affect the variable but would be useful nonetheless), or do something like i++ or i+10.

Many loops only ever have one variable, one condition and one loop, making the for loop a nice way of writing a loop; everything that matters all goes on one single line. Note that the semicolon is used to separate the code sections—this must not be left out, even if the section is empty. Empty conditions evaluate true and will put you straight into an infinite loop if nothing is done to stop it.

To better understand the for loop, compare the code below to the while loop code above:

```
int i; // declaration and initialization of variable

while ( i < 10 ) // condition

{

        cout << i << '\n';

        i++; // variable update

}
```

The for loop does the same thing as the while loop, but in a better way.

Here's a for loop example that does something more than just print a number sequence. This one will print the square of all the numbers from 0 to 9:

```
#include <iostream>

using namespace std;

int main ()
```

```
{
        // The loop goes while i < 10, and i will increase by one every loop
        for ( int i = 0; i < 10; i++ )
        {
                // Remember that the loop condition checks
                // the conditional statement before looping.
                // This means that, when i equals 10 the loop will break.
                // i is updated before the condition gets checked.
                cout<< i << " squared is " << i * i << endl;
        }
}
```

This is a simple example:

First, we set i to zero to initialize the variable.

The condition is checked. i is less than 10 so the body is executed.

The variable is updated to add 1 to i.

The condition is checked and, if true, the loop body will execute again. If not, it will end.

This continues until i is not less than 10.

Do-while Loops

Do-while loops are used for writing loop bodies that happen one or more times. The structure is:

```
do

{

        // body...

} while ( condition );
```

Rather than at the start, the condition gets tested at the end of the body which means the loop body is executed a minimum of one time before the condition gets checked. If the condition evaluates as true, the loop goes back to the start, executes one more time and checks again. It's nothing more than a reversed while loop; where the while loop says to loop for as long as the condition is true, executing the code, the do-while loop says execute it and then check and loop back for as long as it is true.

The following example allows a user to keep inputting a password until they get it right:

```
#include <string>

#include <iostream>

using namespace std;

int main ()

{

        string password;

        do

        {

                cout << "Please input your password: ";

                cin >> password;
```

```
    } while ( password != "foobar" );

    cout << "Welcome, you  got it right";

}
```

The loop body will be executed once, allowing the password to be entered. If it isn't right, the loop goes back and repeats, asking for the password; this continues until the correct one is input.

Note that we have a trailing semicolon following the while part of the code. Other loops don't require this but the while loop does; it is the only loop that should be terminated using a semicolon.

Loop Control Flow

While it's normal to check a loop condition to exit the loop, there may be times when you want to exit early. There's a keyword for that: break. Using a break statement will immediately bring you out of the loop.

Take a look at an example; this gets you out of what could be an infinite loop:

```
#include  <string>

#include  <iostream>

using namespace std;

int main ()

{

    string password;

    while ( 1 )

    {
```

```
            cout << "Please input your password: ";

            cin >> password;

            if ( password == "foobar" )

            {

                   break;

            }

      }

      cout << "Welcome, you got it right";

}
```

Break statements end a loop straightaway, going over everything to the closing bracket. As soon as the right password is input, the loop ends. You can put a break statement anywhere in a loop, including at the end, and that means you can use an infinite loop as an alternative to a do-while; the break statement is the condition check.

These statements are useful when you need to get out of a large loop, but be careful not to use too many—they make your code hard to read.

Another way to control a loop is to use a continue statement to skip over one iteration. When the program comes to the continue statement, the current iteration will end immediately but won't exit the loop.

You could, for example, write a loop that skips printing a number, like 10:

```
int i = 0;

while ( true )

{
```

```
        i++;

        if ( i == 10 )

        {

                continue;

        }

        cout << i << "\n";

}
```

The infinite loop doesn't come to an end; instead, when i gets to 10, the continue statement will send the loop right back to the beginning, skipping the cout call. When you use "continue with" for loops, the update happens after continue.

This statement is useful when there is code in the middle of the body that you want skipped over. You might, for example, want to check on the input and, if it is incorrectly entered, you could skip over the input processing using something like the following example:

```
while ( true )

{

        cin >> input;

        if ( ! isValid( input ) )

        {

                continue;

        }

        // process the input as normal
```

}

Nested Loops

It's common in programming to want to loop over more than one related value. For example, you might want to use one loop to print out some emails and another that prints the author from each of those emails. You could write a second loop to do this but that loop must execute inside the first loop. This is called a nested loop.

The example below is quite simple; we're printing a multiplication table using a nested loop:

```
#include <iostream>

using namespace std;

int main ()

{
        for ( int i = 0; i < 10; i++ )

        {
                cout << '\t' << i; // \t represents the tab character, which nicely
formats the output
        }
        cout << '\n';

        for ( int i = 0; i < 10; ++i )

        {
                cout << i;
```

```cpp
    for ( int j = 0; j < 10; ++j )

    {

            cout << '\t' << i * j;

    }

    cout << '\n';

}

}
```

With nested loops, you will often see terms such as outer loop and inner loop. In the code above, the j variable is the inner loop while the i variable is the outer loop. What you mustn't do is use the same loop variable for both loops, like this:

```cpp
for ( int i = 0; i < 10; i++ )

{

    // oops, redeclared i again here!

    for ( int i = 0; i < 10; i++ )

    {

    }

}
```

You can nest multiple loops in C++, loops within loops within loops and so on.

Choosing the Right Loop

Why do we need all three types of loops? Truthfully, you don't. The do-while loop is rarely used in real programming, with most programmers opting for the for loop and while loop.

Over time you will learn for yourself which loops work better for your code. As you're first learning though, here are a few guidelines.

For loop: if you know exactly how many times you want to loop, or are using multiplication tables, use a for loop. These are also the standard way to iterate over an array, which you will see later. Do NOT use a for loop when a variable needs updating; they work best with single statements

While loop: if your loop condition is complicated, or there is lots of math involved to get to the loop variable value, use a while loop. With these, it's easy to see when the loop will terminate, but they don't make it easy to see what has changed on each loop. If that change is complex, use a while loop. That way, your program reader knows it was more than an update!

As an example, if you have two loop variables that were different:

```
int j = 5;
for ( int i = 0; i < 10 && j > 0; i++ )
{
        cout << i * j;
        j = i - j;
}
```

Not everything that is of any consequence is inside the single for loop line—some turn up at the end of the body. This is misleading and a while loop would be a better fit:

```
int i = 0;

int j = 5;

while ( i < 10 && j > 0 )

{

        cout << i * j;

        j = i - j;

        i++;

}
```

It still doesn't look nice but is at least no longer misleading. While loops are great for almost indefinite looping, an example would be a chess game where each player needs to take a turn until the game ends.

Do-while loops: these won't be used very often. Just about the only time you might use one is if you want something done at least once. The password checker code from earlier is a good example of this, but if you need the body of the loop to be a little different each time it's checked, it isn't the best loop.

Take a look at the following example. How would you write this using a do-while loop?

```
string password;

cout << "Input your password: ";

cin >> password;

while ( password != "xyzzy" )

{
```

```
        cout << "Incorrect password--try again: ";

        cin >> password;
}
string password;

do

    {

    if ( password == "" )

    {

            cout << "Input your password: ";

    }

    else

    {

            cout << "Incorrect password--try again: ";

    }

    cin >> password;

} while ( password != "xyzzy" );
```

The do-while loop only makes this complicated. The body isn't the same each time; although we still read in user input, the message is different each time.

Quiz 4

If the code int x; for(x=0; x<10; x++){} was run, what would the value of x be?

    A. 10
    B. 9
    C. 0
    D. 1

Take an expression of while(x<100); when would the code block after this execute?

    A. When x is less than 100
    C. When x is greater than 100
    D. When x is equal to 100
    E. When it wants to

Which of these isn't a loop structure?

    A. for
    B. do-while
    C. while
    D. repeat until

What is the guaranteed number of times a do-while loop will loop?

    A. 0
    B. Infinitely
    C. 1
    D. Variable

Functions

Loops let you write some cool programs, but right now you can only write them in the main function. This is because if you're to try doing something complex inside main, the function will get too long and will be difficult to read. Along the way, you will come across times when you want to do one thing in several different places, resulting in you having to copy and paste code repeatedly.

Functions save the day here. When you break a program down into functions, you can reuse the code from each function wherever you want without having to copy/paste or rewrite.

Much of what we have gone over so far has been about performing specific actions; on the other hand, functions are about organization and making your code more readable.

Function Syntax

You already know how to create a function; every program discussed so far has had the main function in it. So let's look at a different one:

```
int add (int x, int y)

{

        return x + y;

}
```

This looks much like the main function, but there are two differences:

This one will take two arguments—main took none

This one explicitly returns a value—main also returns a value, but there is no need to manually input the return statement in main.

The line

int add (int x, int y)

first provides the return type and then the function name. The arguments come after the name; if you didn't want to add arguments, you would just use a pair of empty parentheses, like this:

int no_arg_function ()

If you don't want your function to return a value, perhaps one that just prints something, you can declare it as having a void type. This stops you and others from using the function as an expression.

The return statement provides the return value; it has just one line—return x+y—but you can have multiple lines, just like the main function. In this case, the function will stop when the return statement runs, no matter how many lines there are.

Once the function has been declared, you can label it as follows:

add(1, 2); // ignore the return value

And the function can be used as an expression, either by assigning it to a variable or outputting it:

#include <iostream>

using namespace std;

int add (int x, int y)

{

   return x + y;

```
}
int main ()
{
        int result = add( 1, 2 );  // call add and then assign the result to a
variable
        cout << "The result is: " << result << '\n';
        cout << "Adding 3 and 4 gives us: " << add( 3, 4 );
}
```

It probably looks as though cout will output our add function here, but, as it is using variables, cout will actually print the expression result and not the literal phrase. We would have gotten the same if we had run this:

```
cout << "Adding 3 and 4 gives us: " << 3 + 4;
```

Note also that we call the add function more than once, instead of repeating that piece of code over and again. That doesn't really help in a short function like this, but if we want to add more code into the function later, we will only need to change the function, rather than every instance of the code. That's a lot less work!

Local and Global Variables

When a variable is declared inside a function, you provide a name for it. So, what does that name mean in terms of where you can refer to it?

Local

Here's a simple function:

```
int addTen (int x)
```

```
{

        int result = x + 10;

        return result;

}
```

We have two variables here: result and x. The result variable can only be accessed inside the brackets it is defined in; no more than the two code lines inside the add function. You could also write another function that uses the result variable:

```
int getValueTen ()

{

        int result = 10;

        return result;

}
```

And getValueTen could also be used inside addTen:

```
int addTen (int x)

{

        int result = x + getValueTen();

        return result;

}
```

Now we have two variables named result—one in the function called getValueTen and one in addTen. These do not conflict with one another because when each function executes, it can only access its own result variable, not the other.

Variable visibility is known as scope. Variable scope means nothing more than the piece of code the variable name is used for in order to access the variable. When you declare a variable inside a function, it's only available in the function scope (when the function executes). When a variable is declared in one function scope, it can't be accessed by any other functions that may be called while the function executes. And when a function calls another function, the only variables available are those in the new function.

Function arguments also get declared in the function scope. The function caller has no access to these variables, even though the value is provided by the caller. In the addTen function, the x variable is a function argument and can't be used anywhere other than in the addTen function.

And, like any variable that you declare in a function, x can't be used by any of the functions that addTen might call. In the above example, x is an addTen argument and can't be accessed by using the getValueTen function.

Think of an argument as being the stunt double of the variables that get passed to the function; when you change an argument, it won't affect the original variable. To do this, when you pass a variable to a function, it gets copied into the argument:

```
#include <iostream>

using namespace std;

void changeArgument (int x)

{

        x = x + 5;

}

int main()
```

```
{

    int y = 4;

    changeArgument( y ); // y will not be harmed by the function call

    cout << y; // still prints 4

}
```

The variable scope can be much smaller than a function. Every set of curly brackets defines a new, narrower scope. For example:

```
int divide (int numerator, int denominator)

{

    if ( 0 == denominator )

    {

        int result = 0;

        return result;

    }

    int result = numerator / denominator;

    return result;

}
```

The first time result is declared, it's only in the scope of the curly brackets around the if statement. The second time, the scope only ranges from the point it's declared to the end of that function. Generally, a compiler isn't going to prevent you from creating more than variables with identical names, so long as they aren't used in the same scope. Where you have the divide function, for example, if you had several variables with the same name in scopes that are quite similar, it would be confusing to an outsider reading your code.

So, a variable that gets declared in a function scope or in a block is a local variable, but you can also have more widely available variables.

Global

At times, you might have one variable that you want all your functions to have access to. Take a board game, for example. You might want the board as a global variable—that way, several functions can access it without you needing to pass the variable to each one.

A global variable is one that gets declared outside a function and is available at any point in the program after it has been declared.

Here is an example of how to declare and use a global variable:

```cpp
#include <iostream>

using namespace std;

int doStuff () // a small function that demonstrates scope
{
        return 2 + 3;
}

// initialize a global variable like any other variable

int count_of_function_calls = 0;

void fun ()
{
        // the global variable is available here
```

```
        count_of_function_calls++;
}
int main ()
{
        fun();

        fun();

        fun();

        // and it's available here too!

        cout << "Function fun was called " << count_of_function_calls <<
"
times";
}
```

The variable called count_of_function is in scope from just before the function called fun. The function called doStuff can't access the variable because count_of_function was declared after doStuff. The main and fun functions *can* access it because they were declared later.

A warning here:

It might seem easier to use global variables because they can be used by everyone, but they do make your code hard to read. Use a global variable only when something really needs to be available widely. Otherwise, stick with passing arguments to function instead of making it so a function has to access a global variable.

Let's go back to the game board as an example. You could make the function that displays the board access a global variable. But what if you wanted a different board displayed? The function isn't taking the board as the argument; all it does is show one global board.

Make Your Functions Available

The scoping rules that go with variables, like only being able to use them after they have been declared, apply to functions too. For example, the program below will NOT compile:

```
#include <iostream> // needed for cout

using namespace std;

int main ()

{

        int result = add( 1, 2 );

        cout << "The result is: " << result << '\n';

        cout << "Adding 3 and 4 gives us: " << add( 3, 4 );

}

int add (int x, int y)

{

        return x + y;

}
```

If you tried to compile it, you would get a message that tells you "add" wasn't declared in the scope.

The problem here is that the add function wasn't declared at the time it was called, so it isn't in scope. If the compiler spots that you are calling a function you haven't declared, it doesn't like it. One way around this is to place the entire function above where it will be used. Another method is to make sure a function is declared before it is defined.

You might think that declaring and defining functions is much the same, but they have different meanings.

Definitions and Declarations

When you define a function, you're giving the whole function, and that includes the function body. The way the add function was written earlier is an example of defining the function because it showed exactly what the function does. A function definition is a declaration too because, when a function is defined, it needs all of the relevant information provided by the declaration.

Function declarations provide only basic information needed by the caller—the name, arguments, return type. Before a function can be called it has to be declared, either through a declaration or a full definition.

Declaring a function requires you to write the function prototype. The declaration informs the compiler what will be returned by the function, what its name is and what arguments will be passed to it.

A prototype is like a blueprint that tells you how the function will be used:

Return_type function_name (arg_type arg1, ..., arg_type argN);

arg-type is the argument type, i.e. char, int, or double. This is all you would do if you were declaring a variable.

Here's what a function prototype looks like:

int add (int x, int y);

This is specifying that the function named "add" will take two arguments, both of them integers, and an integer will be returned. Use of the semicolon is telling the compiler it's looking at a prototype, not a full function definition.

Here's how to use a function prototype:

```
#include <iostream>

using namespace std;

// function prototype for add

int add (int x, int y);

int main ()

{

        int result = add( 1, 2 );

        cout << "The result is: " << result << '\n';

        cout << "Adding 3 and 4 gives us: " << add( 3, 4 );

}

int add (int x, int y)

{

        return x + y;

}
```

We start with the include files, followed by the add function prototype, not forgetting the semicolon. After this, the add function can be used by any code, including the man function even though the function wasn't defined until after main.

Because the prototype appears above main, the compiler knows that it has been declared; from there it can work out what the arguments are and what the return value is.

Don't forget; while calling a function can be done before it is defined, you must define it at some point, otherwise your code won't compile.

Breaking Down into Functions

Knowing how to write a function is one thing; knowing when to use it is another entirely.

Repetitive Code

Functions are designed for making code reuse easier. If you continually copy and paste, you will get a program that is long, hard to read, and full of repetitive code. Rather than having to keep rewriting or copy/pasting, all you need to do is call the function. Functions save space and time, as well as making your code much nicer to read. Plus, when you need to make a change, you just change the function, not fifty different instances of it scattered throughout your code (and forgetting at least one of them!)

A rule of thumb: if you have written/used one piece of code more than three times, write a function.

Easier Code

To be honest, even if you don't have a need to reuse code, it can be hard to read and understand a long and complicated block. Turning it into a function provides a much easier way of saying, this is the concept I want, and then using it. It is much easier, for example, to read a concept of reading user input when one function does it for you. The code that implements the retrieval of the key presses, and converts them so they can be read into a variable, is complicated; it would be much better if you could just read:

int x;

cin >> x;

than the full details. If you're writing code and struggling to understand the bigger picture, try writing functions to organize things better. That way, you focus on the inputs the function takes and what it outputs rather than all the nitty-gritty details.

And yes, at times you will need to know those details, but not all the time. When you do, just take a look inside the function—everything is there.

Take a menu program for an example. When a user chooses a menu item, the code can be quite complex. There should be a function for each choice in the menu and each choice can easily be understood just by looking at the function. Plus, the main input code is much better structured and easier to read. The very worst programs will have just the main function filled with tons of jumbled-up code; you will see an example of this soon.

Function Naming and Overloading

When you name a function, just like a variable, you need to give it a good name—this will tell you exactly what the function does. When a function is called, the code implementation is not in front of you so your name must describe what the function action is. And that means you may want the same name for more than one function. Take an example of a function finding a triangle's area, based on three coordinates:

int computeTriangleArea (int x1, int y1, int x2, int y2, int x3, int y3);

What if we wanted another function that would give us the area of a triangle area, using the height and width? You could use the name "computeTriangleArea" again because it really does say what you're doing, but would that reuse cause a problem?

No. C++ allows you to overload a function, which means you can use one name for multiple functions so long as each function has a different list of arguments. So, you could write this:

int computeTriangleArea (int x1, int y1, int x2, int y2, int x3, int y3);

and this

int computeTriangleArea (int width, int height);

The compiler can tell the difference because each function, while identically named, takes a different number of arguments. You could have the same number of arguments in both functions too, so long as they are different.

For example, if you write this:

computeTriangleArea(1, 1, 1, 4, 1, 9);

computeTriangleArea(5, 10);

the compiler will know which function needs to be called.

Don't overdo it. Overloading is useful when you have two functions doing the same thing, using different arguments, but you don't want to have too many with the same name.

Quiz 5

Which of these is not a proper prototype?

    A. int funct(char x, char y);
    B. double funct(char x)
    C. void funct();
    D. char x();

Take the function with the prototype of int func(char x, double v, float t); what is the return type?

    A. char
    B. int
    C. float
    D. double

Assuming that the function exists, which of these would be a valid function call?

    A. funct;
    B. funct x, y;
    C. funct();
    D. int funct();

Which of these is a complete function?

    A. int funct();
    B. int funct(int x) {return x=x+1;}
    C. void funct(int) {cout<<"Hello"}
    D. void funct(x) {cout<<"Hello";}

Switch Case and Enums

Let's move on to conditionally executing code. At times, you will have quite a few conditions to check and will write many if-else statements. Let's say, for example, that you read in a user-input key; you might want to check it against five values, or maybe more. If your program is a game, you could be checking it against arrow key presses or the space bar. In this section, we'll go through writing checks for multiple conditions using a switch case statement and we'll also look at creating simple types that work with these statements.

A switch case statement can be used instead of a long if statement, comparing one value to multiple integral values—which is nothing more than a value that may be expressed as an int or a char (an integer type). The variable value in the switch statement will be compared to the individual value for the cases and when a match is found, the program will be executed from the point of the match until the end of the block or a break statement, whichever comes first.

This is the basic layout of a switch statement:

switch (<variable>)

{

case this-value:

    // Code to execute if <variable> == this-value

    break;

case that-value:

    Code to execute if <variable> == that-value

```
        break;

// ...

default:

        // Code to execute if <variable> does not equal the value following
any

cases

        break;

}
```

For the first case that holds the value that goes with the specified variable, the code after the colon gets executed. If none of the given cases run, the default will. You don't have to use the default case, but you should include it; there may be unexpected cases that need handling.

Note that the break keyword is used after each code block. This stops the program from falling through and executing the code from the next case statement—strange behavior, but it happens, so don't forget those break statements.

The values that you provide each of the cases have to be constant integral expressions. So you couldn't do this:

```
int a = 10;

int b = 10;

switch ( a )

{

case b:
```

```
        // Code

        break;

}
```

If you tried compiling this, you would get an error telling you that b can't be a constant expression.

The example below is a program that can be run, showing how a switch case is used:

```
#include <iostream>

using namespace std;

void playgame ()

{}

void loadgame ()

{}

void playmultiplayer ()

{}

int main ()

{

        int input;

        cout << "1. Play game\n";

        cout << "2. Load game\n";

        cout << "3. Play multiplayer\n";
```

```cpp
cout << "4. Exit\n";

cout << "Selection: ";

cin >> input;

switch ( input )

{

case 1: // Note the colon, NOT semicolon after each case

        playgame();

        break;

case 2:

        loadgame();

        break;

case 3:

        playmultiplayer();

        break;

case 4:

        cout << "Thanks for playing!\n";

        break;

default: // Note the colon, NOT the semicolon is used for default

        cout << "Error, bad input, quitting\n";

        break;
```

```
        }

}
```

This one will compile and provides a basic idea of how user input is processed. What you may notice is that the user only has one choice before exiting the program. If the wrong value is input, tough luck. You could fix this by putting the entire switch case block inside a loop, but what would happen with the break statements? Aren't they going to make the loop exit? No, they won't. The break statement will go only to the end of the switch case statement, nowhere else.

Comparing the Switch Case with If-Else

If you are stumped by the switch statement logic, consider that it's much like writing one if-statement for each case statement:

```
if ( 1 == input )

{

        playgame();

}
else if ( 2 == input )

{

        loadgame();

}
else if ( 3 == input )

{

        playmultiplayer();
```

```
}

else if ( 4 == input )

{

        cout << "Thank you for playing!\n";

}

else

{

        cout << "Error, bad input, quitting\n";

}
```

So, why do we need a switch statement if we can do it all with if-else statements? The biggest advantage is that the switch statement makes a program flow more clearly; you have one variable that controls the path of the code. Conversely, if you use several if-else statements, every condition has to be read carefully.

Using Enums to Create Simple Data Types

Occasionally, you will want to use a variable that can take only a small number of values and all those values will be known up-front. Let's say that you want to provide constants for all the possible background colors that a user can choose from. It would be incredibly convenient if we could have the set of constants and a variable type that only holds these constants. And it would be even better if that variable worked with switch case statements because you already know all the values.

The good news is, we can do this with "enumerated types," known as "enums." An enum is a variable type that is created using an enumerated or fixed list of values. A good example would be the colors of the rainbow:

```
enum RainbowColor {

    RC_RED, RC_ORANGE, RC_YELLOW, RC_GREEN, RC_BLUE,
    RC_INDIGO, RC_VIOLET
};
```

There are a couple of important things that you should note:

- We use the enum keyword for introducing new enums
- We give the type its own name – RainbowColor
- We list all possible values for the given type
- And let's not forget our semicolon

Now we can declare the special variable of RainbowColor type:

```
RainbowColor chosen_color = RC_RED;
```

And the code like this:

```
switch (chosen_color)

{

case RC_RED: /* color screen red */

case RC_ORANGE: /* color screen orange */

case RC_YELLOW: /* color screen yellow */

case RC_GREEN: /* color screen green */

case RC_BLUE: /* color screen blue */

case RC_INDIGO: /* color screen indigo */

case RC_VIOLET: /* color screen violet */

default: /* handle unexpected types */
```

```
}
```

Because the type is enumerated, we can be almost certain that all possible variable values have been included.

What values do your enums have? If you don't give a value when you declare an enum, the value will be the value from the last enum plus one. The first enum has a value of 0, so the next would be 1, the next 2 and so on.

You could define values, a useful practice if you need specific values from another system or a piece of code that you want to reuse, and you would name those values:

enum RainbowColor {

  RC_RED = 1, RC_ORANGE = 3, RC_YELLOW = 5, RC_GREEN = 7, RC_BLUE = 9,

RC_INDIGO = 11, RC_VIOLET = 13

};

One of the main reasons enums are so useful is that they let you name a value that would otherwise be hard-coded into the program. Let's say that you want to make a tic-tac-toe game; the Xs and the Os on the board need to be represented. You could use a 0 for a blank square, a 1 for the O and a 2 for the X. To do this you might need code that will compare each board square against the values of 0, 1 and 2:

if (board_position == 1)

{

  / do something, it's an O */*

}

This isn't very easy to read—there is a magic number in the code that has a meaning, but it isn't clear what the meaning is unless you comment the code. With enums, you can name the values:

```
enum TicTacToeSquare { TTTS_BLANK, TTTS_O, TTTS_X };

if ( board_position == TTTS_O )

{

        /* some code */

}
```

Now, if there are any bugs that need fixing in the future, whoever does it can see exactly what should be happening.

Enums are great for when you work with fixed inputs and switch case statements work well with user input. However, neither solve the issue of working with more than just a couple of values at the same time. You might want to read in a long list of football stats and process them, for example. For something like this, you don't need the switch case block—you need a way of storing large amounts of data and manipulating it.

We will get to that in part 3 of this guide, but first, we need to learn more about making programs do things and behave in different ways with small data sets.

Quiz 6

Which of these should follow a case statement?

    A. :
    B. ;
    C. -
    D. A newline

To avoid falling through from one case to another, what should be used?

    A. end;
    B. break;
    C. Stop;
    D. A semicolon

What keyword is used for unhandled possibilities?

    A. all
    B. contingency
    C. default
    D. other

Look at the following code and determine the output:

```
int x = 0;

switch( x )

{

case 1: cout << "One";

case 0: cout << "Zero";
```

```
case 2: cout << "Hello World";

}
```

A. One
B. Zero
C. Hello World
D. ZeroHello World

Randomizing Your Programs

There are two ways that you can make your program do different things whenever you run it:

1. Get different input from the user (or take it from files)
2. Make your program behave in a different way for the same input

For many cases, the first way works well, and for most users, program predictability is just fine. Let's say that you were writing a web browser or a text editor; most likely, whenever a web address or text is input you want to do the exact same thing every time. It wouldn't be any good if your web browser decided which web page you were going to, regardless of input!

Sometimes though, having the same behavior causes massive problems. Many of the computer games we use rely on something called randomness—take Tetris, for example. If the same block sequence fell for every game, users would be able to memorize the sequences and get further just because they know what's coming next. Wouldn't that be fun? Not!

To make a game like Tetris fun, you need to have the tiles selected randomly and for that, a computer has to generate random numbers. A computer will only do what you tell it to; if you ask for something, that is exactly what you get, and that makes random value generation difficult.

Fortunately, it isn't always absolutely critical to have random numbers. Instead, we can generate pseudo-random numbers. For that, the computer requires something called a seed. It will apply math transformations to it, transforming it into another number which becomes the seed for the generator. If the program were to choose a different seed for each run, for all intents and purposes, you wouldn't ever get the same random number sequence.

The math transformations are selected carefully so that the random numbers come up with the same frequency without any obvious patterns. And all of this is provided by C++, so there's no need to worry about the math; you just use functions. All you have to supply is the random seed. This can be as simple as using the current time.

Random Numbers In C++

There are two functions in C++ that are useful—one sets the random seed and the other uses that seed to generate the random numbers:

void srand (int seed);

srand sets the number it takes as the seed and should be called just once at the start of your program. Usually, the way to use srand is to give it the result from the time function; the value returned is a number that represents the current time:

srand(time(NULL));

If you were to continuously call srand, you would end up seeing the random number generator repeatedly and that would result in less randomness.

Using srand requires the use of a header file called cstdlib and, for using the time function, the ctime header is needed too.

```
#include <cstdlib>

#include <ctime>

int main ()

{
        // call once, at the start

        srand( time( NULL ) );

}
```

Now we can get the random numbers. We call the rand function, which has this prototype:

```
int rand ();
```

rand does not take arguments; all it does is gives a number back:

```
#include <cstdlib>

#include <ctime>

#include <iostream>

using namespace std;

int main ()

{
        // call once, at the start

        srand( time( NULL ) );
```

```
        cout << rand() << '\n';

}
```

This will behave in a different way each time it's run—a different number each time!

Okay, it may not be that exciting because the numbers have a very wide range. But you can do more things if you can get the number within a specified range. As it happens, rand returns a value between 0 and the RAND_MAX constant, at least 32,767, which is large. Most likely, you only want a small range. One way to accomplish that is to call rand inside a loop and wait for a number that comes up in the specified range:

```
int randRange (int low, int high)

{

        while ( 1 )

        {

                int rand_result = rand();

                if ( rand_result >= low && rand_result <= high )

                {

                        return rand_result;

                }

        }

}
```

But that's slow, and there's no guarantee of termination—you might not even get the number you want. Luckily, there's a way that guarantees the result.

It's a C++ operation using the modulus operator. This will return the remainder from a division operation, such as 4/3—the answer is 1 with a remainder of 1. Any number that is divided by 4 will always have a remainder of 0 to 3. Divide the random number by the range size and you get a number somewhere between 0 and the range size (not including the size).

Here's an example:

```
#include  <cstdlib>

#include  <ctime>

#include  <iostream>

using namespace std;

int randRange (int low, int high)

{

        // we get a random number, between 0 and the difference

        // between high and low, then add the lowest possible value

        return rand() % ( high - low ) + low;

}

int main ()

{

        srand( time( NULL ) );
```

```
for ( int i = 0; i < 1000; ++i )

{

        cout << randRange( 4, 10 ) << '\n';

}

}
```

"Low" has to be added to the value to ensure we get the right range. Let's say we want a number between 10 and 20; first we need a random number from 0 to 10 and then 10 is added to the range.

Being able to get random numbers in a specified range means you can create all sorts of games.

Quiz 7

If you did not call srand before you called rand, what would happen?

    A. rand would fail
    B. rand would always return 0
    C. Whenever the program runs, rand returns the same number sequence

What would be the purpose of seeding srand with the current time?

    A. To make sure that your program always runs the same way
    B. To generate new random numbers whenever your program is run
    C. To ensure that only real random numbers are generated by the computer.
    D. This is done automatically; all you have to do is call srand if you want the seed set to the same thing each time.

What range of values does rand return?

    A. Whatever range you want
    B. 0 to 1000
    C. 0 to RAND_MAX
    D. 1 to RAND_MAX

What will the expression 11 % 3 return?

    A. 33
    B. 3
    C. 8
    D. 2

When should srand be used?

A. Whenever you need a random number
B. Never. It's nothing more than window dressing
C. Just once, at the beginning of your program
D. Every now and again, just to add some randomness

Chapter 3: Intermediate Guide

Up to this point, we've looked at basic programs that do a few interesting things. We know how to display output, make decisions based on user-input, interact with users, do simple operations repeatedly and so on.

After a while of doing this, you'll get bored of working with small data amounts. Where things get interesting is when we start to work with large data amounts but, right now, you haven't learned enough to be able to do this.

Take a poker game. You have 52 cards—how do you track which have been played? What about shuffling the deck and displaying it? It won't be easy to do. First off, you need 52 variables. Whenever the value is set for a card, every variable has to be checked, to see if the card represented by the variable has been drawn already. By the time you reach the end, you have a long piece of unwieldy code and a strong desire to never set eyes on another code in your life! Thankfully, we have better ways of doing this.

In this part of the guide, we are going to look at everything you need to be able to work with larger data amounts including, how to read, store and manipulate them. The first thing we will look at is a way of storing multiple pieces of data without needing to create many variables. This will solve those problems with the poker game.

Arrays

So, how do you store large amounts of data? Using an array. This is basically a variable with one name that stores lots of values, each indexed with a number. Really, it's a numbered list where each element can be accessed using its number.

In terms of seeing what a variable is like, they are pretty easy:

val0	val1	val2	val3	val4	val5

Each one of those boxes is a separate element and to retrieve one, all you do is ask for the value in a given box.

And that, right there, is where the magic of arrays happens. Because all the array values are stored with one name, you can choose which element you want when it comes to run time. Let's say that you want a five-card poker hand. All five will be stored in an array with a size of five. To pick a card, you simply change which index is being set, instead of having to use a new variable.

As a result, the same code can be used for each card draw—no more having to write separate code for each one. So, instead of doing this:

Card1 = getRandomCard();

Card2 = getRandomCard();

Card3 = getRandomCard();

Card4 = getRandomCard();

Card5 = getRandomCard();

you would do this:

for (int i = 0; i < 5; i++)

{

> *card[i] = getRandomCard();*

}

That's for five cards—think of that in terms of a deck of 52!

Basic Array Syntax

Declaring an array requires the name, type and size to be specified:

int my_array[6];

This would declare an array that has six elements, all integers. Note that the array size is put inside square brackets and follows the variable name.

To get to those elements, brackets are used again, but, rather than the array size, you provide the element index:

my_array[3];

my_array is the whole array and my_array[0] is the first element, my_array[4] is the fifth element. And no, that wasn't a mistake. Array indexing is zero-based—that means it starts at zero. The first element will always be 0, the second element will always be 1 and so on. So for an array of size five, the indexes are 0, 1, 2, 3 and 4.

Once you have decided which index you want to access, it's much like any variable. The element can be modified like this:

int my_array[4]; //declare the array

my_array[2] = 2; // set the third element of the array to 2

So, what can we use arrays for?

- **Storage of orderings**

Back to the beginning, how do you shuffle a deck of 52 cards? Part of the issue lies in needing a way of representing all those cards. We solved that— an array. The next part is, how do we show the order the cards are in? Good news there too; because an array is numerically accessed, the elements are treated as the natural card order. So, if you were to randomly assign 52 unique values to an array, you could say that index 0, the first one, is the top card and index 51 is the last card.

- **Storage of sorted values**

What if you had 100 values that you wanted to read in? Forgetting about sorting for now; you would represent the order by placing the values into the array, again using the array's natural ordering to your advantage.

- **Using multidimensional arrays to represent grids**

We can also represent multidimensional data using arrays—think of the aforementioned chessboard. All this means is that there is more than one index for a piece of data. For a two-dimensional array, each dimension must be provided in the declaration:

int tic_tac_toe_board[3][3];

This is what the board would look like:

[0][0] [0][1] [0][2]

[1][0] [1][1] [1][2]

[2][0] [2][1] [2][2]

Because two-dimensional arrays are rectangular in shape, you must use two indices to access it: row and column. All you then need are the values for each.

When you have an array shaped like a grid it's much easier to organize the data. Take the tic-tac-toe board from earlier—all you would need to do is set each array element value to match the current position on the board.

Using Arrays With For Loops

Arrays work very well with for loops; you initialize a variable to 0 to access an array and the variable is incremented until it is as large as the array size. That pattern perfectly fits the for loop model.

Take a look at an example program that shows the for loop being used to create a multiplication table and then storing the results within a two-dimensional array:

```cpp
#include <iostream>

using namespace std;

int main ()
{
    int array[ 8 ][ 8 ]; // Declares an array that looks just like a chessboard
    for ( int i = 0; i < 8; i++ )
    {
        for ( int j = 0; j < 8; j++ )
        {
            array[ i ][ j ] = i * j; // Set the element to a value
        }
    }
    cout << "Multiplication table:\n";
    for ( int i = 0; i < 8; i++ )
    {
        for ( int j = 0; j < 8; j++ )
        {
```

```
                    cout << "[ " << i <<" ][ " << j <<" ] = ";

                    cout << array[ i ][ j ] <<" ";

                    cout << "\n";

            }

        }

}
```

Passing Arrays to Functions

It won't take you long to learn that many features of a program will interact with one another. For example, with your newfound knowledge of arrays, you might ask how an array can be passed to a function. In terms of syntax, it's quite simple; when you call a function, just use the array name:

int values[10];

sum_array(values);

When you declare the function, the array name then looks like this:

int sum_array (int values[]);

Hold on. We didn't give an array size. You don't need to for one-dimensional arrays. You only need to provide the size when the array is defined, so that the compiler can create enough space. When an array is passed into a function, only the original array goes in— because we aren't making a new one, we don't need to give the size.

If you make modifications to an array that you have passed into a function, any modifications will stick once the function has returned. We saw earlier that a normal variable gets copied; when a function takes an argument and the variable that holds the argument value is modified, the original value isn't affected.

However, unless the function knows the size of the array, in order to use it, the function will need a second parameter that gives the array size:

```
int sumArray (int values[], int size)

{

        int sum = 0;

        for ( int i = 0; i < size; i++ )

        {

                sum += values[ i ];

        }

        return sum;

}
```

If, on the other hand, a multidimensional array is passed in, you will need to provide all of the sizes, with the exception of the first int check_tic_tac_toe (int board[][3]);

Weird? Yes. But for now, all you have to remember is that the first dimension is included. If you do add it in, don't worry—it will just be ignored.

When we get to the section on pointers, we'll talk more about passing arrays to functions and I will also talk about what's going on under the hood. So don't worry if you don't understand it fully yet; you will later.

Here's a full program that shows the sum_array function in action:

```
#include <iostream>
```

```cpp
using namespace std;

int sumArray (int values[], int size)
{
        int sum = 0;
        // this array stops when i == size because the last element is size -
1
        for ( int i = 0; i < size; i++ )
        {
                sum += values[ i ];
        }
        return sum;
}
int main ()
{
        int values[ 10 ];
        for ( int i = 0; i < 10; i++ )
        {
                cout << "Enter value " << i << ": ";
                cin >> values[ i ];
        }
        cout << sumArray( values, 10 ) << endl;
```

}

Think about how this would be written if you didn't use an array. There wouldn't be a way of storing the values, so you would need to keep a running total; each time an input was entered by the user, you would need to add it immediately. You wouldn't be able to track all the numbers very easily, if you wanted them to later show, for example, which ones were added.

Writing Off the End

Although you're pretty free to do what you want with the array elements, one thing you shouldn't do is write any data past the last array element. For example, if you had an array of 10 elements and you tried to write to index 10:

int my_array[10];

my_array[10] = 4; // tries writing an eleventh element

The array only has 10 elements and the last index is nine. If you tried to use an index of 10, you could find your program crashes; you'll see why when we talk about memory. The commonest scenario for this is when you write a loop over an array:

int vals[10];

for (int i = 0; i <= 10; i++)

{

> *cin >> vals[i];*

}

There are 10 elements in the array, but the loop condition is looking to see if i is equal to or less than 10. It will write the data into vals[10], which it shouldn't do. The compiler won't tell you that this is a problem; instead, you'll only know when your program does strange things or crashes because the changed value is in use by another piece of code.

Sorting Arrays

You have 100 values and want to sort them—how do you do it? To start off, you need a loop that will read in 100 user-input integer values:

```
#include <iostream>

using namespace std;

int main ()
{
        int values[ 100 ];
        for ( int i = 0; i < 100; i++ )
        {
                cout << "Enter value " << i << ": ";
                cin >> values[ i ];
        }
}
```

That's the easiest bit. The data has been read in, so how do we sort it? The natural way is to find the lowest value and move it to the start; then find the next lowest and move it to the second position and so on.

In visual terms, if you were sorting a list of:

3, 1, 2

The 1 would be moved to the start of the list:

1, 3, 2

Then the 2 would be moved to the next spot:

1, 2, 3

Using the C++ features that you've seen already, could you write some code to do that? Don't you think it looks like a loop? You start at the first element, loop over the array and find the smallest element from the remainder of the array to decide which value to use. That value is swapped with the current index element value.

We can start like this, using a top-down approach:

```cpp
void sort (int array[])

{

        for ( int i = 0; i < 100; i++ )

        {

                int index = findSmallestRemainingElement( array, i );

                swap( array, i, index );

        }

}
```

Next, we think about how we can implement the helper methods in this code—swap()— and findSmallestRemainingElement(). Let's start with findSmallestRemainingElement. It needs to iterate over the array starting from index i and find the smallest element. Another loop, right? Each array element is looked at and, if it is smaller than the smallest so far, that index is used as the index for the smallest element.

```
int findSmallestRemainingElement (int array[], int index)

{

        int index_of_smallest_value = index;

        for (int i = index + 1; i < ???; i++)

        {

                if ( array[ i ] < array[ index_of_smallest_value ] )

                {

                        index_of_smallest_value = I;

                }

        }

        return index_of_smallest_value;

}
```

That looks good, doesn't it? Or did you spot a problem? You should have.
Consider: when should the loop stop? The function arguments don't
indicate the size of the array, so we need to add it. We also need to add in
the size of the function call to findSmallestRemainingElement. This
scenario is one where using a top-down approach to coding means going
right back to the start of the code and modifying it. This is common and
you will do it a lot. We also want to fix things so that the code we have for
sorting doesn't contain a value of 100 for the array size hard-coded in:

```
int findSmallestRemainingElement (int array[], int size, int index)

{

        int index_of_smallest_value = index;
```

```
    for (int i = index + 1; i < size; i++)

    {

            if ( array[ i ] < array[ index_of_smallest_value ] )

            {

                    index_of_smallest_value = i;

            }

    }

    return index_of_smallest_value;

}

void sort (int array[], int size)

{

    for ( int i = 0; i < size; i++ )

    {

            int index = findSmallestRemainingElement( array, size, i );

            swap( array, i, index );

    }

}
```

Lastly, the swap function has to be implemented. Because the original array can be modified by a function it's passed to, all we need to do is exchange the values and hold the first overwritten value using a temporary variable:

```cpp
void swap (int array[], int first_index, int second_index)

{

        int temp = array[ first_index ];

        array[ first_index ] = array[ second_index ];

        array[ second_index ] = temp;

}
```

Because the array that was originally passed into the swap function can be directly modified, that's all we have to do.

If you want proof that this really does work, just fill up the array with data that is randomly generated and sort it.

Here's the full program:

```cpp
#include  <cstdlib>

#include  <ctime>

#include  <iostream>

using namespace std;

int findSmallestRemainingElement (int array[], int size, int index);

void swap (int array[], int first_index, int second_index);

void sort (int array[], int size)

{

        for ( int i = 0; i < size; i++ )

        {
```

```
        int index = findSmallestRemainingElement( array, size, i );

        swap( array, i, index );

    }

}

int findSmallestRemainingElement (int array[], int size, int index)

{

    int index_of_smallest_value = index;

    for (int i = index + 1; i < size; i++)

    {

        if ( array[ i ] < array[ index_of_smallest_value ] )

        {

            index_of_smallest_value = i;

        }

    }

    return index_of_smallest_value;

}


void swap (int array[], int first_index, int second_index)

{

    int temp = array[ first_index ];
```

```cpp
        array[ first_index ] = array[ second_index ];

        array[ second_index ] = temp;

}

// just a small helper method that displays the before and after arrays

void displayArray (int array[], int size)

{

        cout << "{";

        for ( int i = 0; i < size; i++ )

        {

                // this pattern is quite common for formatting
                // lists—just check that we are past the first element, and
                // if we are, append a comma
                if ( i != 0 )

                {

                        cout << ", ";

                }

                        cout << array[ i ];

        }

        cout << "}";

}
```

```
int main ()

{

        int array[ 10 ];

        srand( time( NULL ) );

        for ( int i = 0; i < 10; i++ )

        {

                // smaller numbers are far easier to read!

                array[ i ] = rand() % 100;

        }

        cout << "Original array: ";

        displayArray( array, 10 );

        cout << '\n';

        sort( array, 10 );

        cout << "Sorted array: ";

        displayArray( array, 10 );

        cout << '\n';

}
```

That sorting algorithm is called insertion sort, but it isn't the fastest one you can use for number sorting. It does have one distinct advantage though—it's easy to understand and implement. If you had an extremely large dataset to work on, you might consider a faster algorithm, but implementing those isn't so easy. That's just one trade-off you will come across on your programming journey and, most of the time, the case will be that the easiest algorithm is also the best. If you have a website, on the other hand, that sees millions of daily visitors, that easy algorithm won't do the trick. Your job is to make the right decision based on the data amount and how important speed is to a particular project.

As you see, arrays are very powerful. We can now work with a good deal more data and organize it efficiently, but we haven't solved all the problems. What about if we had dozens of different values, all related, in one place? How would we associate them? While arrays are great for organizing distinct data, they can't help us to organize related data. That is something we will cover next, when we discuss structures.

Another problem is in memory—the array will provide as much fixed memory as you need, but that amount is determined right at the start when you define and declare your array. What if you want to work with and store unlimited data? Fixed-size arrays won't work for that either, but again, we will come up with the solution for that shortly. For now, on to the next quiz.

Quiz 8

Which of these is the correct way of declaring an array?

A. int anarray[10];

B. int anarray;

C. anarray{ 10 };

D. array anarray[10];

In an array of 29 elements, what is the index number of the last element?

A. 29

B. 28

C. 0

D. Programmer-defined

Which of the following is a two-dimensional array?

A. array anarray[20][20];

B. int anarray[20][20];

C. int array[20, 20];

D. char array[20];

Which of these is the correct way to access the seventh element of an array called foo with 100 elements?

elements?

A. foo[6];

B. foo[7];

C. foo(7);

D. foo;

Which of these is the correct way of declaring a function that will take a two-dimensional array?

A. int func (int x[][]);

B. int func (int x[10][]);

C. int func (int x[]);

D. int func (int x[][10]);

Structures

Now that you know how to store single values in arrays, you can start thinking about writing code that deals with multiple values. As you start working with more data, you will come across scenarios where lots of pieces of data are associated with one another. For example, you might have screen coordinates, or x and y values, for video game players that you want to store along with their names. At the moment, you would have these three arrays:

int x_coordinates[10];

int y_coordinates[10];

string names[10];

The problem is, you need to remember which array matches another. If you move an element position in one array, the associated element in the other arrays needs to be moved too. And if you have a fourth value to work with, things get even trickier. A further array will be needed and will have to be kept synced to the others.

Surely there is a better way of doing this.

There is, and it's called structures. With a structure, it's possible to store different values inside variables, all stored under one variable name. These are incredibly useful when you need to group several data values together. The syntax for defining a structure is:

struct SpaceShip

{

    int x_coordinate;

int y_coordinate;

string name;

}; // <- Note that semicolon; don't forget to include it

In this example, the structure is named SpaceShip. We have defined our own type and can use it for declaring a variable, like this:

SpaceShip my_ship;

The type has two fields: x_coordinate and y_coordinate. But, hold on a minute, what's a field? Right, what we have done is created a compound type. This is a variable that will store multiple associated values, like first and last names, screen coordinates and so on. You can determine the variable you want by giving the name of the field that you want to access. Think of it as being similar to having two variables, each with a different name, but grouped together with a consistent way of giving them names.

A structure is very much like a form that you fill in. It has fields for each separate piece of data but each data file is related to all the other ones. You declare a structure by defining the form and then declaring a variable of the structure type. This creates a copy of the form that can be filled out and used for storing the data.

Accessing the fields requires the variable name (NOT the structure—each of the variables will have separate values for its own fields) followed by a dot and then the field name:

// declaring the variable

SpaceShip my_ship;

// use it

my_ship.x_coordinate = 40;

my_ship.y_coordinate = 40;

my_ship.name = "USS Enterprise (NCC-1701-D)";

As you see, a structure can have as many fields as you need and they can all be different types.

The following example shows the names of five game players being read in (we haven't included the game) and this is a combination of arrays and structures:

```
#include <iostream>

using namespace std;

struct PlayerInfo

{
        int skill_level;

        string name;

};

using namespace std;

int main ()

{
        //as you can with a  normal variable type, arrays can be made of structures

        PlayerInfo players[ 5 ];

        for ( int i = 0; i < 5; i++ )

        {
```

```
            cout << "Please input the player name: " << i << '\n';

            // first access the array element, using standard

            // array syntax; then access the structure field

            // using the '.' syntax

            cin >> players[ i ].name;

            cout << "Please input the skill level for " <<
        players[ i ].name

<< '\n';

            cin >> players[ i ].skill_level;

        }

    for ( int i = 0; i < 5; ++i )

    {

            cout << players[ i ].name << " is at skill level " << players[ i
].skill_level << '\n';

    }

}
```

The structure named PlayerInfo is declaring two fields—the player name and skill level. Because PlayerInfo can be used just like any variable type, an array of players can easily be created. When an array of structures is created, each element is treated as if it were a single instance of a structure; accessing a field in the first structure would be players [0.] name. This would give the player name from the first element.

What this program is doing is taking full advantage of the useful ability to combine structures and arrays. This lets us read in the information for five separate players, each with two pieces of data in one for loop, and then print the information in another for loop. We don't need to write related arrays for each individual bit of data and you certainly don't need to have separate arrays for player_names and player_skill_level.

Passing Structures

More often than not, you will want a function that will either take a structure as one of its arguments or return a structure as the result. For example, say you have a small game that has spaceships moving around. You can have a function that initializes a structure for a brand-new enemy:

struct EnemySpaceShip

{

> *int x_coordinate;*

> *int y_coordinate;*

> *int weapon_power;*

};

EnemySpaceShip getNewEnemy ();

With this example, when getNewEnemy is called, we should get a value returned that has all the values inside the structure initialized. This is how it could be written:

EnemySpaceShip getNewEnemy ()

{

> *EnemySpaceShip ship;*

```
        ship.x_coordinate = 0;

        ship.y_coordinate = 0;

        ship.weapon_power = 20;

        return ship;

}
```

The function makes a copy of the local variable (called ship) that is returned. What that means is that every single field in the structure is copied into a new variable, one at a time. You might think it would slow things down, having to copy one field at a time, but on most occasions, your computer will be fast enough that you won't notice. Where it will matter is when you're working with many different structures. When we discuss pointers in the next chapter, we'll talk about avoiding extra copies.

Receiving the variable that gets returned involves this kind of code:

```
EnemySpaceShip ship = getNewEnemy();
```

Now the ship variable can be used just like any of the other structure variables.

To pass a structure in, do this:

```
EnemySpaceShip upgradeWeapons (EnemySpaceShip ship)

{

        ship.weapon_power += 10;

        return ship;

}
```

When you pass a structure into a function, it gets copied (the same as happened when a structure was returned), and any modifications to the structure inside the function are lost. This is why we need the function to return a copy of that structure once the structure has been modified—that way, the original hasn't been touched.

So, if we wanted to modify EnemySpaceShip using upgradeWeapons, we would do this:

ship = upgradeWeapons(ship);

When we call the function, the ship variable gets copied into the function's argument. When that function returns, the returned EnemySpaceShip variable gets copied back to the ship variable and that will overwrite the original fields.

This is a simple program showing you how to create one enemy ship and upgrade it:

struct EnemySpaceShip

{

      int x_coordinate;

      int y_coordinate;

      int weapon_power;

};

EnemySpaceShip getNewEnemy ()

{

      EnemySpaceShip ship;

      ship.x_coordinate = 0;

```
        ship.y_coordinate = 0;

        ship.weapon_power = 20;

        return ship;

}

EnemySpaceShip upgradeWeapons (EnemySpaceShip ship)

{

        ship.weapon_power += 10;

        return ship;

}

int main ()

{

        EnemySpaceShip enemy = getNewEnemy();

        enemy = upgradeWeapons( enemy );

}
```

You could be wondering how you can create a supply of enemy ships with no limits and track every one of them through the course of the game. To make the new enemy ship, you will call getNewEnemy; that's simple enough, but what about tracking them all? Storing them? At the moment, all we have is a fixed-size array, and yes, you can create an array that contains objects of the EnemySpaceShip type. Something like

```
EnemySpaceShip my_enemy_ships[ 10 ];
```

All that does is give you 10 enemies, no more. What if that isn't enough? In the next section we will talk about pointers, which will be the start of solving this problem.

Quiz 9

Which of these is used to access a variable in structure b?

A. b->var;

B. b.var;

C. b-var;

D. b>var;

Which of these is a properly defined structure?

A. struct {int a;}

B. struct a_struct {int a};

C. struct a_struct int a;

D. struct a_struct {int a;};

Which is the correct way of declaring a structure variable, type foo, called my_foo?

A. my_foo as struct foo;

B. foo my_foo;

C. my_foo;

D. int my_foo;

What will be the final value this code outputs?

```
#include <iostream>

using namespace std;
```

```cpp
Struct MyStruct
{
int x;
};
void updateStruct (MyStruct my_struct)
{
my_struct.x = 10;
}
int main ()
{
MyStruct my_struct;
my_struct.x = 5;
updateStruct( my_struct );
cout << my_struct.x << '\n';
}
```

A. 5

B. 10

C. This will not compile

D. 20

Introduction to Pointers

Until now, we have been working with fixed memory amounts. This is an amount decided on before the program was started. When a variable is declared, a certain amount of memory is allocated under the hood to hold the stored information in the variable. The amount is chosen at compile time and cannot be changed, nor can you add to it when the program is running.

So far, we have created data arrays to get multiple variables, thus giving us a large amount of memory. But the number of elements in those arrays must be specified when they're created and that limits us once again to the amount of memory. In this section we will discuss how we can access more memory than we started with. Then, continuing with our spaceship program, we'll learn how we can create unlimited enemies.

To gain access to an almost unlimited amount of memory, what we need is a variable type that refers to the memory that stores those variables directly. We call this type of variable a pointer and the name is very apt.

A pointer is a variable that points to specific locations in the memory. It's much like a hyperlink that points to a specific web page which is located on a web server. If you want to send that page to someone, you don't copy the entire page and send it; you send a link. That's precisely what pointers do: they let you send or store links to variables, structures or arrays instead of copying them.

Pointers also store the location or address of other bits of data. Because of this, you can use a pointer to store memory from the operating system. In basic terms, your program is able to request more memory and uses pointers to access it.

You saw an example of a pointer earlier; we passed an array to a function without copying the array. The original was passed in instead and that can only work with pointers.

Before we move on, we need to have a short discussion about memory.

What is Memory?

One of the easiest ways of visualizing the memory your computer system has is to think of a spreadsheet in Excel. A spreadsheet is nothing more than a collection of cells, each of which can store data. That is all computer memory is—multiple sequential cells of data. However, whereas Excel spreadsheet cells can store large amounts of data, computer memory 'cells' can only store one byte of memory each, providing 256 possible values for each byte. And, where Excel stores data in a grid fashion, computer memory stores it linearly. If it helps, think of your computer memory as being one long array of chars.

If you are familiar with Excel, you will know that each spreadsheet cell can be located using the column letter, row number and cell location as its address. That address is the value stored by the pointer when the memory location is held. In Excel, the pointer is a cell that holds another cell's name; for example, cell B2 holds the string A4.

Below you can see a diagram depicting how a small memory chunk might be visualized. It's very much like an array:

0	4	8	12	16	20
??	16	??	??	??	??

Each number represents one location in memory where you can store data. The numbers are representing the memory addresses and these are how locations in memory are identified. We use steps of four because most of the variables that are stored in memory will take four bytes—what you see above is the memory that is associated with six variables, each one four

147

bytes. As an example, the address of four is storing a value of 16, which could well be the address of another location in memory.

The memory at that address of four belongs to one of the pointer variable and the values indicated by ?? are telling you that, at the moment, they don't have a known value. Though they still hold something, until that's initialized, the value isn't very useful because it could be anything.

Variables Vs. Addresses

Is there a distinction between variables and addresses? Variables represent values that are stored at a specific location in the memory, at a specific address. To implement those variables in your program, the compiler will use the memory addresses. The pointer is a special variable type that you can use to store an address that points to another variable.

What's cool is that, as soon as you can use a variable address, you can then go to it and get the data that has been stored within. So, if you have a very large piece of data that you need to be passed into a function, when your program is running it's more efficient to pass the location rather than copying every data element. This same approach can be used when you want to pass a structure into a function. All you do is take the address where the data that goes with the structure variable is stored and pass it to the function—no need to copy all that structure data.

The single most important function of any pointer is to let you obtain more memory from the operating system when you need it. But how do you get it? The operating system itself will tell you what the memory address is and you will then store that address in a pointer. When you need more memory, you ask for it, and change the value being pointed to. As a result, the pointer allows us to forget about the limitations of fixed memory by letting us decide how much we want at run time.

Terms

When we use the word 'pointer,' we are referring to one of two things:

1. A memory address

2. A variable that stores the memory address

Normally, the distinction between the two isn't all that important. If a pointer variable is passed into a function, all you are passing in is the memory address or the value the pointer stores.

For the sake of clarity, from here on, if I'm talking about memory addresses, that's what I will call them (or just "addresses"). But, if I'm talking about variables that store the memory addresses, I'll call them pointers. For example, if we have a variable storing the address of another variable, I will tell you that the first variable is pointing to the other variable.

Memory Layout

So where does the memory come from? Why do we need to ask the operating system for it? Going back to the Excel spreadsheet, what you have is a big group of cells, each of which can be accessed. With computer memory, there's also a lot of memory, but it's far more structured. Some of the memory is already being used by other things.

One bit of the memory used for storing the variables declared in running functions is called the stack. The name is derived from the fact that if multiple function calls are made, each function's local variables stack up, one on top of the other, in that section of memory. So far, every variable we have worked with has been stored on the stack.

Another bit of the memory is called the free store or, more commonly, the heap. This is where unallocated memory is stored, allowing you to request it in chunks. It's managed by the operating system and when a bit of memory has been allocated, it should be used only by the code that originally allocated that memory or by the code to which the memory allocator provides the address.

Having access to this memory is a powerful thing, but that comes with a great deal of responsibility. Memory is not an abundant resource, not as hard to come by as it once used to be, but it isn't unlimited. Every piece of memory that is allocated from the heap eventually has to go back there when it isn't needed by your program anymore. The bit of code that has the responsibility of releasing a specified piece of memory is known as the owner of the memory. When the owner doesn't need the memory any longer, for example when an enemy ship is destroyed in a space game, the piece of code that has ownership of the memory should send it back to the heap so that it can be used by other code. If the memory is not returned, your program will run out of memory and, at best, will slow down. Worst case, your program will crash.

You might have heard people say that a web browser is using far too much memory; you might even have experienced it yourself. The reason it does this is because memory wasn't freed up when it should have been and this causes a memory leak.

The concept behind ownership of memory is not an explicit part of the C++ language; it has more to do with the interface between users and functions. When a function that takes a pointer is written, it's down to you, the programmer, to indicate clearly whether the function will take on ownership of the memory. The language isn't responsible for tracking this and unless you make an explicit request for it to do so, the language won't free up memory that was explicitly allocated by you.

There's a good reason why you can't just grab memory whenever you want it. Only specific code should use specific memory; let's say that you generate a random number and then treat that number as a memory address. Technically this can be done, but it isn't a good idea because there's no way of knowing who was responsible for allocating the memory;

it could have been the stack, for all you know. And if you then modify the memory, that data in use will be ruined. To protect against this, the operating system will protect the memory that isn't already being used. That memory will be classed as invalid and if you try to access it, your program will crash. That's not a bad thing because it allows you to detect the issue.

Wait, did I just say that crashing is a good thing? In some situations, yes, it is. When a crash happens because of invalid memory, it's very easy to diagnose compared to a bug that occurs if bad data is written into valid memory. Usually, you will be able to locate the source of these crashes fairly quickly because the issue occurs immediately. But if you modify valid memory that isn't owned by you, the bug won't happen until code that does have ownership of the memory attempts to use it.

This might happen sometime later on down the line, a long time after the memory has been written. At that point, good luck with trying to find what went wrong! That said, later on we will be discussing using Code::Blocks to debug and part of that will be about debugging crashes that are a result of bad memory.

Invalid Pointers

Valid memory can be used accidentally if you use pointers without initializing them. When a pointer is declared, initially it will have some random data in it. It's pointing to a location in memory that might or might not be valid. Regardless, using it is dangerous and almost like a random number has been generated. If you use that value, one of two things can happen: your data will be corrupted or your program will crash. Always, always remember that a pointer must be initialized before it's used!

Memory and Arrays

Remember what I said earlier about how you shouldn't write past the end of an array? We know more about memory now, so you should be able to see why this would cause a problem. Arrays have set amounts of memory associated to them, based on the array size. If you try to access an element that is beyond the end of that array, you're trying to access memory that doesn't have anything to do with the array. It isn't the array, but what it is, is dependent entirely on the code and the way the compiler has been implemented. That doesn't matter; what does matter is that it is NOT part of the array, and if you try to use it, there will definitely be problems.

Advantages and Disadvantages

You now have a pretty good idea of what pointers are all about. Later, we will look at how to use them. For now, we'll go over the trade-offs that come with using pointers. It will help you to know that hyperlinks and pointers both have the same disadvantages and advantages:

- No need to make copies

Much like a web page, if the data held in memory is too large and complicated, it can be very difficult and slow to copy it properly—more about this later. With pointers, there's no need for that.

- Latest values always available

When a web page is updated, you will always get the up-to-date copy. The same thing goes with the pointers to memory; if the value stored at the memory address is updated, the pointer will always have the correct value.

There is one main disadvantage:

- The memory may have been returned

Sometimes, a web page gets deleted or moved and you can't find it. With pointers, you might find that the memory has already been returned to the operating system but the pointer hasn't been removed. The only way to avoid this is for the code that has ownership of the memory to track whether the memory is in use by anyone else.

I don't want to overload you. So, to keep things simple, just keep in mind that a pointer is a special kind of variable. In the next section, we'll talk about using the variables. For now, move on to the quiz and see how much you've learned about pointers in general.

Quiz 10

Which of these isn't a good reason to use a pointer?

A. You want a function to be able to modify an argument that was passed into it

B. You don't want to copy large variables and you want to save some space

C. You want access to more operating system memory

D. You want quicker access to variables

What is a pointer used for storing?

A. The name of another variable

B. An integer value

C. The address of another variable in memory

D. A memory address, but it may not be another variable

When your program is executing, where should you get more memory from?

A. You can't get anymore

B. The stack

C. The free store

D. Through the declaration of another variable

What could go wrong when you are using pointers?

A. You may access memory that can't be used and this will cause your program to crash

B. You may access the wrong memory address, which will corrupt data

C. You might forget that the memory has to be returned to the OS and the program will run out of memory

D. All of the above

When you declare a normal variable in a function, where does the memory come from?

A. The free store

B. The stack

C. A normal variable doesn't use memory

D. The program's own binary

Once memory has been allocated, what do you do with it?

A. Nothing, you can keep it forever

B. When you've finished with it, you return it to the OS

C. You see the value that is being pointed to as 0

D. The value 0 is stored in the pointer

Getting to Grips with Pointers

You now know what memory is an how you should think about or visualize it. Now it's time to look at writing code that can make use of the memory. We'll start by looking at the syntax required to work with a pointer and then move on to examples that show you how they work using real code. Later, in the next section, we'll look at accessing memory from the heap.

First, let's look at the syntax.

Declaring a Pointer

C++ provides us with specific syntax that we use to declare a variable as a pointer. This will indicate not just that the value is a pointer but also the memory type that is being pointed to.

A pointer declaration will look like this:

<type> *<ptr_name>;

So, for example, you could be declaring a pointer that will store an integer address and the syntax will look this:

int *p_points_to_integer;

Note that we use the * in the syntax. That symbol is the real key to pointer declaration. Place it right before the name of the variable and you are indicating that the variable is, in fact, a pointer. The C++ language doesn't necessarily require the p_ prefix, but it does help clarify that a variable is a pointer. However, if you declare more than one pointer on the same line, each variable name must have the * prefacing it:

// one pointer, a regular int

int *p_pointer1, nonpointer1;

// two pointers

int *p_pointer1, *p_pointer2;

So, why isn't there an easier way to do this? Why can't we just write something like this:

pointer p_pointer

There's a good reason: for the memory address to be used, the compiler has to know the data type stored at the address. If it doesn't, it can't possibly interpret it properly. An example would be that the same bytes in memory mean something different for ints and doubles. Instead of having separate names for pointers to different data types, for example, char_ptr, int_ptr, and so on, we simply use the * symbol together with the name of the type to get the pointer.

Getting the Variable Address

We can make use of a pointer to hold new memory, but first, we'll look at how pointers work with variables that already exist. To retrieve the address of a variable, the ampersand (&) sign must be placed right before the name of the variable. The & symbol is the address-of operator and is used to return the variable's memory address:

int x;

int p_x = & x;

*p_x = 2; // initialize x to 2

Here's an easy trick to help you remember to use the & symbol to get your variable address: both the name of the symbol (ampersand) and address-of start with the letter 'a.' It's as simple as that!

Really, it should make sense that you need to do something different to get the location in memory of a variable because, at the end of the day, mostly all you will want out of a variable is its value.

Using a Pointer

When you use a pointer, you need additional special syntax. Why? Because when it comes to pointers, you need to be able to do two different things:

1. Ask for the memory location being stored by the pointer, and
2. Ask for the value that is stored at the memory location.

When pointers are used like normal variables, the memory location you get is the one that the pointer stores.

In the code snippet below, we're printing the address that (stored in) p_pointer_to_integer points to:

int x = 5;

int *p_pointer_to_integer = & x;

cout << p_pointer_to_integer; // prints the address of x

// the equivalent of cout << & x;

So, we're printing the address of variable x, stored in p_pointer_to_integer.

If you wanted access to the value at that location in memory, you would need to use the * symbol. In the next example, you can see the initialization of a pointer that points to a different variable:

int x = 5;

int *p_pointer_to_integer = & x;

cout << *p_pointer_to_integer; // prints 5

// the equivalent of cout << x;

What the code line *p_pointer_to_integer is saying is that we should follow that pointer and retrieve the value that the pointed-to memory stores. In the case of the above code, because p_pointer_to_integer is pointing to x which has a value of 5, we print 5.

There's an easy way of remembering that the * symbol is used for retrieving the pointed-to value: pointer variables are much like any normal variable; getting the value that the variable holds is all about using the variable name. The value held by the variable is a memory address, and if you want to do anything out of the ordinary, like getting the value the memory address stores, a special syntax is required.

Using the * symbol to get the value at the address that was pointed to is known as "dereferencing the pointer." The name is derived from the fact that, when you get the value, you're following a reference to a memory address.

Dereferencing also allows you to set values into memory addresses:

int x;

*int *p_pointer_to_integer = & x;*

*p_pointer_to_integer = 5; // x is now 5!

cout << x;

It isn't always easy to remember when the * or the & needs to be added, so use the following as a reference:

Action	Punctuation needed	Example
Declaring a pointer	*	int *p_x;
Getting the address of the pointer		

holds	Nothing	cout << p_x;
Setting the address stored in the pointer =	Nothing	int *p_x; p_x = /*address*/;
Getting the value at that address *p_x;	*	cout <<
Setting a new value to that address *	*p_x = 5;	
Declaring a variable	Nothing	int y;
Getting the value stored in a variable << y;	Nothing	int y; cout
Setting the value stored in a variable	Nothing	int y; y = 5
Getting the address of a variable *p_x; p_x = &	&	int y; int y;
Setting the address of		

a variable	N/A cannot change addresses	variables

There are two easy rules that you should learn:

1. Pointers store addresses; when the bare pointer is used, you will get the address back. If you want to retrieve or modify the value that has been stored at the address, something else is needed, like the asterisk symbol.
2. Variables store values. When the variable is used, you will obtain its value. If you want the variable address, you need to use the ampersand.

Take a look at a program that shows you these features and then let's analyze exactly what happens in memory:

```cpp
#include <iostream>

using namespace std;

int main ()

{

        int x;        // A standard integer

        int *p_int;     // A pointer to an integer

        p_int = & x;     // Read it, "assign the address of x to p_int"

        cout << "Please input a number: ";

        cin >> x;      // Place a value in x, we could use *p_int here as
well

        cout << *p_int << '\n'; // Note that we use the * to retrieve the
value
```

```
*p_int = 10;

cout << x;  // 10 is output again!
```

}

So, the first cout will output the value that is in x. Why? To answer that, we'll look at how the program works and the effect it has on memory.

We begin with an integer named x and a pointer that goes to an integer called p_int.

In terms of visualizing it, we have a pair of variables, most likely side by side, with values that we don't yet know:

??   ??

x   p_int

Next, the memory location for x is stored in pointer p_int. This is done by using the & operator to retrieve the variable address:

```
p_int = & x;       // Read it, "assign the address of x to p_int"
```

Now, visually, you could draw a line between the p_int variable and the x variable; this would indicate that p_int is pointing to x.

??

x   p_int

Next, the user would input a number which would then be stored in the x variable—the same location that p_int points to:

```
cin >> x;       // Place a value in x, we can also use *p_int here
```

So, imagine that the user has input a five. Visually, you would have this:

5

x   p_int

The next code line would then be *p_int to cout. *p_int is dereferencing p_int; it will look at p_int to see the stored address, will go to that address and will return the value from it.

*cout << *p_int << '\n'; // Note that we use the * to get the value*

The last couple of code lines demonstrate that, when you modify a pointer, the original variable is also modified.

The code line below is storing a value of 10 in the memory that p_int points to; this is also the memory where the x value is stored:

*p_int = 10;

The memory state will now be:

10

x   p_int

You now know what happens when working with pointers. If you ever get confused, map the initial memory state out and then walk through the code, one line at a time, to see how the memory state changes.

When a pointer changes the location it points to, a new line can be drawn. When a variable modifies its value, the value must be updated. If you do this visually, you will be able to see exactly what happens, even in the most complex of programs and systems.

Uninitialized Pointers and NULL

In the example above, we initialized p_int so it pointed to a certain memory address before it could be used. If we didn't do this, it could point anywhere, and this would result in negative consequences such as overwriting the memory another variable holds, or a program crashing. To avoid this, and any other unpleasant behavior, pointers must always be initialized before they are used.

However, there will be times when you need to say that the pointer has explicitly not been initialized. Luckily, C++ has a value for that, and you can use it to mark that pointer as explicitly uninitialized. That value is NULL; if your pointer points to NULL, it has not been initialized. When you create new pointers, set them to NULL first; you can look later to see if they have been set to something that can be used or not. Otherwise, you don't have any way of testing a pointer to see if it is usable without your program crashing:

int p_int = NULL;

// code that may set p_int, it may not

if (p_int != NULL)

{

> **p_int = 2;*

}

Visually, if you added NULL pointers to your memory diagram, all you do is write the word NULL; no need for any lines to be drawn pointing to it:

NULL

p_int

Pointers And Functions

Pointers let you pass local variable addresses into functions and these can them modify that local variable. The easiest way to illustrate this is with a pair of functions that try to swap the values that two variables store:

#include <iostream>

```cpp
using namespace std;
void swap1 (int left, int right)
{
        int temp;
        temp = left;
        left = right;
        right = temp;
}
void swap2 (int *p_left, int *p_right)
{
        int temp = *p_left;
        *p_left = *p_right;
        *p_right = temp;
}
int main ()
{
        int x = 1, y = 2;
        swap1( x, y );
        cout << x << " " << y << '\n';
        swap2( & x, & y );
```

```
        cout << x << " " << y << '\n';

}
```

Take a good look at the above code. Which function do you think will swap the two variables correctly?

This isn't the main value that pointers bring; there is another feature in C++ that makes writing swap functions simple, without having to use the full power of pointers. That feature is called references.

References

Occasionally, you will want to use some pointer features, for example, not wanting to make extra copies of large data chunks. But, at the same time, you don't want all the power offered by pointers. For this, you can use a reference.

References are variables that are used to refer to other variables both sharing the same piece of backing memory. Think of a reference as being a pointer that has been stripped down without the need to use the * symbol and the & symbol for the value being referred to or when the reference is assigned. Unlike the pointer, references always have to point to memory that is valid and we use the & syntax to declare them:

int &ref;

However, that is an illegal declaration. Why? Because a reference must always be initialized. i.e., it always has to refer to an address that is valid:

int x = 5;

int &ref = x; // note that the ampersand (&) is not needed before x!

A reference can be visualized in much the same way that a pointer is visualized, with one difference: when references are used, the referenced memory value is returned and not the address that goes with that memory:

int x = 5;

int &ref = x;

Here, the actual reference variable memory is holding a pointer to the x variable memory. When a plain reference is written, the compiler will know that you want the value that is being pointed to. You can think of the reference as a pointer that has the opposite behavior of what happens when a variable name is written.

We can also use the reference to pass a structure into a function without needing to pass the entire structure or concern ourselves with NULL pointers:

struct myBigStruct

{

      int x[100]; // big struct with a lot of memory!

};

void takeStruct (myBigStruct& my_struct)

{

      my_struct.x[0] = "foo";

}

Because a reference is always referring to the original object, you get away with not having to copy and the original object passed in can be modified. In the above example, you can see how my_struct.x[0] was set so that the original structure that gets passed in and has 'foo' in it when the function is returned.

Now that we've discussed how to write swap functions using pointers, let's see just how much easier it gets using a reference:

void swap (int& left, int& right)

{

      int temp = right;

      right = left;

      left = temp;

}

This is a much simpler way of doing it. References are really nothing more than stand-ins for the original variables. When the compiler implements a reference, it's to use pointers for storing references—all the dereferencing is done for you.

References vs. Pointers

A reference can be used instead of a pointer when a variable needs to be referred to by several names. For example, when you want arguments passed to a function without having to copy them or need a function's parameters modified in a way that the caller can see.

References are not as flexible as pointers, simply because they always have to be valid. You can't indicate a NULL or use references to say that you don't have something valid. References were not designed for this and because they can't represent NULL, there's no way to use references for building complex data structures. We'll talk more about data structures in the coming sections. When we do, for each example, ask yourself if the same thing could be done using references.

One more difference between references and pointers is that, as soon as you initialize a reference, the memory it's referring to can't be changed. References will always refer to the same variable, all the time, and this makes them somewhat inflexible when it comes to complex data structures.

Throughout the rest of this guide, references will be used only where it is appropriate to do so, and that will usually be when a structure or class instance is passed as a function argument. The pattern for that will almost always be something like this:

void (myStructType& arg);

For now, take a break, take the quiz, and then we'll move on and discuss dynamic memory allocation.

Quiz 11

Which of these is the correct declaration of a pointer?

A. int x;

B. int &x;

C. ptr x;

D. int *x;

Which of these will give the memory address of integer variable a?

A. *a;

B. a;

C. &a;

D. address(a);

Which of the following gives the memory address of a variable pointed to by pointer p_a?

A. p_a;

B. *p_a;

C. &p_a;

D. address(p_a);

Which of these will give the value stored at the address pointed to by the pointer p_a?

A. p_a;

B. val(p_a);

C. *p_a;

D. &p_a;

Which of these is the correct way of declaring a reference?

A. int *p_int;

B. int &my_ref;

C. int &my_ref = & my_orig_val;

D. int &my_ref = my_orig_val;

Which of these is not a great time for using a reference?

A. For storing addresses that have been allocated dynamically from the free store or heap

B. So you don't need to copy a large variable when you pass it to a function

C. So you can force parameters passed to a function never to be NULL

D. So that a function can access the original variable that was passed to it without needing to use pointers.

Dynamic Memory Allocation

If you came through the last sections unscathed and you understand it all, well done. If not, please go back and review what you don't understand before you move on to this next section.

Now we will get to the really good bit about pointers: using them as a way of resolving real-world problems. We'll learn how we can access an almost unlimited amount of memory while our programs run by using dynamic memory allocation.

What this means is that we can request what we want, however much or little it is, while our programs run. The program itself will work out how much it needs rather than having to work with a fixed number of variable of a specified size. In this section we'll discuss allocating memory. In future sections, we'll cover taking full advantage of dynamic allocation.

First, we need to know how to get more memory. We use a keyword, new, for initializing pointers with memory from the heap. Remember: the heap is a store of unused memory that we can ask to access. The basic syntax for this is:

int *p_int = new int;

What the "new" operator has done is take an example variable; from this, it works out the size for the requested memory. In our case, it has taken an integer and returned sufficient memory to hold a value of integer type.

We set p_int to point to the memory and both p_int and the code associated with it will take ownership of the memory. At some point, p_int needs to return the memory to the heap in a process known as "freeing then memory." Until it has been freed, the memory is marked as being in use and will not be allocated anywhere else. If you continue to allocate the memory and don't free it, eventually the memory will run out.

Returning memory to the heap is as simple as using the delete keyword. This frees up any memory that was allocated using the new keyword. This is how p_int would be freed:

delete p_int;

After a pointer has been deleted, you should set it so points to NULL:

delete p_int;

p_int = NULL;

This isn't strictly necessary, but once you delete a pointer, the memory it was pointing to can no longer be read or written to because it has been returned. Therefore, if you set the pointer to point to NULL, your program will crash immediately if the code attempts to dereference the pointer. This is a lot better than not discovering the problem until later on.

References And Dynamic Allocation

As a rule, you shouldn't store the memory that was allocated in a reference:

*int &val = *(new int);*

Why? Because references don't give you immediate access to raw memory addresses. You get them by using the & syntax, but references should really provide an extra variable name rather than storage of dynamically allocated memory.

Pointers and Arrays

Right, so how do we use "new" to obtain more memory if all we can do is initialize a pointer with it? Well, since a pointer can also point at a sequence of values, that means we can't create it in a similar fashion to an array. After all, an array is a series of sequential values stored in memory. Because memory addresses are stored by pointers, the address for the first element in an array can also be stored. Accessing each element is accomplished by taking a value that is a set distance from the beginning of the array.

This is useful because it means you dynamically create arrays from the heap, this allowing you to work out how much memory you will need at runtime.

Arrays can be assigned to pointers without needing to use the address-of operator:

int numbers[8];

int* p_numbers = numbers;

Now p_numbers can be used as if it were an array:

for (int i = 0; i < 8; ++i)

{

      p_numbers[i] = i;

}

When you assign the numbers array to a pointer, it will act like a pointer. An array is NOT a pointer, but it can be assigned to one. The compiler knows how to convert arrays to pointers that will point to the array's first element. And we can dynamically allocate an array of memory, using "new," and then assign a pointer with the memory:

int *p_numbers = new int[8];

The array syntax is used as the argument and lets the compiler know how much memory is required; here, we want enough for an integer array or eight elements. Now, p_numbers can be used just as though it were pointing to an array. However, unlike the array, the memory that p_numbers points to must be freed, whereas you don't want to free up pointers that point to arrays that are statically declared. Freeing memory requires a special syntax using the delete operator:

delete[] p_numbers;

The square brackets let the compiler know that the pointer is pointing to an array of values and not just one value.

The following example shows how to dynamically determine the amount of memory you need:

int count_of_numbers;

cin >> count_of_numbers;

int *p_numbers = new int[count_of_numbers];

This code asks a user how many numbers are needed and then uses the resulting variable to work out what size the dynamically allocated array is. We don't need to know this number beforehand; the memory can be reallocated each time the number grows.

Let's analyze a program showing this in action. The program will read in user-input numbers and, if too many numbers are input, the array will need to be resized:

#include <iostream>

using namespace std;

int *growArray (int* p_values, int cur_size);

int main ()

{

       int next_element = 0;

```
int size = 10;

int *p_values = new int[ size ];

int val;

cout << "Please input a number: ";

cin >> val;

while ( val > 0 )

{

        if ( size == next_element + 1 )

        {

                // now we implement growArray

                p_values = growArray( p_values, size );

        }

        p_values[ next_element ] = val;

        cout << "Please input a number (or 0 to exit): ";

        cin >> val;

    }

}
```

Let's consider how we can grow the array. We can't extend what memory we already have, so we need to ask for more and copy the old values over.

How much do we need? It would be terribly inefficient if we extended the array one integer at a time! There would be a lot of unnecessary reallocations and, while you wouldn't run out of memory, it would make things slow. The best method is to take the current array size and double it. That way, we won't waste much space if no new values get read in, and we won't be reallocating memory all the time. So, we need the current array size and the original array to copy from:

```
int *growArray (int* p_values, int cur_size)

{

        int *p_new_values = new int[ cur_size * 2 ];

        for ( int i = 0; i < cur_size; ++i )

        {

                p_new_values[ i ] = p_values[ i ];

        }

        delete p_values;

        return p_new_values;

}
```

Note that the p_ value is deleted once the data is copied from the array; if not, the memory would be leaked because we have overwritten the pointer that stores the array when it is returned from growArray.

Multidimensional Arrays

It can be useful to be able resize a large array, but what if you have more than one that you need to work with? We mentioned multidimensional arrays earlier, but wouldn't it be great if we could choose what size we want them to be? We can! This is a great exercise to help you gain a much better understanding of pointers. However, this does require more background knowledge, so over the next couple of sections we'll go over that background and then show you how multidimensional data structures can be dynamically allocated.

Pointer Arithmetic

Take a deep breath. We're going to dive deeper into the pointer. While the content in this section may challenge you initially, everything will eventually start to make sense; don't worry if you don't grasp this the first time around—just go back over it. Take your time; if you can understand all of this, the rest of the guide will be a whole lot easier!

Let's start with memory addresses. A pointer represents a memory address, which is nothing more than a number. So, that means we can do arithmetic operations: we can add a pointer and a number or subtract a pointer from a pointer. Why? Sometimes you will write a block of memory and know exactly which index you want a value placed at. You've come across this already in arrays.

So, when you write:

int x[10];

x[3] = 120;

you are actually doing pointer arithmetic so the third memory slot is set to 120. The bracket operator does nothing more than make it look simpler, and you could do the exact same thing, like this:

*(x + 3) = 120;

What's going on here? Not what you might think. Three is NOT being added to the x value; 3 * sizeof(int) is being added instead. sizeof is one of the special keywords in C++. This one provides the byte size of a variable of the byte type. You will need to do this quite a bit when you work with memory. Pointer arithmetic doesn't treat a pointer like a number; it adds memory "slots." This is the same as the manner in which array brackets let you access a specific array element. By adding increments of the size of the variable, you can't accidentally use the arithmetic to read or write between a pair of values. Most of the time, you will just use the array syntax instead of trying to get the arithmetic correct.

When you do pointer arithmetic, it isn't always easy to keep the math straight, and it's very easy to forget that memory slots aren't being added rather than single bytes. However, having a grasp of this arithmetic will stand you in good stead for more complex concepts, such as those we'll review later, and it will give you a good understanding of how multidimensional arrays are dynamically allocated.

Two-Dimensional Arrays

Before we move on to talk about dynamic allocation of multidimensional arrays, you need to understand what a multidimensional array really means. Again, pay close attention here, because it will pay off in the long run.

We'll start with something odd. When a function is declared that will take a two-dimensional array as an argument, the size of the second part of the array MUST be provided.

You can do it like the example below demonstrates, providing both array sizes:

int sumTwoDArray(int array[4][4]);

Or you can also do it this way, with just one size:

int sumTwoDArray(int array[][4]);

But you can't leave both sizes out:

int sumTwoDArray(int array[][]);

And you can't provide only the first size:

int sumTwoDArray(int array[4][]);

We only need specific sizes to do pointer arithmetic. A two-dimensional array is laid flat in memory; the compiler allows the programmer to treat it like it's a square memory block though, really, it's nothing more than a linear address collection. The compiler does this by taking an array access, such as array[3][2], and turning it into a position in memory.

Consider this visualization of an array:

□□□□

□□□□

□□□□

□□□□

But, in memory, it's laid out like this:

□□□□□□□□□□□□□□□□

To use array [3][2], the compiler will need access to memory that is three rows down and two columns across. Because each row is the width of four integers, going three rows down means going 4 * 3 slots and then adding two more slots. So, to put it simply, the arrays of [3][2] will be transformed into the following pointer arithmetic:

**(array + 3 * <width of array> + 2)*

The array width is needed because the math doesn't work without it. And that width is the second dimension of any two-dimensional array. The same can't be done with the height because of the way the data is physically laid out in memory. Because of all this, an array can be passed as a function argument having a variable length for the height— but with the second dimension ALWAYS fully specified. For any multidimensional array, the sizes must be specified for all dimensions, with the exception of the height. If it helps, consider a one-dimensional array to be a special array with just a height.

When you declare a two-dimensional array, because you need a hard-coded width, you need another feature of C++ for dynamic allocation. That feature is called pointers-to-pointers.

Pointers-to-Pointers

A pointer can also point to another pointer, not just to normal data. After all, like any variable, a pointer contains an address that can be accessed. Declaring a pointer to a pointer is done like this:

int **p_p_x;

So, p_p_x is pointing to an address in memory where there is a pointer to an integer. We used the p_p prefix just to indicate that this is a pointer to a pointer. That means you need to give it the memory address of a pointer:

int *p_y;

int **p_p_x;

p_p_x = & p_y;

Then we use p_p_x to assign p_y with a pointer:

*p_p_x = new int;

Pointers-to-pointers can be used for making two-dimensional arrays in much the same manner that a single pointer can be used for making arbitrary one-dimensional arrays.

The best way to think about it is this: you have a one-dimensional pointer array; each pointer in the array points to another one-dimensional array. The first one is pointing to a collection of pointers and each of those points to a row on our tic-tac-toe board from earlier. To allocate a data structure like this, we need to do the following:

int **p_p_tictactoe;

// note that we use int*, because this is an array of pointers being allocated

p_p_tictactoe = new int*[3];

// each pointer needs to store the address of an array of integers

for (int i = 0; i < 3; i++)

{

    p_p_tictactoe[i] = new int[3];

}

Now the allocated memory may be used like a two-dimensional array. For example, the entire tic-tac-toe board can be initialized using two for loops:

for (int i = 0; i < 3; i++)

{

    for (int j = 0; j < 3; j++)

    {

        p_p_tictactoe[i][j] = 0;

    }

}

Freeing the memory requires us to go in the opposite direction in which the array was initialized. Each row is freed first and the pointer holding the row is also freed.

```
for ( int i = 0; i < 3; i++ )

{

        delete [] p_p_tictactoe[ i ];

}

delete [] p_p_tictactoe;
```

Typically, this is not the approach you would use when the memory size required is already known. In this case, for example, creating the tic-tac-toe board, you would simply do this:

```
int tic_tac_toe_board[ 3][ 3 ];
```

If, on the other hand, you wanted to create a larger game board, you would need to use the more complex approach.

Two-Dimensional Arrays and Pointers-to-Pointers

Note that when a pointer-to-pointer is used for holding a two-dimensional array, it isn't laid out in memory in the same way that a two-dimensional array is. The latter is contiguous memory, whereas the pointer-to-pointer approach isn't. Each row is one set of data and may be stored on memory that is some way off from all the other memory, not sequential.

There is a consequence to this for functions that take arguments of arrays. You already know that an array can be assigned to a pointer:

int x[8];

int *y = x;

What you can't do is assign a pointer-to-pointer with a two-dimensional array, like this:

int x[8][8];

int **y = x; // this won't compile

With the first case, we can treat the array as a pointer to a memory block containing all of the data. However, in the second case, the array is nothing more than a pointer to a memory block.

Perhaps the most important consequence of the layout difference is that a pointer-to-pointer can't be passed into a function that is expecting a multidimensional array:

```
int sum_matrix (int values[][ 4 ], int num_rows)
{
        int running_total = 0;
        for ( int i = 0; i < num_vals; i++ )
        {
                for ( int j = 0; j < 4; j++ )
                {
                        running_total += values[ i ][ j ];
                }
        }
        return running_total;
```

}

If a pointer-to-pointer were allocated and passed to the function below, the compiler would not be happy:

*int **x;*

// allocate x so it has 10 rows

sum_matrix(x, 10); // this will not compile

With the one-dimensional array, both of the operations will go to a specified index that comes from the pointer address. In the two-dimensional array, when you use the pointer-to-pointer approach, you need two pointer dereferences; one to locate the correct row and the other to get the right value out of it. For the array, the pointer arithmetic is used for getting the right value. Because the pointer math isn't done by the pointer-to-pointer, the compiler won't allow a pointer-to-pointer to be passed in a two-dimensional array, even if the code is written to look the same.

Taking Stock

You might feel like pointers are incredibly confusing, but they are relatively easy to understand. Don't worry if you haven't got it all; just go back through these sections as often as you need to. Take the quiz, assess any mistakes you make, and review the material again. The most important thing to understand is the syntax needed for working with pointers and initializing them, as well as the way memory is allocated.

In the next section, we will look at data structures and linked lists.

Quiz 12

Which of these is the right keyword to use for allocating memory in C++?

A. new

B. malloc

C. create

D. value

Which of these is the right keyword to use for deallocating memory in C++?

A. free

B. delete

C. clear

D. remove

Which of these is a true statement?

A. Pointers and arrays are the same

B. You can't assign an array to a pointer

C. You can treat pointers like arrays, but they are not arrays

D. Pointers can be used like arrays but cannot be allocated like arrays

What will the final values in x, p_int and p_p_int be in this code?:

```
int x = 0;

int *p_int = & x;

int **p_p_int = & p_int;

*p_int = 12;

**p_p_int = 25;

p_int = 12;

*p_p_int = 3;

p_p_int = 27;
```

A. x = 0, p_p_int = 27, p_int = 12

B. x = 25, p_p_int = 27, p_int = 12

C. x = 25, p_p_int = 27, p_int = 3

D. x = 3, p_p_int = 27, p_int = 12

How do you indicate that a pointer doesn't have a valid value that it points to?

A. Set it as a negative number

B. Set it as NULL

C. Free the memory that is associated with the pointer

D. Set the pointer as false

Introduction to Data Structures and Linked Lists

You should now know how to dynamically allocate an array using the ability to allocate that all-important memory. Now we are going to look at more ways we can use dynamic memory allocation. The one good thing about having so much memory is that it gives you many more places to store your data. But that leads to another question: how do we store the data quickly and in a way that makes it easy to access as needed? That's what we're going to discuss here.

First, a data structure is a method of organization for data stored in memory. An array, for example, is a data structure. It's a simple one, storing data linearly, and every item in that array is an item in a data structure. Two-dimensional arrays that are implemented with pointers-to-pointers are also data structures, albeit more complex.

The problem with arrays is that you can't add one that has no slots empty. As you saw earlier, you have to start over; a new array has to be created and then the items in the existing array must be copied over to it. This is what is known as an 'expensive' operation and that means, as far as your computer processor is concerned, it takes too long. These kinds of operation might be nothing as far as users are concerned, especially if you don't do many of them; after all, most computer processors are fast these days. But, in some cases, expensive operations are a problem.

The second problem is that you can't insert data easily between the existing elements. Let's say that you want to add a new element in between element one and element two. You have 1000 items in your array and that means you have to move every element from two right up to 1000. That is mega-expensive. The data structure is all about efficient data storage, keeping things moving at a decent pace and not holding up your users.

Another reason for making use of different structures is that they let you start thinking about your programming at higher levels. Instead of loops, you'll start thinking about lists. The data structure gives you a logical and efficient way of storing data along with a shorthand communication method. For example, if you want a list, you need to be clear that you have data that you want to be stored in a way where it can be efficiently added and removed. As you begin to understand data structures, you will start seeing your programs in terms of data and how it needs to be organized.

Now let's turn to linked lists.

Remember that, with an array, you need to copy existing elements into a new array. How helpful would it be if you had a data structure where each data item told you where the next one was? That way, it would be easy to add elements at the end just by making the last one point to the new one. It would also be easier to insert an element between two others by changing the location one element pointed to.

Let's use our space game example. You might want to have a list of all the space enemies. In that list, every element is its own structure that stores all the information about each enemy. You also want to be able to add and remove the information quickly. And what if each of those enemies also contained information about the next one?

We can see this in visual terms, each of the elements having x and y coordinates and a weapon that has a specific power:

x_coordinate

y_coordinate   y_coordinate

weapon_power   weapon_power

p_next_enemy

We have a structure called EnemySpaceShip that is linked to the next structure using a pointer. So each of the ships contains a pointer to the next one:

struct EnemySpaceShip

{

     int x_coordinate;

     int y_coordinate;

     int weapon_power;

     EnemySpaceShip* p_next_enemy;

};

And yes, before you ask, it's perfectly okay to use EnemySpaceShip in the EnemySpaceShip structure definition; C++ is more than capable of handling it.

What would be a problem is if you did this in the structure:

EnemySpaceShip next_enemy;

What that gives us is a structure that will repeat itself ad infinitum. Declaring just one ship will take all the system memory. But, did you notice that we're using a pointer to EnemySpaceShip and not an actual EnemySpaceShip? Pointers are not required to point only to valid memory. Because of that, we don't need a never-ending list of spaceships. All we need is one ship that might or might not point to another one. If it does, you need more memory. But, until that happens, the only memory in use is whatever the pointer takes up. All a pointer is doing is suggesting that more valid memory may be pointed to and all it needs is enough memory to store the address.

When an EnemySpaceShip is declared, you need sufficient space to hold four things: x_coordinate, y_coordinate and weapon_power, along with one last pointer.

Let's look more closely at using pointers with structures.

Pointers and Structures

Accessing the structure fields using a pointer is done using the -> operator rather than the dot (.) operator:

p_my_struct->my_field;

Each structure field has its own memory address and this is normally no more than a few bytes off from the beginning of the structure. The arrow syntax (->) works out the exact index needed to access the specified field. All the other pointer properties are still applicable and the arrow syntax is the same as writing this:

*(*p_my_struct).my_field;*

If a pointer to a structure is passed to a function as an argument, the function can make modifications to the memory at the address that goes with the structure and that means it can modify the actual structure. It works the same as an array is passed to the structure.

We can see an example of this in our EnemySpaceShip structure:

// we require this header for NULL; normally it would be included by

// other header files, but we don't need to use any other headers this time

// #include <cstddef>

struct EnemySpaceShip

{

```
        int x_coordinate;

        int y_coordinate;

        int weapon_power;

        EnemySpaceShip* p_next_enemy;
};
EnemySpaceShip* getNewEnemy ()
{
        EnemySpaceShip* p_ship = new EnemySpaceShip;

        p_ship->x_coordinate = 0;

        p_ship->y_coordinate = 0;

        p_ship->weapon_power = 20;

        p_ship->p_next_enemy = NULL;

        return p_ship;
}
void upgradeWeapons (EnemySpaceShip* p_ship)
{
        p_ship->weapon_power += 10;
}
int main ()
{
```

EnemySpaceShip* p_enemy = getNewEnemy();

upgradeWeapons(p_enemy);

}

We have used new in getNewEnemy to allocate memory for another ship. And, in upgradeWeapon, we can directly modify p_ship because it is pointing to a memory block that contains all the structure fields.

Creating Linked Lists

Now that we know what syntax to use to work with pointers to structures, we can move on to creating lists. Whenever you use a structure that has a pointer to the following element to create your list, it is known as a linked list.

Identifying the list means we have a way of holding the beginning of the list; using our previous example, we can add a method to hold spaceships:

struct EnemySpaceShip

{

    int x_coordinate;

    int y_coordinate;

    int weapon_power;

    EnemySpaceShip* p_next_enemy;

};

EnemySpaceShip* p_enemies = NULL;

We have a variable called p_enemies where the list of enemies will be stored. Whenever a new enemy is added to the game, we will put it in this list. More importantly, it will be added to the front of the list, like this:

```
EnemySpaceShip* getNewEnemy ()

{

        EnemySpaceShip* p_ship = new EnemySpaceShip;

        p_ship->x_coordinate = 0;

        p_ship->y_coordinate = 0;

        p_ship->weapon_power = 20;

        p_ship->p_next_enemy = p_enemies;

        p_enemies = p_ship;

        return p_ship;

}
```

At the start, p_enemies is NULL (its empty). When a new enemy is created, it is updated so it points to the last first element of the list, which is stored in p_enemies, and then p_enemies is set to point to the new enemy. Basically, every new element is added at the beginning of the list by pushing all the others down. No copying is needed; all we do is modify a pair of pointers.

Are you confused? We'll walk through it twice:

First Time

p_enemies begins as Null: we have no enemies. (NULL will always be used as an indicator for the end of a list)

1. We allocate a new ship called p_ship, giving us an enemy named SHIP 1. This is not in our linked list yet and is pointing to unknown memory.
2. The p_next_enemy field in SHIP 1 is set so it is pointing to the current enemy list (NULL, at the moment).
3. Next, we update p_enemies so it points to the new ship.
4. The function will return p_ship to the caller and p_enemies gives us access to the whole list, which has just one element right now.

Second Time

When we go through it again, we start with p_enemies pointing to the new ship:

1. The new ship, called p_ship, gets allocated, giving us two enemies. The second also has a field of p_next_enemy, which is also pointing to unknown memory
2. p_next_enemy then gets set so it is pointing to the current enemy list; this is the enemy that was created on our first walk-through.
3. p_enemies is updated so it points to the new ship (the second ship we created, which points to our first ship).
4. The function will return p_ship back to the caller and p_enemies will allow us access to the whole list.

Really, all we're doing is pushing the elements one step down the list whenever a new one is inserted. There isn't any need to copy the list as you would with arrays; all you do is update the relevant pointer so it points to the new first element. You will normally have one pointer that always points to the first element, known as the "head" (p_enemies, in our case). When the function ends, p_enemies and p_ship are both pointing to the same place; before we got to that stage, the p_ship pointer needed to hold the new memory so that p_next_enemy could be modified to point to the last head of the list, in p_enemies.

We've used a global variable in the function but you could write it so it takes the head; that way it will work on any list and not just one global list. This could look like this:

EnemySpaceShip* addNewEnemyToList (EnemySpaceShip* p_list)

{

      EnemySpaceShip* p_ship = new EnemySpaceShip;

      p_ship->x_coordinate = 0;

      p_ship->y_coordinate = 0;

      p_ship->weapon_power = 20;

      p_ship->p_next_enemy = p_list;

      return p_ship;

}

Note that this is different from the getNewEnemy function because a pointer is returned to the list and not the new enemy. Because the function is unable to modify an associated global variable, and it also can't modify the pointer that is passed into it, we need to give it a way of letting the caller have the new beginning of the list. Then, the caller can write:

p_list = EnemySpaceShip* addNewEnemyToList(p_list);

when it needs to add a new item.

The interface we have here for addNewEnemyToList allows the caller to choose which base list to use and where the returned list should be stored. To imitate what we had before, when we had the global variable called p_enemies, we would write this:

p_enemies = EnemySpaceShip* addNewEnemyToList(p_enemies);

Traversing Linked Lists

Ok, we're getting there; we now know how stuff gets stored in lists. But how do we use that list to do something? We know how to get access to all the elements in an array by iterating over it with a for loop, and we can do the same thing with a linked list, using a technique called traversal.

Getting to the next element in the list requires nothing more than having the current item and writing a loop that has a pointer to the current element, performs some operation on the element and then updates it so it is pointing to the next element.

We can see how that might work in an example where we upgrade every enemy weapon:

```
EnemySpaceShip *p_current = p_enemies;

while ( p_current != NULL )

{

        upgradeWeapons( p_current );

        p_current = p_current->p_next_enemy;

}
```

Well, that was a bit short! And that's all it takes. The variable called p_current is tracking the current item and begins by pointing to the first element of the list, whatever p_enemies is pointing to. p_current isn't a NULL, but we still upgrade the current enemy weapons and then update p_current so it becomes the next in the list.

All p_current does is change what it is pointing to. Then p_enemies, along with everything else, carries on pointing to the same place. That's how powerful pointers are. You can move through data structures just by changing where the pointer points and without having to make copies. You only need one copy of each of the ships at any time. This way, you can upgrade the weapon code so the original ship can be modified, rather than a copy of it.

Taking Stock

Linked lists let you add new memory easily to your data structures without needing to copy memory and shuffle your arrays around. You can also do other operations, like adding elements anywhere in the list, or even removing them. In order to properly implement any linked list, you need to be able to do all of this.

But linked lists have a bit of a secret: the chances of you ever having to implement one yourself are very small. Instead, you can make use of the STL, or Standard Template Library, which we'll be covering very soon. However, the importance of learning linked lists is that you will make use of similar techniques to come up with some pretty interesting structures. What you learned here is not a waste. Even if you never have to write your own list, having an understanding of how you implement them allows you to understand the trade-offs of using arrays or linked lists.

Arrays vs. Linked Lists

Linked lists have one main advantage over arrays: they can be added to or have their size changed easily without having to move every element. Adding a new node, for example, is very easy.

What about keeping your list organized while adding new elements? Let's say you have a list of numbers—1, 3, 5, 9, 11, 13—and want to add another one—6. It should go in between 5 and 9 and you'll need to resize the array so there's room for the new element. Then, every element after 9, right up to the end of the list, will need to be moved. While in a small list, that isn't an issue, you could have a list of thousands of elements. How time-consuming would that be? With linked lists, all you do is modify the element o 5 so it is pointing at the new element and the new element is modified so it points to 9. That's it! It doesn't matter how large the list is; the operation will always take the same amount of time.

The main advantage of using an array is that you can choose an element quickly, simply by giving the element index. With the linked list, you need to look at every element until you come to the right one. To gain the advantage of using the array, the index should be related to the value that is stored in the item collection. Otherwise you will need to go through the entire collection anyway.

For example, an array can be used to create a tally for votes; the voters will use the numbers from 0 to 9 to vote for a specific candidate and the array index will then correspond to a candidate. The value of the array at that point will be the number of votes a candidate earns. In terms of inherent relationships, there isn't one between the candidate and the number, but, by assigning a number to each candidate, you can easily make one. Then that number will be used to retrieve information about a specific candidate.

The following implementation uses an array to demonstrate this:

#include <iostream>

using namespace std;

int main ()

{

     int votes[10];

     // ensure the election hasn't been rigged (by clearing out the array)

     for (int i = 0; i < 10; ++i)

     {

```cpp
            votes[ i ] = 0;

    }

    int candidate;

    cout << "Vote for your choice of candidate, using numbers: 0)
John

1) Billy 2) Marie 3) Suzanne 4) Millie 5) Ellie 6) Alexander 7) Timmy 8)
Michael 9)

Eileen" << '\n';

    cin >> candidate;

    // input votes until the user exits by entering a non-valid
candidate  number

    while ( 0 <= candidate && candidate <= 9 )

    {

            // note that a do-while loop cannot be used because we
            must

            // check that the candidate is in the correct range before

            // the array is updated/ a do-while loop requires the
            candidate value

            // to be read in,, checked and then the vote incremented

            votes[ candidate ]++;

            cout << "Please input another vote: ";

            cin >> candidate;
```

```
        }

        // display the votes

        for ( int i = 0; i < 10; ++i )

        {

                cout << votes[ i ] << '\n';

        }

}
```

See just how easy it is for the count to be updated for a specified candidate? We could get a bit more complex here and have an array of structures. Each structure can have the candidate names and the vote count. Doing it this way will make it a lot easier to print the names and votes.

Now think about how things would go if you tried this using a linked list. The code would need to go through each individual element until it got to the specified candidate. So, a vote for candidate 4 would need the loop to go from candidate 0 to candidate 1, then on to 2 and so on—you can't go into the middle of the list.

The time taken to use an index to access an array element is constant; it will not change with the array size. However, the time taken for finding an element in a linked list is proportional to whatever size the list is. As the list gets bigger, the time gets slower.

One very important thing to consider is the amount of space a data structure will use, especially if it is a large one. You won't see a great deal of difference with smaller structures, but for very large ones, the amount of space could be an issue.

Arrays don't take up as much space per element. Linked lists need both the list item and the pointer to the next list element which means they need around twice as much space for each element to start with. However, if you have no idea how many elements are going to be stored, the linked list can, initially, take up less space. Rather than having to allocate a massive array and leave it mostly empty, you simply allocate new nodes when needed so you never allocate memory that you won't use.

And let's not forget that the array may also be multidimensional. It would be easy to represent a chessboard using an 8 x 8 array, but trying to do it with a linked list would require one list made up of other lists. And good luck trying to get a specific element from that!

There are some rules of thumb for when you should use a linked list or an array:

- When you require constant time for accessing elements by their index and know the number of items needed to be stored up-front or you need to keep the space per element to a minimum, use an array.
- If you need to be able to keep on adding new elements or want to insert data into the middle, use the linked list.

Do the quiz that follows this section. Go back over anything you didn't understand, and then we'll move on to discussing recursion.

Quiz 13

What is the advantage of using a linked list over an array?

A. Linked lists don't take up so much space per element

B. Linked lists can grow dynamically so they can hold individual new elements without needing to copy the existing elements

C. Linked lists are faster than arrays at finding specified elements

D. Linked lists can hold structures as their elements

Which of these statements is true?

A. There is no good reason for using an array

B. Both arrays and linked lists have the exact same characteristics for performance

C. Both arrays and linked lists allow constant time access to an element by index

D. You can add an element to the middle of a linked list much faster than you can an array

When would a linked list normally be used?

    A. When you only have a single item to store
    B. When you know, at compile time, the number of items to be stored
    C. When you need to dynamically add elements and remove them
    D. When you need to have instant access to an item in a sorted list without doing any iteration

Why is it okay to declare a linked list that has a reference to the list item type?

(struct Node {

Node* p_next; };)

    A. It isn't, and you can't do this
    B. Because the compiler can work out that you don't need the memory for items that are self-referencing
    C. Because the type is a pointer and you only need the space to add a single pointer. The memory for the next real node will be allocated at a later time
    D. It's okay only if you don't need to assign p_next so that it points to another structure

Why should you have a NULL at the end of the linked list?

A. Because it's the only way of indicating that the list has ended

B. It stops the code from using memory that hasn't been initialized

C. It's used to help with debugging—go too far down the list and the program will crash

D. If a NULL is not stored, the list will require infinite memory; this is down to the self-reference

In what way are arrays and linked lists similar?

A. Both let you quickly add new elements to the middle of the current list

B. Both let you store and access data sequentially

C. Both can incrementally add elements to grow much larger

D. Both give you quick access to all the elements on the list

Recursion

Over the course of this guide, you have seen several algorithms with a basis in looping, or repeating something over and again. You can repeat code over and again without using loops; instead, you can use repeated function calls. We call this recursion, a technique whereby an operation is expressed in terms of itself. What that means is, the function will call itself.

Recursion is much like looping, but far more powerful, and, when it comes to writing programs that are virtually impossible to write using loops, recursion makes them simple. It's most powerful when you apply it to linked lists and binary trees, which we will discuss soon. In the next couple of sections you will learn the basics behind recursion and see a few examples of when it is useful

How to Think of Recursion

The best way of thinking about recursive function is as a process whereby one instruction is simply repeated. This makes it similar to the loop, but using recursion makes it far easier to express an idea in which the recursive call result is required for the task to complete. Of course, there will be times when the recursive call is not needed for a process to be completed.

Think of an example whereby you build a wall. It's 10 feet in height, so you build a nine-foot wall and then add the last foot of bricks. As a concept, this is the same as saying a function called buildWall will take an argument of height and, if it is more than one, the function will call itself to build the lower wall and then add the rest.

Let's see if we can clarify that with a simple structure. It does have a couple of flaws that we can discuss later, but what is important is that building the wall can be expressed in terms of a smaller wall:

```
void buildWall (int height)

{

        buildWall( height - 1 );

         addBrickLayer();

}
```

There is a problem here: when will the code stop calling buildWall? Never, but the solution is easy—the recursive call needs to be stopped when the wall is at height 0. When we have a height of 0, a layer of bricks is added without the smaller wall being built.

```
void buildWall (int height)

{

        if ( height > 0 )

        {

                buildWall( height - 1 );

        }

        addBrickLayer();

}
```

The condition where the function doesn't call itself is called the function's base case. In our example, the function called buildWall will know that, if we get to the ground, a layer of bricks can just be added to build the wall (the base). Otherwise, a small wall will still need to be built and a layer of bricks added on.

If you are struggling to follow the code, think in terms of a physical wall. Start with the idea of building the wall to a specific height. Then tell yourself that, to put a brick in this place, your wall must be one brick smaller. Eventually, you will say that you don't need a wall that is smaller; you can just build from the ground up—that's your base case.

So, our algorithm reduces the problem down to a smaller one and then resolves that small problem. Soon enough, the small problem becomes small enough that we don't have to go any further; the simple case can be solved immediately.

In the real world, that means we get the wall built. In C++, it means the function stops making those recursive calls at some point. This is very much like the top-down program design that we saw earlier, where the problem is broken into smaller ones. Functions were created for the subproblems and then those functions were used to build up the entire program. With recursion, the problem is broken down into small versions of the same small problem.

When a function has finished calling itself, it can move to the line following the call site, after the call has returned. When a recursive call is returned, the function will continue to perform operations and will carry on calling other functions. In our wall-building case, once the small wall is built, the function carries on executing by adding another layer of bricks.

Let's see a real-world example, where real output can be seen. Let's say that you want to print the numbers 1234567899987654321. How will the recursive statement be written? We start by writing a function that will take a number. Print it twice—once before the recursion and once after.

#include <iostream>

```cpp
using namespace std;

void printNum (int num)
{
        // the calls in the function to cout will surround an inner
        // sequence that contains the numbers (num+1)...99...(num+1)
        cout << num;
        // While begin is lower than 9, we must print the sequence
        // recursively for (num+1) ... 99 ... (num+1)
        if ( num < 9 )
        {
                printNum( num + 1 );
        }
        cout << num;
}
int main ()
{
        printNum( 1 );
}
```

The recursive function call of printnum(num + 1) prints a sequence (num+1)...99...(num+1).

When you print num on both sides of the printnum(num+1) call, you create a kind of sandwich. num gets printed on each side of the (num+1)...99...(num+1) sequence and that makes it (num)(num+1)...99...(num+1)(num). If num is 1, then what you have is 12...99...21.

There is another way to think of this function. First, each time printnum is called, it will print the sequence of 1 through 9. When it gets to the base case, printnum will return each of the recursive calls and the numbers will be printed in the order the functions were returned in; because the last function was called using the number 9, it will print as soon the base case is reached and won't call the function again.

When the call is returned, it is returned to the call where 8 is the value of num and that means 8 is printed. It returns, 7 is the value of num and so on, all the way through the numbers until 1 is printed.

Recursion And Data Structures

There are data structures that lend themselves very nicely to the recursive algorithms because the structure composition is best described as having small versions of one single data structure. Because recursive algorithms work by taking problems and turning them into smaller versions of themselves, they work extremely well with data structures that contain small versions of one data structure; the linked list is one of these.

Up to now, we have described linked lists as lists whereby more nodes can be added at the beginning. Another way of thinking of them is that they consist of a first node which points to a much smaller linked list. So, the linked list is made up of individual nodes with each one pointing to another at the beginning of "the rest of the list."

This is important because it provides us a useful property to work with— we can write code that works with linked lists by handling the current node or the rest of the list. As an example, if you wanted to find a specified node in the list, you would use a basic algorithm like this:

If we reach the end of the list, NULL is returned.

Else if the current node is the target, return it.

Else repeat the search on the rest of the list.

In code, that would look like this:

```
Struct node
{
        int value;
        node *next;
};
node* search (node* list, int value_to_find)
{
        if ( list == NULL )
        {
                return NULL;
        }
        if ( list->value == value_to_find )
        {
                return list;
        }
```

```
        else

        {

                return search( list->next, value_to_find );

        }

}
```

We've talked about called functions doing work in recursive calls. What a function will do, depending on the input, is called the function's contract. The contract is a summary of what a function does. For example, a search function contract says that it finds a specified node in a list. This is implemented by saying, if the current node is what we want, it is returned; if not, look through the remainder of the list. The search function must be called on the rest of the list, not the entire list again.

Recursion only works if you are able to :

1. Work with the answer toward a small version of the main problem to find a way of solving the big problem
2. Solve the base case

The search function will solve a possible two base cases:

- Either we are at the end of the list, or
- We got the node that we wanted

If neither case matches, the search function is used to solve a small version of that problem. That is the key point of recursion: it works when you can solve smaller versions of a problem in a way that can be used to solve the big problem.

On occasion, the value that the recursive call returns is used instead of being returned immediately. Here's an example, using the factorial function:

Factorial(x) = x * (x - 1) *(x - 2)...*1

Or, put another way:

Factorial(x) =

If (x == 1) 1

Else x * Factorial(x - 1)

What this means is that we solve factorial by taking the current value and multiplying it by the current value multiplied by the factorial form, which is a smaller value.

In this case, we use the value that the recursive call returns and multiply it by another value:

That looks like this:

```
int factorial (int x)
{
        if ( x == 1 )
        {
                return 1;
        }
        return x * factorial( x − 1 );
}
```

We can solve the base case or solve the small factorial problem and then the result is used to compute the factorial once more. Again, each call results in x being smaller, and we will eventually get to the base case.

Note that the subproblem is solved first and then something is done with the result.

When we search a linked list, all we do is solve the subproblem and return the result. You can use recursion in two ways: make a recursive call that hands over full responsibility of solving the problem, or take the result from the subproblem solution and use it to do more work.

Loops And Recursion

There are cases where recursive algorithms can be expressed as loops with the same structure. For example, we could write searching the list like this:

```
node *search (node *list, int value_to_find)

{

    while ( 1 )

    {

        if ( list == NULL )

        {

            return NULL;

        }

        if ( list->value == value_to_find )

        {

            return list;

        }

        else
```

```
        {

                list = list->next;

        }

    }

}
```

We use the exact same checks so you can see how it compares with the recursive version. There's just one difference between the two: rather than recursion, we use a loop here. And, rather than a recursive call, the list is set to point to "rest of the list" so it shortens each time. This is one of those situations where both loops and recursion work well.

Generally, it's not difficult to write loops as recursive algorithms and vice versa when the result from the recursive function call doesn't require anything done with it. We call this tail recursion. The recursive call is the absolute last thing done by the function, right at the tail end, and isn't any different from moving to the next step in a loop. Once the next call has completed, nothing is needed from the previous call. One good example of tail recursion is the list search example.

You should also consider the factorial. Turning this into a loop based on recursive implementation could cause a problem:

```
int factorial (int x)

{

        while ( 1 )

        {

                if ( x == 1 )

                {
```

```
            return 1;

        }

        // what should we put here??

        // return x * factorial( x – 1 );

    }

}
```

Something has to be done with the factorial (x-1) result so a loop isn't an option. Really, the subproblem needs to be solved before we can work this out.

However, it turns out that the factorial is quite simple to transform into a loop; all you need to do is rethink the original problem. Here's the definition we started with:

Factorial(x) = x * (x - 1) *(x - 2)...*1

If we track the current value, the factorial can be computed. But what about storing the running result from the multiplication of x*(x-1) *)x-2) ...

```
int factorial (int x)

{

        int cur = x;

        while ( x > 1 )

        {

                x--;

                cur *= x;
```

```
        }

        return x;

}
```

Instead of taking the subproblem result to solve this, do the multiplication the opposite way. Let's say that we compute the factorial of five; the recursive solution will then perform the multiplication like this:

1 * 2 * 3 * 4 * 5

Conversely, the iterative or loop solution will do it the opposite way around:

5 * 4 * 3 * 2 * 1

Either way will work, but they have different structures. When you rethink the algorithm structure, you can write that same factorial as a loop. This is a simple example though; it won't always be so easy. Ultimately, whether you opt for recursion will depend on the ease with which you can rethink the structure in iterative terms. With the factorial it's quite easy, but other cases won't be. Shortly, we'll show you some examples.

The Stack

Let's go back to function calls and how they work. Once you understand them, you will find recursion much easier to follow and should have some grasp of why some algorithms are far easier to write as recursion than loops.

Every piece of information used by a function gets stored on the stack. Think of a stack of plates; you can add to or remove from the top. The stack works the same way. Only, rather than plates, we have stack frames. When a function gets called, a new stack frame is placed on the top of the stack and that stack frame is used by the function to store all local variables that are going to be used.

When another function is called, the space for the stack frame is retained and another added on top; this gives the new function space to store its variables. The function that is currently executing will always use the top frame.

In the very simplest of cases, when the main function is executing, the stack will look like this:

Variables in the main func

Here, we have just one function, the main one, and the stack contains only the variables for that function.

If main calls another function, the new one creates a stack frame which goes to the top, and it looks like this:

Variables in the second func
Variables in the main func

Now the current function can store its variables so it can work with them and not interfere with the main function variables. If this function calls one, the stack will look like this:

Variables in the third func
Variables in the second func
Variables in the main func

Again, the new function will have a stack frame of its own. Each function call will create a stack frame and, when the function is returned from, the stack goes back to how it was before:

Variables in the second func
Variables in the main func

And when the second function returns, the stack reverts to just one frame:

Variables in the main func

The active frame, the one at the top, will always be associated with the function being executed at the time.

Along with the function variables, function arguments are also stored on the stack, as is the code line the function should return. So, the stack frame is used for storing the function location and everything the function uses. When you call a function recursively, a new stack frame gets created even it's for the same function. That's why recursion really does work; each function call has its own frame with its own variables and arguments. Because of this, a function can work quite easily on a small version of a bigger problem.

When a function has returned, it will remove its own stack frame from the stack and return to the point in the caller where it executed. When the stack frame is removed, it's restored to the caller for further use.

One very important thing to note is that the stack frame stores the location for the function to return to. Once the function has completed, that location is removed. If the correct stack frame isn't there, the current function can't execute as it should once the called function returns because it won't have the right values for its own local variables.

Think of it like this: when a function gets called, everything that the previous function requires to keep on executing correctly is retained. Let's say that you're working on a thesis and really need to eat. You write a few notes so you can remember where you stopped and then, after dinner, you can pick up where you left off. The stack lets the computer keep those notes and they're a good deal more complex than anything you could write!

The following is a stack demonstrating a series of three recursive calls to the buildWall function. We start at height 2, where you can see that the frame stores the new value for height passed into the function. Note that the function call with 0 as a value is the top one; this would be the bottom of the wall in physical terms:

height = 0
height = 1
height = 2

You will often see this kind of approach to drawing stacks abbreviated as:

buildWall(x = 0)

buildWall(x = 1)

buildWall(height = 2)

main( )

Every function is shown above the function that called it and you can see the function arguments too. This is a good technique to use to help you understand the way a recursive function might work.

The Stack's Power

Recursion's key value is a stack of function calls and not just one stack frame. A recursive algorithm will take full advantage of all the additional information in each stack frame; the loop will get just one set of variables instead. That means recursive functions can make way for recursive calls to return and pick up exactly where they were before. If you want to write a loop that works like this, you'll need to try and implement a version of a stack.

Downsides to Recursion

Stacks are fixed in size and that means limitless recursion is not an option. There will come a point when room for new stack frames runs out. The code below demonstrates recursion that could, in theory, go on forever:

```
void recurse ()

{

        recurse(); // Function will call itself

}

int main ()

{

        recurse(); // Sets off the recursion

}
```

In time though, the space on the stack gets used up and you get a stack overflow, causing the program to crash. Stack overflows happen when space on the stack runs out and no more function calls are possible or the program will crash. While they don't happen very often, when you see a stack overflow error, it will usually be a recursive function that has a bad base case. As an example, the factorial we used earlier wasn't quite right— there were no checks for negative numbers in the base case. If -1 had been passed in by the caller, the stack would have overflowed.

Next we have a simple example of the number of recursive calls needed to use up all the stack space for a tiny function. It's worth bearing in mind that the bigger the stack frame is for a function, the less recursive calls can be made. However, where the base case is right, this will rarely present a problem:


```
#include <iostream>

using namespace std;

void recurse (int count) // Each call will have its own count

{

        cout << count << "\n";

        // There is no requirement to increment count because each function's

        // variables are separate (and the count in each of the stack frames will

        // be initialized as one greater than the previous count)

        recurse( count + 1 );

}

int main ()

{

        recurse( 1 ); // First function call, so it begins at one

}
```

Debugging Stack Overflows

When you try debugging stack overflows, the most important thing you have to work out is which function or functions are adding new frames repeatedly. For example, if you used a debugger, you would see from the example above that, when the program crashed, the stack looked like this:

recurse(10000);

recurse(9999);

recurse(9998);

...

recurse(1)

main()

This one is easy to work out because there's only a single function; it should be clear that some kind of base case is missing, likely related to a failure to stop when the recursive argument gets to a certain size.

On occasion you may get two functions calling each other. This is known as mutual recursion. The example below uses the factorial, with two functions computing it; one does odd numbers while the other does even:

```
int factorial_odd (int x)

{

        if ( x == 0 )

        {

                return 1;

        }

        return factorial_even( x – 1 );

}
```

```
int factorial_even (int x)

{

        if ( x == 0 )

        {

                return 1;

        }

        return factorial_odd( x – 1 );

}

int factorial (int x)

{

        if ( x % 2 == 0 )

        {

                return factorial_even( x );

        }

        else

        {

                return factorial_odd( x );

        }

}
```

In this case, the base cases are not guarding against inputs that are negative and, if you call factorial (-1), the call stack will look like this:

factorial_even(-10000)

factorial_odd(-9999)

factorial_even(-9998)

factorial_odd(-9997)

Just from that, you should be able to determine that the base case is where the problem lies and the functions are just calling one another. So, your next step should be to examine the code and work out which one should have a check built into the base case for negative numbers. For factorial computations, the sensible thing would be to have separate base cases for both functions, each base case with the same check. There will be other cases where only one function will need the final base case.

Whenever you find yourself having to debug a complex recursive call, try to find a series of repeating functions. In our case, it's just the two functions calling each other —factorial_odd and factorial_even—but, in other cases, it may be that there is a long period between the repetition and you need to find an entire set of repeating function calls. Then you have to work out why.

Taking Stock

With recursion, you can create algorithms to resolve problems; this is done by breaking a problem down into smaller clones of the original problem. Recursion is more powerful than loops; the recursive functions keep the current state of each individual recursive call in the stack and that means the function can carry on executing after the subproblem result is returned.

Recursive algorithm implementation will often feel more correct than loop implementation. In the next chapter, you will see more examples covering binary trees. As you continue to develop code, you will start to find that recursion gives you more scope for wider ranges of problems than looping can solve.

In conclusion, here a couple of rules that you should use to determine whether to use recursion or looping.

Recursion should be used when:

- A solution requires the original problem to be broken down into small versions of itself and writing a loop isn't an obvious choice
- You're working with linked lists or other recursive data structures.

Loops should be used when:

- It's obvious that a loop can solve the problem, i.e., a list of numbers is being added
- The data structure you're using is number indexed, i.e., an array.

Quiz 14

What is tail recursion?

A. When you call your dog to you

B. When a function calls itself

C. When a recursive function calls itself and this is the last thing it does before it returns

D. When a recursive algorithm can be written as a loop

When should recursion be used?

A. When the algorithm can't be written as a loop

B. When an algorithm is more naturally expressed in terms of a subproblem than a loop

C. Never, it's far too hard

D. When you work with linked lists and arrays

What elements are required from a recursive algorithm?

A. A recursive call and a base call

B. A base case and a method of breaking the problem down into a smaller version

C. A way of recombining all the smaller versions

D. All of the above

What might happen if you don't have a complete base case?

A. The algorithm might finish before it should

B. The compiler will detect it and won't like it

C. This won't be a problem

D. You could have a stack overflow

Binary Trees

Binary trees are one of the most useful of all the basic data structures and are by far the most interesting. They are the perfect example of how recursion and pointers can be used to do some very useful things.

Though binary trees aren't hard to work, it's critical that you understand recursion and the concepts behind the linked list. If you find that difficult, go back over pointers, linked lists and recursion and try the quizzes again before you return to this section.

One of the best techniques for creating lists of things is the linked list, but finding an element in the list can take a while. And, if you have a large amount of unstructured data, an array won't help much either. You can try sorting the array but, even so, inserting items into it will still be difficult. If you have an array that you want to keep sorted, inserting new elements will take a lot of shuffling! And trying to find things in a list as quickly as possible is quite important, especially in scenarios like these:

- You're building an MMORPG game and players need to be able to sign in quickly—that involves quickly looking players up

- You're building software to process credit cards and millions of transactions need to be handled hourly—credit card balances need to found very quickly

- You're using a low-power device, such as a tablet or smartphone, and showing your users an address book. You don't want your users kept hanging because your data structure is slow.

This section will discuss the tools needed to overcome these problems and more.

The idea of the solution is to be able to store elements in a structure like a linked list, using pointers to help structure the memory, but in an easier way than the linked list. Doing this requires that the memory have more structure than a simple list.

So what does structuring data mean? When we started this journey, we only had arrays, but these never really gave us the ability to use data structures other than sequential lists. Linked lists use pointers to grow sequential lists incrementally but don't use the flexibility of the pointer to build more sophisticated structures.

What are these more sophisticated structures in memory? Structures that hold more than a single next node at any given time are a good example. But why would you want this? Simple. If you have two "next nodes," one can be used to represent elements that are more than the current element. This is called a binary tree.

These are named because there are always one or two branches from every node. Each of the next nodes is a child and the node that links to the child is the parent node.

This is what a binary tree might look like:

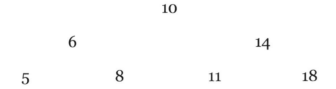

In the tree, the left child on each of the elements is smaller than the element and the right child is larger. 10 is the parent node for the whole tree and the child nodes of 6 and 14 are both parent nodes to their own small trees, called subtrees.

Binary trees have one very important property: each child is an entire tree. Combine this with the rule of the left child being smaller and the right child being larger, and you have an easy way of defining algorithms that locate specific nodes in the tree.

First, look at the current node value. If it equals the search target, it's done. If it's more than the search target, go left; otherwise, go right. This works because each node to the left of the tree is less than the current mode value and each on the right is more.

In an ideal world, your binary tree will be balanced with the exact same number of nodes on both sides. In such cases, every child tree is roughly 50 percent of the entire tree and, when you search the tree for a value, the search can eliminate 50 percent of the results each time it gets to a child node. So, if you had a tree of 1000 elements, 500 would be immediately eliminated. Search that tree again (it only has 50 elements now) and you can cut it by about 50 percent again. That way it doesn't take long to find the value you want.

So, how many times must a tree be subdivided before you get to one element? The answer to that is $\log_2 n$ (n is the number of elements the tree has). This is a small value, even if your tree is large—if your tree had, say, 32 billion elements, the value would be 32; almost 100 million times faster than a search of a linked list of four billion elements, where every single one has to be assessed.

If the tree isn't balanced, you won't be able to eliminate roughly half of the elements; worst case, each node only has one child and that makes the tree nothing more than a linked list with a few extra pointers, thus requiring you to search all elements.

So, when a tree is balanced approximately, it's much faster and easier to search for nodes than the same search on a linked list. This is because you can structure the memory how you want it.

Implementing a Binary Tree

To implement a binary tree, begin by declaring the node structure:

struct node

{

      int key_value;

      *node *p_left;*

      *node *p_right;*

};

The node can store values as a simple integer, key_value, and has two child trees— p_left, and p_right.

There are some common functions that you want on your binary tree: inserting, searching, removing and destroying:

node insert (node* p_tree, int key);*

*node *search (node* p_tree, int key);*

void destroyTree (node p_tree);*

*node *remove (node* p_tree, int key);*

Inserting

We'll use a recursive algorithm for inserting into the tree. Recursion is fantastic for trees because there are two small trees for each tree; that makes the entire tree recursive by nature. The function takes a key and a tree that already exists (even an empty one) and returns a new tree that has the inserted value.

```
node* insert (node *p_tree, int key)

{

        // base case--we have got to an empty tree and our new node

        // needs to be inserted here

        if ( p_tree == NULL )

        {

                node* p_new_tree = new node;

                p_new_tree->p_left = NULL;

                p_new_tree->p_right = NULL;

                p_new_tree->key_value = key;

                return p_new_tree;

        }

        // decide – left subtree or right subtree for the insertion

        // depending on the what the node value is

        if( key < p_tree->key_value )

        {

                // build a new tree from p_tree->left, and add in the key

                // replace existing p_tree->left pointer with a pointer

                // to new tree. Set the p_tree->p_left pointer
```

```
            // in case p_tree->left is NULL. (If it isn't NULL,,

            // p_tree->p_left won't change but it set it just

            // to make sure.)

            p_tree->p_left = insert( p_tree->p_left, key );

      }

      else

      {

            // Insertion into the right side is symmetric to the

            // insertion in the left

            p_tree->p_right = insert( p_tree->p_right, key );

      }

      return p_tree;

}
```

The basic logic here is this: if you have an empty tree, you create a new one. If not, the value for insertion goes to the left subtree if it's more than the current node and the left subtree is then replaced with the new one. Otherwise, insert it into the right subtree and replace.

When it comes to seeing it in action, build an empty tree into a tree with a couple of nodes. If the value 10 is inserted in the empty tree (NULL), immediately we will hit base case and the result will be a tree of:

```
1
```

And both of the child trees will point to NULL.

Then insert 5 into the tree and make the following call:

insert(a tree with a parent , 5)

Because 5 is lower than 10, the call onto the left-subtree is recursive:

insert(NULL, 5)

insert(a tree with a parent , 5)

The call of

insert(NULL, 5)

creates and returns a new tree

   5

When the returned tree is received, insert(,5) links the trees. In this example, 10's left child was NULL before. Therefore, the left child of 10 is established a new tree:

                 1

   5

If we now add 7, we get:

insert(NULL, 7)

insert(a tree with a parent, 7)

insert(a tree with a parent , 7)

So, first off,

insert(NULL, 7)

will return a new tree:

7

And then

insert(a tree with a parent, 7)

will link to the subtree of 7 in this way:

5

7

Lastly, the tree gets returned to:

insert(a tree with a parent , 7)

And this will link it back:

10

5

7

Because there was already a pointer from 10 to the node with 5, it isn't really necessary to relink 10's left child to the tree with 5 as the parent, but it does eliminate one conditional check to see if the subtree is empty.

Searching

Now we look at the implementation of a tree search. Basic logic will be much the same as insertion. Check the base cases to see if you got the node or an empty tree. If you don't have the node, work out which subtree needs to be searched.

*node *search (node *p_tree, int key)*

```
{
        // if we get to the empty tree, we know it's not here!
        if ( p_tree == NULL )
        {
                return NULL;
        }
        // if we got to the key, we're finished!
        else if ( key == p_tree->key_value )
        {
                return p_tree;
        }
        // otherwise, look in the left or right subtree
        else if ( key < p_tree->key_value )
        {
                return search( p_tree->p_left, key );
        }
        else
        {
                return search( p_tree->p_right, key );
        }
```

}

So, this search function checks the base cases first; you either have the key or are at the end of the tree branch. Either way, you return the tree if you got the key, or NULL if you got to the end of the tree.

If you're not on a base case, the problem is reduced to looking in a child tree for the key; the value will dictate whether it is left or right. Note that whenever a recursive call is made, the tree size is cut by roughly 50 percent, as described at the start.

Destroying

This should also be a recursive function. Before deleting the current node, the algorithm destroys both of the subtrees that are at the current node.

void destroy_tree (node *p_tree)

{

> *if (p_tree != NULL)*

> *{*

>> *destroy_tree(p_tree->p_left);*

>> *destroy_tree(p_tree->p_right);*

>> *delete p_tree;*

> *}*

}

As a way of better understanding this, let's say that the value of the node was printed before the node was deleted:

void destroy_tree (node *p_tree)

```
{

    if ( p_tree != NULL )

    {

            destroy_tree( p_tree->p_left );

            destroy_tree( p_tree->p_right );

            cout << "Deleting node: " << p_tree->key_value;

            delete p_tree;

    }

}
```

As you can see, the tree is deleted from the bottom up. Nodes 5 and 8 go first, then 6, before moving to the other side and deleting 11 and 18, followed by 14. Lastly, 10 will be deleted. The tree values aren't important; what matters is where the node is. In the following binary tree, rather than the node values, we use the order of deletion:

It can be helpful to walk through the code manually on a few trees, so you can see it much clearer.

Deleting from trees is a great example of a recursive algorithm that's not easy to do as an iterative implementation. First, you need a loop that can deal with both sides of the tree at the same time. You need to be able to delete a subtree while simultaneously tracking the next one, and that needs to be done for every level. With the stack, you can keep your place much more easily. The best way of visualizing this is to say that each stack frame will store the tree branch that has been deleted or destroyed already:

destroy_tree( )

destroy_tree( ) – knows whether the subtree was the left or right

Each of the stack frames knows which bits of the tree have to be destroyed because it knows what point in the function execution should continue. When the first call to destroy the tree is made, the program is notified by the stack frame to continue executing when the second call is made to destroy_tree. When that second call is made, the program is told to continue with delete tree. Because every function has a stack frame of its own, it can track the entire state of the tree's destruction at the current time, one tree level at a time.

To implement this in a non-recursive way would require having a data structure that retains the same amount and type of information. You could, for example, write a function that holds a linked list as a way of simulating the list. That linked list would have subtrees that were being destroyed and trees left for destruction. Then a loop-based algorithm could be written to add the subtrees to the list and remove them after they were destroyed fully. Basically, recursion lets you use the stack data structure built-in rather than needing to write your own.

Removing

This algorithm is more complex. The structure is much like the pattern we saw earlier; if we get an empty tree, we're finished. If the value to be removed is in the subtree on the left, the value is removed from that tree and vice versa for the right side. If the value is found, it's removed.

```
node* remove (node* p_tree, int key)
{
        if ( p_tree == NULL )
        {
                return NULL;
        }
        if ( p_tree->key_value == key )
        {
                // what to do?
        }
        else if ( key < p_tree->key_value )
        {
                p_tree->left = remove( p_tree->left, key );
        }
        else
        {
                p_tree->right = remove( p_tree->right, key );
        }
        return p_tree;
}
```

But one of these base cases isn't going to be straightforward. What do you do when you find the value to be removed? Remember that binary trees have to maintain this condition:

- Every tree value on the left of the current node has to be less than the key value. And, on the right, all values must be more than the key value.

There are a couple of basic cases that need to be considered:

- The node to be removed doesn't have any children
- The node to be removed has only one child
- The node to be removed has two children

The first case is the easiest. If a node being removed doesn't have any children, just return NULL.

The second case isn't that difficult either; with just one child, that child is returned.

The third case is the hardest because you can't promote one of the two children. What would happen if you took the node on the left of the element being removed? If you did that, what would happen to the elements on the right of the node?

Let's go back to the tree we looked at earlier:

```
                    10

        6                       14

    5           8           11          18
```

What would happen if you removed 10? If you tried to put 6 in its place, you would have a tree that looked like this:

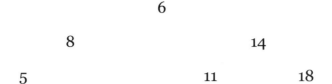

Now 8 is on the left of 6 despite 8 being greater than 6. This breaks the tree; if a search was made for 8, it would look on the right side of 6 and never find 8.

In the same way, and for the same reason, you couldn't take the element on the right:

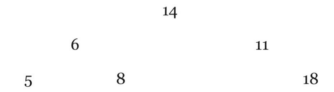

Obviously, 11 is less than 14, but it's on the right side—a big no-no. You can't promote nodes up a binary tree just for the hell of it!

So, what do we do? Anything to the left must be of a lesser value than the current node, so why don't we just find the biggest value on the left of the node being removed and promote that to the top? Because it's the biggest value on the left we can easily replace the current node with—it will always be bigger than any other node on its left and, because it was on the left right from the start, it will always be smaller than any of the nodes on the right side.

In the example we're using, we want the final tree to look like this because 8 is the largest value on the left:

8

| | 6 | | 14 | |
| 5 | | 11 | | 18 |

To do this, we require an algorithm that will locate the largest value on the left side and be a find_max function. This can be implemented by making use of the property that the greatest values are on the right side so all we need to do is look through the right side until we get to NULL. In other words, with a straightforward find_max function, where we take the tree and return the max value, the tree is treated just like a linked list full of right tree pointers:

```
node* find_max (node* p_tree)
{
        if ( p_tree == NULL )
        {
                return NULL;
        }
        if ( p_tree->p_right == NULL )
        {
                return p_tree;
        }
        return find_max( p_tree->p_right );
}
```

Note that two base cases are required: one for when we don't have a tree and one for getting to the end of the child trees on the right. For a pointer to be returned to the last node, we should be looking one node ahead while the pointer is still valid.

So, can we write a remove function using this? If find_max returns NULL in the base case, we will know that the left tree can be used to replace the mode we removed because there won't be any greater value. If not, the removed node needs to be replaced with the find_max function:

node* remove (node* p_tree, int key)

{

*   if (p_tree == NULL)*

*   {*

*   return NULL;*

*   }*

*   if (p_tree->key_value == key)*

*   {*

*   // the first two cases will handle either having zero or just one child node*

*   if (p_tree->p_left == NULL)*

*   {*

*   node* p_right_subtree = p_tree->p_right;*

*   delete p_tree;*

*   // this could return NULL if there are no child nodes,*

```
                // but that is the result we want

                return p_right_subtree;

        }

        if ( p_tree->p_right == NULL )

        {

                node* p_left_subtree = p_tree->p_left;

                delete p_tree;

                // this is always going to return a valid node,
                because we know

                // it isn't NULL from the last if statement

                return p_left_subtree;

        }

        node* p_max_node = find_max( p_tree->p_left );

        p_max_node->p_left = p_tree->p_left;

        p_max_node->p_right = treep_->p_right;

        delete p_tree;

        return p_max_node;

}

else if ( key < p_tree->key_value )

{

        p_tree->p_left = remove( p_tree->p_left, key );
```

```
        }

        else

        {

                P_tree->p_right = remove( p_tree->p_right, key );

        }

        return p_tree;

}
```

But does this really work? There's a bug in here: we didn't remove max_node from its starting point in the tree. That means somewhere in that tree, a pointer to max_node is pointing up the tree and the original max_node child trees are not available any longer.

max_node has to be removed and, as we know it doesn't have a right subtree, it's one of the easier cases to deal with. All we need to do is modify the max_node parent so it points to the max_node subtree on the left.

A simple function can be written that, given the head of the tree with max_node in it and the pointer to max_node, will return a tree that removes max_node properly. We're relying here on the fact that there is no right subtree for max_node.

```
node* remove_max_node (node* p_tree, node* p_max_node)

{

        // defensive coding--shouldn't hit this

        if ( p_tree == NULL )

        {
```

```
        return NULL;

}

// we found the node, now it can be replaced

if ( p_tree == p_max_node )

{

        // we can only do this because know that

        // p_max_node->p_right is NULL so we don't lose

        // any information. If p_max_node doesn't have a left sub-
        tree,

        // then we just return NULL from the branch, and this

        // will result in p_max_node being replaced with an empty
        tree,

        // which is the result we want.

        return p_max_node->p_left;

}

// every recursive call will replace the right sub-tree tree with a

// new one that doesn't have p_max_node.

p_tree->p_right = remove_max_node( p_tree->p_right,
p_max_node );

return p_tree;

}
```

Using that helper function, it's now easy to modify the remove function so that max_node can be removed from the left subtree before the node being removed is replaced with max_node.

```
node* remove (node* p_tree, int key)

{

        if ( p_tree == NULL )

        {

                return NULL;

        }

        if ( p_tree->key_value == key )

        {

                // the first two cases will handle either having zero or just
        one child node

                if ( p_tree->p_left == NULL )

                {

                        node* p_right_subtree = p_tree->p_right;

                        delete p_tree;

                        // this could return NULL if there are no child nodes,

                        // but that is the result we want

                        return p_right_subtree;

                }
```

```
if ( p_tree->p_right == NULL )

{

        node* p_left_subtree = p_tree->p_left;

        delete p_tree;

        // this is always going to return a valid node,
        because we know

        // it isn't NULL from the last if statement

        return p_left_subtree;

}

node* p_max_node = find_max( p_tree->p_left );

// because p_max_node came from the left sub-tree, it has
to be

// removed from that sub-tree before the subtree can be
relinked from the subtree

// back to the rest of the tree

p_max_node->p_left =

        remove_max_node( p_tree->p_left, p_max_node );

p_max_node->p_right = p_tree->p_right;

delete p_tree;

return p_max_node;

}
```

else if (key < p_tree->key_value)

{

      p_tree->p_left = remove(p_tree->p_left, key);

}

else

{

      p_tree->p_right = remove(p_tree->p_right, key);

}

return p_tree;

}

Using our example tree, the code will do this:

```
                    10

        6                       14

    5        8            11         18
```

If 10 is removed, the 'found' function is immediately hit by the remove function; it finds that there are subtrees on the left and right and locates the node that has the maximum value in the subtree that 6 heads up. The node is 8 and the left subtree for 8 is then linked to point to the subtree that 6 heads as long as it doesn't have 8 in it.

It's easy to remove 8. We start with a subtree of:

6

5   8

The first remove_max_node call will see that 6 isn't the right node for removal so it's recursively called on the subtree that 8 heads up. We're looking for node 8 so its subtree on the left, which is NULL, is returned, and the right pointer for 6 is modified to point to NULL. Now we have this tree:

6

5

In the remove call, the tree that remove_max_node returned is now set in the 8 node's left pointer, making the tree:

8

6

5

Lastly, 8's right pointer is set in the right subtree that 14 heads and the tree is rebuilt:

8

6   14

5   11   18

Thus, the original 10 node is freed.

Real-World Uses for Binary Trees

I've talked quite a bit about searching quickly for values, so you might be asking yourself, just how important is it to quickly find a specific value in a data structure? I mean, computers are fast enough anyway. When would you need to be doing so many lookups?

Generally, you will come across two cases where speed is important. The first case is when you want to check for a specific value. For example, you may have written a game where users can register their own username and, when a new user registers, you need to check if a username has already been taken. Depending on what that game is, something like *World of Warcraft*, for example, you need to search millions of usernames very quickly. And, because usernames are strings and not integers, comparisons take longer because each letter has to be compared. While this won't slow things down for just a few names, when you're doing millions of comparisons, it will be noticeable. In this case, a binary tree for storing the usernames would make things much quicker for your game players.

Another situation would be when you have extra data associated with the stored value. We call this kind of structure a map and it stores keys and associated values. That value can be one piece of data or a list, map, entire data structure and so on.

Take *World of Warcraft* again; any huge online multiplayer game needs a map from the player username to the password for handling login and stats. Every time a player logs in using their username and password, the map is searched for the username and the password is compared against the user input. If valid, the information is retrieved and the player can continue. Binary trees can be used to implement maps like this; the tree inserts nodes using the key and the value is stored beside the key in the same node.

Maps show up everywhere. Take a credit card company, for example. It needs a map of some kind because whenever a purchase is made on a credit card, account data needs to be changed. There are hundreds of millions of credit cards in the world and scanning that many numbers for every single transaction would bring commerce to its knees across the globe. The idea is that, given a card number, an account balance should be checked incredibly quickly. A binary tree can be used for this to build maps from each number to the associated balance. Now when a credit card transaction is done, a simple tree search and update to the balance can be done.

Let's say that you have one million card numbers. Using a balanced tree, the lookup will examine an average $\log_2 1000000$ nodes, about 20. That works out 50,000 times better than a linear scan.

Obviously credit card companies will have incredibly complex and sophisticated data structures. For a start, the information has to be permanently stored in databases and not in memory. They also probably have far more sophisticated structures than a map. The key point to understand is that a binary tree and map are building blocks for creating bigger and better structures.

After the quiz, we will move on to the Standard Template Library (STL).

Quiz 15

Name the binary tree's primary virtue

A. It uses pointers

B. Arbitrary amounts of data can be stored in it

C. It lets you do fast data lookups

D. You can easily remove from the binary tree

When would a linked list be better than a binary tree?

A. When data needs to be maintained in a way that makes it easy to do fast lookups

B. When you want access to the elements in sorted order

C. When you need to have the ability to add to the front or end quickly without ever accessing the middle items

D. When you don't need to free up the memory in use

Which of these is true?

A. You can change the structure of a tree by changing the order you add items

B. Items should be inserted in a binary tree in sorted order for the best structure

C. Linked lists are faster than binary trees for locating elements if the elements have been inserted in random order

D. Binary trees can't be reduced to a structure like a linked list

Which of the following is the right way of describing why a binary tree can find nodes so fast?

A. They're not that fast; two pointers means more work needs to be done in traversing the tree

B. Each node has a pair of subtrees whose creation is based on whether the items in them are of lesser or greater value than the current node's value

C. They're no better than a linked list

D. A recursive call on a binary tree is faster than a loop over a linked list

The Standard Template Library

It's good to be able to write your own data structures. However, as you might have picked up, it isn't really all that common. But you didn't work through all the previous content for no reason. You've now learned quite a bit about building data structures as necessary, along with some of the more common structures that you might need when writing a data structure.

However, C++ has a cool feature; a huge library of code that can be reused. It's called the Standard Template Library (STL) and contains the most common data structures, including those built on the binary trees and linked lists. These structures let you specify what data type they will store at the time you create them, so they can be used for anything—structured data, strings, ints and so on.

Because you have this flexibility, the STL will, in many cases, eliminate the need for you to build structures of your own. In fact, using it can raise your code level in these ways:

1. You can start thinking of your code in terms of the structures required rather than having to think about building and implementing them yourself
2. You have free and easy access to the best data structure implementations, with space use and performance optimized for most problems
3. You no longer have to concern yourself with the allocation and deallocation of memory for your data structures.

However, as with everything, using the library comes with its trade-offs:

1. You need to learn the STL interfaces and how they should be used
2. When you get compiler errors from using the STL, they are incredibly difficult to read and understand
3. You won't find all data structures in the library

Thoroughly discussing the STL would require an entire book, so I will only give you an overview of the most common data structures that you will use from the STL.

Vectors

Contained in the STL is an array replacement—the vector. This is much like an array but is resizable automatically; you no longer have to worry about allocating memory and moving the other elements around. However, the vector syntax is different from that of a standard array.

The array syntax is:

int an_array[10];

whereas the vector syntax is:

#include <vector>

using namespace std;

vector<int> a_vector(10);

Clearly, the vector header file must be included along with the namespace std. This is because, like cout and cin, the vector is a part of the standard library.

Furthermore, when a vector is declared, you must provide the data type being stored in the vector. This is done using angled brackets<>:

Vector<int>

This makes use of a C++ feature known as templates. Vector code is written in such a way that any data type can be stored. All you have to do is tell the compiler what type a vector is storing. What this really means is that we have two types here: the data structure type, which dictates the way data is organized, and the data type held in the data structure. Using a template lets you combine different data structure types with different data types within the data structure.

Finally, when the vector size is provided, it must be placed in a set of parentheses, rather than brackets:

vector<int> a_vector(10);

This is the syntax used for the initialization of certain variable types. For this, the value of 10 is passed to the initialization, called the constructor, and that sets the vector with the size ten. As we go through the guide, you will learn about constructors and objects that have constructors.

Once the vector is created, individual elements can be accessed in the same way as an array:

for (int i = 0; i < 10; i++)

{

      a_vector[i] = 0;

      an_array[i] = 0;

}

Calling a Method on a Vector

A vector provides you with much more than the functionality for an array. You can do all sorts of things, such as adding elements beyond the vector end. The vector provides functions to help with this sort of thing, but the function syntax isn't the same as the syntax we used before.

A vector uses a C++ feature known as a method. This is a function that you declare with the data type. Calling methods requires new syntax, as in this example:

a_vector.size();

This is calling a method size on a_vector and it returns that size. It's much like accessing a structure field but, instead, you're calling a method that goes with the structure. Although something is being done to a_vector by the method, a_vector doesn't need to be passed as an argument to the method. The syntax already knows that a_vector is to be passed as an implicit argument into the size method.

The syntax below

<variable>.<function call>(<args>);

can be thought of as calling a function that goes with the type for the variable. In other words, it's a bit like writing:

<function call>(<variable>, <args>);

In the example:

a_vector.size();

it would be like:

size(a_vector);

Over the next few sections, we will discuss more methods, including ways to declare and use them. For now, it's enough for you to understand that there are several methods that can be called on a vector, using the right syntax. The special method syntax is the only way of making that type of function call. You couldn't, for example, write this:

size(

a_vector).

Other Vector Features

A vector also makes it very easy to up the number of items held without needing to allocate memory. For example, adding extra items to the vector would be written like this:

a_vector.push_back(10);

This adds another item of 10 at the end of the vector. The vector will take care of the resizing. If you wanted to do this with an array, the memory would have to be allocated, the values copied over and the new item added in. While a vector does do memory allocation and copying, it does it intelligently, in a manner in which it doesn't have to resize itself every time a new item is added.

However, although you can use push_back to add items to the end of the vector, using the brackets on their own wouldn't be the same. Brackets let you work only with data that has already been allocated, mainly so that memory allocation isn't done without you being aware.

So, a code like this:

vector<int> a_vector(10);

a_vector[10] = 10; // the last valid element is 9

wouldn't work and would likely result in the program crashing. Not to mention, it's dangerous. Writing it like this:

vector<int> a_vector(10);

a_vector.push_back(10); // add a new element to the vector

works to resize the vector.

Maps

We mentioned maps a little while ago—using a value to look up another value. This is common in programming such as when you want to implement an address book for emails where addresses are looked up by name or a program where you look up an account using an account number, or letting users login to their games.

The STL gives us a map type that lets us specify the key type and value. An example would be a data structure that holds an email address book; this could be implemented as follows:

#include <map>

#include <string>

using namespace std;

map<string, string> name_to_email;

We have to tell the structure that there are two types: string, for the key, and another string for the value, an email address in this case.

One of these maps' helpful features is that when a map is used, the syntax can also be used as an array. If you want to add value, it's much like an array, except the key type is used instead of an integer:

name_to_email["Billy Bunter"] = "billybunter@thisemailaddress.com";

and getting value from a map is much the same:

cout << name_to_email["Billy Bunter"];

You get the simplicity that goes with an array, but with the ability to store whatever type you want. And what's even better is that, unlike the vector, the map size doesn't have to be set before the [] operator is used to add an element.

Removing items from maps is just as easy. Let's say that you fell out with Billy Bunter and want him removed from your address book. You can do that using the erase method:

name_to_email.erase("Billy Bunter");

And you can use the size() method to check what size a map is:

name_to_address.size();

And the empty() method to see if a map is empty:

if (name_to_address.empty())

{

   cout << "The address book is empty. I bet you wish you hadn't deleted Billy.";

}

Do not confuse this with how you make a map empty. That's done using the clear() method:

name_to_address.clear();

Because of the consistency in the naming conventions in the STL, the same methods can be used on vectors.

Iterators

As well as data storage and the ability to access elements individually, you can also go through all the items in a data structure. With arrays or vectors, this is just a case of reading each element using the array length. But with maps, because they have both numeric and non-numeric keys, you can't always iterate through using a counter variable.

To get around this, the STL provides us with an iterator, which is a variable that lets you access the elements of a data structure sequentially, even if the data structure doesn't usually have a good way of doing that. We'll start by looking at using iterators with vectors and then move on to using one with the map elements. The idea is that the iterator will store the position in a structure so that you can use that position to access the element. Then you call a method on the iterator to move on to the next element.

Some unusual syntax is required for declaring an iterator. For a vector of integers, it would look like this:

vector<int>::iterator

What this says is that you have the vector and want an iterator that will work for the specific type, which is why we used the ::iterator. Because the iterator marks the position in the structure, the iterator is requested from the data structure:

vector vec;

vector<int> vec;

vec.push_back(1);

vec.push_back(2);

vector<int>::iterator itr = vec.begin();

The begin method call will return an iterator that allows you to access the vector's first element.

Iterators can be considered similar to pointers—you speak of element locations in the structure or use it for getting the element. In our case, we read the vector's first element using this syntax:

*cout << *itr; // print out the vector's first element*

We use the * operator in the same we do with a pointer; makes sense when you consider that both store locations.

If you want the next element, the iterator is incremented:

itr++;

This lets the iterator know it needs to move on to the next element.

The prefix operator can also be used:

++itr;

You can see if you have reached the end by doing a comparison with the iterator and the end iterator; to do this, call:

vec.end();

If you want code that will loop over a whole vector, it would look like this:

for (vector<int>::iterator itr = vec.begin(); itr != vec.end(); ++itr)

{

      cout << *itr << endl;

}

This is saying that an iterator should be created and the first element retrieved from the given vector of integers. So long as the iterator does not equal the end iteration, it will continue to iterate. What we don't want to do is call vec.end() each time through the loop:

vector<int>::iterator end = vec.end();

for (vector<int>::iterator itr = vec.begin(); itr != end; ++itr)

{

```
        cout << *itr << endl;

}
```

To make the code easier to read, you can also add several variables into the first part of the for loop:

```
for ( vector<int>::iterator itr = vec.begin(), end = vec.end(); itr != end;

++itr )

{

        cout << *itr << endl;

}
```

We can loop over a map using a similar approach, but remember that the map doesn't store single values; it stores key/value pairs. When you dereference an iterator, it has two fields—one for key and one for value:

```
int key = itr->first; // get the key from iterator

int value = itr->second; // get the value from iterator
```

Below is some code that will display a map's content in an easy-to-read format:

```
void displayMap (map<string, string> map_to_print)

{

        for ( map<string, string>::iterator itr = map_to_print.begin(),
end =

map_to_print.end();

                itr != end;
```

```
        ++itr )

  {

        cout << itr->first << " --> " << itr->second << endl;

  }

}
```

This code is very similar to what is used for iterating over a vector; the only difference is that the map data structure is used along with the first and second fields on the iterator.

Checking a Map for a Value

Sometimes you want to be able to see if a given key has been stored in a map. Let's say you're looking for someone in your address book. You use the find() method to see if the specified value is there and, if it is, retrieve it. An iterator is returned and will either have the object location with the specified key or will be an end iterator if the object wasn't found.

map<string, string>::iterator itr = name_to_email.find("Billy Bunter");

if (itr != name_to_email.end())

{

*   cout << "How it is to see Billy again. His email is: " << itr->second;*

}

If you just want to access an element that isn't in the list, use the standard brackets:

name_to_email["John Doe"];

An empty element will be inserted by the map if the value isn't there already.

Taking Stock

I have really only touched on the basics of the STL, but you now have enough information to use some of the foundational types in the library. The vector can be used to replace arrays altogether and, if you don't want to take the time to insert and modify, vectors can also be used in place of linked lists. With the vector type at your fingertips, there are very few reasons why you would want to use an array and most of those reasons are advanced, such as when you work with file I/O, which we will discuss at the end of the guide.

The single most useful data type is the map. Using maps makes it easy to write sophisticated programs without having to worry too much about data structure creation. Instead, your attention can be focused on solving problems. In some ways, the map can replace a basic binary tree. Most of the time you'll want to go into binary tree implementation unless it's for certain performance requirements or you specifically need a tree structure.

That's where the STL's true power lies: around 80 percent of the time, it gives you the core structures you need, leaving you free to write the code that solves the problems. The rest of the time, you will need the knowledge to build and implement your own data structures.

There are programmers who prefer using their own code instead of ready-built code. Most of the time, you should NOT use your own data structures; the built-in ones are faster, better and more complete. However, knowing how to build does give you much better insight into using them.

So, when might you want to use your own structures? Let's say you want a calculator that allows arithmetic expressions to be input by users and then evaluates the inputs with the correct order of operations. An example would be something like 4*9+8/3, evaluated in a way that the division and multiplication are done before the addition.

This kind of structure can easily be thought of in terms of a tree. You could express 4*9+8/3 like this:

```
                    +


        *                       /


  4           *          8           3
```

Each node is evaluated in one of two ways:

1. If the node is a number, the value is returned
2. If the node is an operator, the values of the two subtrees are computed and the operation is performed.

To build a tree like this will require a raw data structure; you can't just use a map. If you only have the STL, you will struggle with this. However, once you understand recursion and binary trees, it becomes a lot easier.

In the next section, after the quiz, we will delve deeper into strings.

Quiz 16

When is it appropriate to use a vector?

A. When you need an association between a key and a value stored

B. When you're changing to a collection of items and need to maximize performance

C. When you don't want to have to worry about the details involved in updating the data structure

D. Vectors are appropriate all the time

How do you remove all the items from a map at once?

A. You set the item as an empty string

B. Call erase

C. Call empty

D. Call clear

When should you implement a data structure of your own?

A. When you need something incredibly fast

B. When you need something a bit more robust

C. When you need to take advantage of the data's raw structure, such as when you build an expression tree

D. You will probably never implement your own data structures

Which of these is the correct way of declaring an iterator that can be used with a vector?

A. iterator<int> itr;

B. vector::iterator itr;

C. vector<int>::iterator itr;

D. vector<int>::iterator<int> itr;

Which of these will access the element key that an iterator over a map is currently on?

A. itr.first

B. itr->first

C. itr->key

D. itr.key

How can you tell if an iterator can be used?

A. You compare it with NULL

B. You compare it to the result of calling end() on the container that is being iterated over

C. You check it against 0

D. You compare it with the result of calling begin() on the container that is being iterated over

Let's Talk Strings

If you've managed to work your way through the last couple of sections and fully understand them, well done. For this section we're going to take a break from new data structures and go back to a type that you've already seen: the string.

Though they're very simple data structures, strings are used everywhere. In fact, some programs are written just for reading in and modifying strings. Often you will want strings read in so you can display them to a program user, but there will be times when you will also want some meaning from the string. For example, you may need a specific value from a string so that a search function can be implemented. You might want to come up with an interface for a text-based game, implement a list of high scores or read some tabular data, all comma-separated.

Probably the most common app in use every single day, the web browser is pretty much just one huge string processor of HTML pages. All these require you to do more with a string than just read it in and print it.

Strings can get big, holding many characters in the memory, and that means we can use some of the features we've learned recently, in particular the reference, to create programs that are efficient, even when strings are being passed between functions. In this section we will discuss different operations that can be used with strings as well as ways to keep your program running at optimal speed when you use them.

Reading Strings In

Sometimes, when you're reading strings into a program, you might want to read the whole string and not use a space separator to read one word at a time. A function called getLine will help you do this. The function will take an input stream and read a specified line of text from it. One of the best examples of an input stream is cin. This is what is used for reading one word at a time. It might interest you to know that cin is actually an object of the input stream type and the method that reads the data in is cin>>.

Take a look at a simple example showing one line from a user being read:

```
#include <iostream>

#include <string>

using namespace std;

int main ()

{

        string input;

        cout << "Please input a line of text: ";

        getline( cin, input, '\n' );

        cout << "You typed in " << '\n' << input;

}
```

This is reading a character sequence into the string input, not stopping until it reaches the newline character, when Enter is pressed by the user. The newline is discarded, but if you want to have one in the string, you will need to add it in yourself. Any character can be used as the marker to indicate when reading stops; you don't have to use the newline. getLine won't return until the user has pressed Enter, but the only text read will be up to the point of the character or delimiter.

Here's an example of reading in text that has been CSV-formatted (comma-separated value):

Sonny, Jim, 40 Carrot Top Road, New York, New York, USA

Every section of data is separated with a comma, so what we want is a program that will read user-input CSV data, storing a list of players in a game, using this format:

<player first name>,<player last name>,<player class>

Later, when you get to the file I/O section, you can modify this program and read CSV files in from disk; for now, we'll stick with reading user-input values. The program ends when the first name reads empty:

```cpp
#include <iostream>
#include <string>
using namespace std;
int main ()
{
    while ( 1 )
    {
        string first_name;
        getline( cin, first_name, ',' );
        if ( first_name.size() == 0 )
        {
            break;
        }
```

```cpp
        string last_name;

        getline( cin, last_name, ',' );

        string player_class;

        getline( cin, player_class, '\n' );

        cout << first_name << " " << last_name << " is a " <<
player_class << endl;

    }

}
```

Note that we used the size() method on string; this lets us see if there is an empty string and is just one method that can be used on strings.

String Length and Individual Elements

If you want to find out what length a string is, use the size or length function we just discussed above. These functions belong to the string class and both will return the number of characters a string contains:

string my_string1 = "ten chars.";

int len = my_string1.length(); // or .size();

There isn't any difference between these two methods, so just use whichever one you're comfortable with.

Indexing a string can be done numerically, as with the array. For example, iteration over all the string characters is possible, accessing each of them using the index just as if the string were an array. This is great if you need to work with the individual string characters, such as if you're looking for a particular character like a comma. It's important to remember that, as with arrays, the size of length function is used to stop you from going beyond the end of the string.

Here's another example showing you how to loop over a string so it can be displayed:

```
for( int i = 0; i < my_string.length(); i++ )

{

        cout << my_string[ i ];

}
```

Searching and Substrings

There are three methods you can use with strings for simple searches and substring retrievals: find(), rfind() and substr(). The first, find(), will take both a given substring and a position from the string and will search from the given position for the first instance of the substring. The result will be one of two things—the first instance index or string::npos, which is a special integer value indicating a substring couldn't be found.

The code below shows each instance of the string "dog" within a specified string, counting how many instances there are:

```
#include  <iostream>

#include  <string>

using namespace std;

int main ()

{

        string input;
```

```
    int i = 0;

    int dog_appearances = 0;

    cout << "Please input a line of text: ";

    getline( cin, input, '\n' );

    for ( i = input.find( "dog", 0 ); i != string::npos; i = input.find(
"dog", i ) )

{

            dog_appearances++;

            i++;  // Go beyond the last instance found so we don't

            // find the string again

    }

        cout << "The word dog appears " << dog_appearances << " in the
string

" << "" << input << "";

}
```

If you want to start from the end of the string to find a substring, the rfind() function can be used in much the same way, except the search will be in reverse; going back instead of forward from the given starting point. String matches still run left to right, so if you use rfind() to look for dog, it will not match the string "god."

The substr() function will create a brand-new string that has a slice of the original string of a specified length, starting at a specified position:

// sample prototype

string substr (int position, int length);

For example, if you want to extract a slice of the first 10 characters in a string, you can write:

#include <iostream>

#include <string>

using namespace std;

int main ()

{

    string my_string = "abcdefghijklmnop";

    string first_ten_of_alphabet = my_string.substr(0, 10);

    cout << "The first ten letters of the alphabet are "

        << first_ten_of_alphabet;

}

Passing by Reference

Strings can be small or very large, with lots of data in them. Generally, the best practice is to take the string parameters by reference:

void printString (string& str);

As a reminder, reference parameters are much like pointers—instead of the string variable being copied, the reference to the original is passed instead:

string str_to_show = "there is one x in this string";

printString(str_to_show);

Here, instead of copying the variable called str_to_show, printString has taken the variable address and the str parameter is used as the original string would be.

Passing references does have a potential downside; remember that the reference will take the original variable address so the variable can be modified by the function. It's unlikely that you will do this accidentally when writing your first function, but when you go back to maintain it (add some new functionality), don't forget that the variable that has been passed in can't be modified.

There's a mechanism in C++ that prevents accidental reference parameter modification. The function is able to specify that the reference is a constant and, in C++, we have a special keyword for that: const. Const references can only be read, not modified:

```
void print_string (const string& str)

{

        cout << str; // legal, doesn't modify str

        str = "abc"; // not legal!

}
```

Whenever a reference parameter is added to a function, you should carefully consider whether you want the function modifying the reference. If you don't, make sure it's marked as const—that way, the function can't modify it.

This isn't limited to just references. The same thing can be done with memory that a pointer points to. You could do something like this:

```
void print_ptr (const int* p_val)

{
```

if (p_val == NULL) //memory p_val points to not modified

{

      return;

}

*cout << *p_val; //memory access is OK*

**p_val = 20; // This is not ok, memory p_val points to is modified*

p_val = NULL; // This is ok, not modifying memory, only the pointer

}

Don't forget that your compiler is quite clever. It can tell very easily whether a value is being assigned to the memory that is pointed to or not. It can go beyond looking to see if a pointer has been dereferenced and see exactly what is happening with the reference. The pointer can be modified because the value of the pointer has been copied. If you changed p_val, it would not affect the variable passed into the function.

Const can also be used to both document and enforce that a specified variable won't change. If you attempt to modify it, the compiler will warn you.

When a const variable is declared, it must be immediately assigned:

const int x = 4; // This should be assigned at the time the variable is created

x = 4; // this is not ok, because x cannot be modified.

Using const wherever you can is good C++ style. When you declare a variable as const, the rest of your code is easier to read because nobody can modify it; you know that the variable can't change later down the line.

Tracking whether that variable takes another value or not isn't important; it leaves you free to focus on the non-const variables and whether they get modified or not. It also means you can't modify that variable by mistake and change the way the code behaves.

Let's say that you have a piece of code that asks a user to input a first and last name; a string is created to contain the full name of the user and the variable that holds the full name should be declared as const because it should not be modified in any way.

Const Propagation

Once a variable has been declared as const, there is no way of passing it by references to any method that takes non-const references. You also can't pass it by a pointer to any method that takes non-const pointers because the method may try using the pointer to modify the value. const X* is not the same type as X* and const X&, which is a reference declared to an X, is not the same type as X&.

X* can be converted to const X* and X& can be converted to const X&, but not vice versa. If you write a method like the one below, for example, it won't compile:

void print_nonconst_val (int& p_val)

{

cout << p_val;

}

const int x = 10;

print_nonconst_val(x); // won't compile because const int can't be passed to any function that takes a non-const reference

However, only pointers and references have this restriction because they share the original value. If you copy a variable, for example, when you pass it by value, there is no need for the function parameter to be made const:

void print_nonconst_val (int val)

{

> *cout << val;*

}

const int x = 10;

print_nonconst_val(x); // fine, x is copied, so it doesn't matter that val

// this isn't const because it is local to the function called print_nonconst_val

As soon as a variable is declared as const, you might find that you have to make other variables const too, specifically the reference and pointer function parameters.

It can be tricky to use const when you're working with helper methods or libraries that don't use const. Conversely, if you're building helper methods or libraries of your own, const should be used to ensure that any code using your methods can take full advantage of it.

The standard library in C++ was built so that const variables can be used safely in code and with the standard library. From now on, const variables will be used where needed.

Note that variables can be declared as const in loops, even if a variable is reset every loop:

for (int i = 0; i < 10; i++)

{

```
        const i_squared = i * i;

        cout << i_squared;

}
```

We can declare i_squared as const even though it gets reset on every loop. The reason for this is scope: the i_squared scope is entirely inside the body of the loop. On every loop, as far as the compiler is concerned, the variable is being recreated.

Const and the STL

When we looked at the STL we saw a function that displays a map. The map is passed by value, so to get passed into the displayMap function, the entire map has to be copied. Let's see that function once more:

```
void displayMap (map<string, string> map_to_print) // map is copied!

{

        for ( map<string, string>::iterator itr = map_to_print.begin(),
end =

map_to_print.end();

                itr != end;

                ++itr )

        {

                cout << itr->first << " --> " << itr->second << endl;

        }

}
```

References would be really useful here; we could make the map a reference so we don't have to copy it. Even better would be if it were a const reference, making it very clear that this is nothing more than a display function and doesn't edit the map:

```
void displayMap (const map<string, string>& map_to_print)

{

        for ( map<string, string>::iterator itr = map_to_print.begin(),
end =

map_to_print.end();

                itr != end;

                ++itr )

        {

        cout << itr->first << " --> " << itr->second << endl;

        }

}
```

If you were to do this though, all you would get is a whole heap of errors at compile time. Why? Because when you make the map a const, you are effectively barring anyone from modifying any of the elements. The problem is, an iterator will let modifications be made.

You could write:

```
if ( itr->first == "Billy Bunter" )

{

        itr->second = "billybunter@thisemailaddress.com"
```

}

to change that particular address in the address book. Thankfully, STL is also const-friendly and every STL container has a special iterator—the const_iterator. This can be used in the same way as a standard iterator with the exception that the container being iterated over can't be modified by writing to the const_iterator:

```
void displayMap (const map<string, string>& map_to_print)

{

        for ( map<string, string>::const_iterator itr =
map_to_print.begin(),

end = map_to_print.end();

                itr != end;

                ++itr )

        {

                cout << itr->first << " --> " << itr->second << endl;

        }

}
```

The const_iterator must be used whenever you're iterating over a const container or when an iterator is required for data access, but not to modify the container.

Take the quiz and see how you do. In the next section, we'll discuss using Code::Blocks for debugging.

Quiz 17

Which of these is valid code?

A. const int& x;

B. const int x = 3; int *p_int = & x;

C. const int x = 12; const int *p_int = & x;

D. int x = 3; const int y = x; int& z = y;

Which of these function signatures will allow the code snippet below to compile?

int x = 3; fun(

x);

A. void fun (int x);

B. void fun (int& x);

C. void fun (const int& x);

D. A and C

Which of these is the best way of telling if a string search failed?

A. Compare the result position to 0

B. Compare the result position to -1

C. Compare the result position to string::npos

D. Check to see if the result position is greater than the string length

How is an iterator for a const STL container created?

A. By declaring the iterator const

B. By using indices and not an iterator to loop over it

C. By using a const_iterator

D. By declaring the template types to be const

Debugging with Code::Blocks

You've learned quite a few of the more powerful techniques for C++ programs, but locating bugs in a program is another matter entirely, especially is a program is complicated. That's where debugging tools come into play. Debuggers let you check your program as it runs, making it easy to see exactly what is going on. One of the biggest mistakes made by new programmers is not learning how to use debuggers because they don't see them as necessary. Learning how to use a debugger so you can use it on your code is time well-spent because it will save you a lot of frustration and hard work down the line.

If you used Code::Blocks to set your environment up, then the debugger is already installed. If you're using a different debugger, don't worry, because most are pretty much the same. The important thing is that you have one.

This section will introduce you to many programs with bugs so you can see how it all works. I would suggest that you start a new Code::Blocks project so you can follow along.

The program we have below is meant to be computing interest rates. These are compounded on an annual basis and the amount of money is specified. This code has bugs in it and therefore the wrong value will be printed:

#include <iostream>

```cpp
using namespace std;

double computeInterest (double base_val, double rate, int years)

{

        double final_multiplier;

        for ( int i = 0; i < years; i++ )

        {

                final_multiplier *= (1 + rate);

        }

        return base_val * final_multiplier;

}

int main ()

{

        double base_val;

        double rate;

        int years;

        cout << "Input a base value: ";

        cin >> base_val;

        cout << "Input an interest rate: ";

        cin >> rate;

        cout << "Input the number of years to compound: ";
```

```
    cin >> years;

    cout << "After " << years << " you will have " << computeInterest(

base_val, rate, years ) << " money" << endl;

}
```

The result of this is:

Input a base value: 100

Input an interest rate: .1

Input the number of years to compound: 1

After 1 you will have 1.40619e-306 money

Clearly, that's a mistake. 1.40618e-306 is most definitely not the figure we want. It's obvious there's a bug in the program, so let's run it in our debugger and see what comes up.

To start with, we need to make sure that we have configured Code::Blocks properly and to do this, we need debugging symbols. These symbols allow the debugger to work out the code line that is being executed at any given time so you always know where in the program you are.

To make sure the symbols are properly set up, open Code::Blocks and go to the Project Menu. Click on Build and make sure that, in Debug, the option for "Produce Debugging Symbols" is enabled.

Then go to the Build Menu and click on Select Target -> Debug and make sure it is selected as the project target. This ensures that the program is built using the symbols that you set up. The easiest thing to do when you set up a Code::Blocks program is to accept the defaults.

Now you're ready to start debugging. If your program was already built but the configuration was changed, rebuild it before you start.

Breaking into the Program

A debugger allows you to see what is going on in your program—which piece of code is being executed and the variable values. In order to do this, the debugger needs to break into the program, which means it needs to pause the execution. This is done by adding a breakpoint into the program and then running it using the debugger. The program is executed up to the breakpoint and then you can examine the program or go through it one line at a time and see the effect each line has on your variables.

We'll set our breakpoint quite early, at the beginning of the main function, so we can see how the whole program executes. Find the line in the code that reads:

double base_val;

Put your cursor on the line and press the F5 key (or go to Debug -> Toggle Breakpoint.) A red dot will appear in the sidebar beside the code line, indicating the breakpoint. Now the program can be executed, so click on Debug -> Start or press F8.

The program will now execute as normal until it gets to the breakpoint which, in this case, will be very early. The debugger will open and you will see, under the red dot, a small yellow triangle. This tells you which line is next to execute.

There should also be another window open called "Watches." Look carefully for it, as it may be hidden. This window displays all the variables that are currently available, local or function arguments, and you can see their values. These look like complete nonsense right now, but that's only because they haven't been initialized—we'll do that shortly. You need the debugger to move to the next executable line, so press the F7 key. This executes the line with the yellow triangle and the cout statement is then run; a message will be output on the screen requesting a value be input.

Don't try typing anything in. It won't work because the program is in the debugger.

Press F7 again and the program will wait for user input—the cin function has not yet been returned because user input is required first. Type in a value of 100 so it matches the bug report and then do the same for the next two variables, using the values from earlier: .1 for interest and 1 for the compounded years number.

Now you get to this code line:

*cout << "After " << years << " you will have " <<
computeInterest(base_val,*

rate, years) << " money" << endl;

You need to check that the inputs were correctly handled, so look at the Watch window and see what the local variable values are.

So far, everything should be correct. The base is 100, the rate is .1 and years is 1. Hold on! The rate isn't .1—it's actually .1000000000000001. But that's just the quirkiness of floating point numbers. They're not entirely precise, but as the difference is so small, it really doesn't matter.

Okay, everything so far is fine. Now you want to see what's happening in the computeInterest function. You need another debugger command here, called "step into." This will go into the function that is going to be called on the line you're on and is used when you want to do your debugging inside the function. So that's what you need to do: step into computeInterest. But wait a minute! This line has a whole load of function calls:

*cout << "After " << years << " you will have " <<
computeInterest(base_val,*

rate, years) << " money" << endl;

The debugger is smart enough to know not to step into any function from the standard library. All it will do is go straight to computeInterest, so let's do that right now.

The first thing to do is verify that the arguments are right; you might have gotten them mixed up. Go to the Watch window and expand the section for Function arguments. It should all look right.

Do the same with the local variables, however, and you should see a problem. Neither final_multiplier nor i look too good. Remember though, you looked at this earlier and the values were just nuts because they hadn't been initialized. If you press F7, the initialization for the loop will be executed. Do it now and see what happens. Check the variables again; i looks fine, but there's still something off about final_multiplier—it hasn't been properly initialized.

Plus, the code line you're currently on is about to use that variable:

*final_multiplier *= (1 + rate);*

This line is saying that you should multiply final_multiplier * (1 + rate) and then get the value assigned to final_multiplier. The problem is, final_multiplier is off, so you would get a fake value from the operation.

Can you see how this should be fixed?

Final_multiplier must be initialized on the code line where it was declared and initialized to 1. Fix it and it will all work fine.

Debugging Crashes

Another kind of bug you will come across is a crash, and these are, quite often, very scary for a new programmer because they seem kind of extreme. As time goes by, these will become your favorite bug to work out because you will know exactly where the problem occurred. Bad data is what causes the crash, and the program can be stopped at the exact crash point so you can work out what the problem was and where it originated.

Below is a simple program that creates nodes in a linked list, printing each of the list values. And, of course, it has bugs:

```cpp
#include <iostream>

using namespace std;

struct LinkedList

{

        int val;

        LinkedList *next;

};

void printList (const LinkedList *lst)

{

if ( lst != NULL )

{

        cout << lst->val;

        cout << "\n";

        printList( lst->next );

        }

}

int main ()
```

```
{
        LinkedList *lst;

        lst = new LinkedList;

        lst->val = 10;

        lst->next = new LinkedList;

        lst->next->val = 11;

        printList( lst );

        return 0;

}
```

When this program is run, it won't work. Instead, it will do one of two things: crash, or enter an infinite loop, indicating that there's something wrong. You'll need to run the code in the debugger to find out what.

Press F8 and the debugger will cause a message to pop up almost immediately. This tells you that there's a Segmentation Fault or a segfault which is using invalid pointers. Basically, the program has tried dereferencing an invalid pointer or a NULL pointer. What's happening is the program is trying to get into memory that it just doesn't have access to.

How can you work out where the invalid pointer came from? The debugger breaks on the line where the program crashed. Click on OK in that message box and look for the yellow pointer on the code line that crashed:

```
cout << lst->val;
```

This line has just one pointer called lst. Go to the Watch window and see what the lst value is. You should see a value of 0xbadfood, which is a special value the compiler uses for initializing memory at the time of allocation. This is used only when the program is running in a debugger and is why you often see behavior different to what you would see outside of the debugger. The debugger will use a consistent value that, if accessed, will cause a segfault; that way, if uninitialized pointers are used, they show up immediately.

We now know that lst wasn't initialized, but why not? We can use another of the debugger features here, the call stack. This will show you all of the functions that are currently being executed and it has a number of columns. Nr is a number that references each of the stack frames, while Address is the function address. Function is the function name and the function arguments. You will see lst=oxbadfood in the call stack. There are also columns for file and line number, so you can easily locate the code line that was executing.

The function at the top of the call stack is the currently executing function while the function underneath that is the current function. The function at the bottom is the main function, the one that starts off the program.

You should be able to see that printList was called three times; the first two have pointer values that are valid and the third has the oxbadfood value. Remember, two list nodes were created by the main function and the first two calls are using those list nodes. The third uses a pointer that hasn't been initialized, Now you know that you need to look again at the code initializing the list and, there, you can see that the next value to NULL wasn't set for the end node.

Because the memory isn't predictable and may even look as though it's valid, the program can behave in a strange way and be hard to find. Instead of crashing immediately, for example, it could read fake memory and then, later, when it uses the memory, it will crash. Using the debugger makes things easier because the behavior becomes consistent and the program crashes as early as it can, putting you as near as possible to the problem.

This particular problem is now resolved, but there will be times when you want some more information about other stack frames. The debugger context can easily be switched to any of the stack frames to see the local variables. To do this, go to the stack frame you're interested in and right-click on it. Choose 'switch to this frame' and the yellow arrow will move to indicate the function call in the chosen stack frame. You can use the Watch window to look at the local variables for that stack frame.

Breaking into Hung Programs

Sometimes, a problem won't be a simple crash; on occasion you might be dealing with a stuck program. It could be an infinite loop or have a slow system call. When you come up against a scenario like this, the program can be run in the debugger. Then when you get to the problem code, you can request that the debugger break into the program.

Here's another example showing how this works:

```
#include <iostream>

using namespace std;

int main ()

{

        int factorial = 1;

        for ( int i = 0; i < 10; i++ )

        {

                factorial *= i;

        }

        int sum = 0;
```

```
for ( int i = 0; i < 10; i++ )
{
        sum += i;
}
// factorial w/o two
int factorial_without_two = 1;
for ( int i = 0; i < 10; i++ )
{
        if ( i == 2 )
        {
                continue;
        }
        factorial_without_two *= i;
}
// sum w/o two
int sum_without_two = 0;
for ( int i = 0; i < 10; i++ )
{
        if ( i = 2 )
        {
```

```
            continue;

        }

        sum_without_two += i;

    }

}
```

When you run this program it won't exit because it's stuck somewhere. To find out where, run the program in the debugger, wait until it gets stuck, and then break in and look around.

Build the program and run it in the debugger by pressing F8. When it runs and doesn't exit, click on Debug and then on Stop Debugger. This makes the debugger break in so you can see what is happening at the point of execution. Once the program is stopped, you can see the call stack and it should look a bit weird. What you see is not your code, so what's the issue?

What you see is the result of what happens when you break into a program that is running. The top of the call stack is named ntdll!DbgUiConnectToDbg. So, ntdll is a core DLL in Windows and DbgUiConnectToDbg is the function that is being called. This function is what breaks into running processes, but what happened to the code that was supposedly being executed? It turns out that, when you break into running processes, the debugger creates a separate thread, which is a way of simultaneously executing code.

To break into a running process, the debugger has to execute code at the same time the original code is executing. This is done by creating a new thread for executing the break-in code. This thread wasn't there in our last examples because we already had a breakpoint set: the debugger had sufficient control to break in without having to create a new thread. This time, we didn't want to break in at a set line of code; we wanted to get in at a certain point in time. So, to locate the code we were executing, all we have to do is get into the correct thread. Click Debug -> Debugging Windows and then click on Running Threads.

The Thread window opens and you should see both threads. In the Active column, the current thread is shown by a * - this is the thread that broke in. You want the second thread, so right-click it and choose 'Switch to this thread'.

Go back to the call stack and the information is now much better. You can see the appropriate code and the yellow indicator is on line 29—the next code line to be executed—which is this code:

for (int i = 0; i < 10; i++)

{

    if (i = 2)

    {

        continue;

    }

    sum_without_two += i;

}

Because the program got stuck and was right in the middle of a loop, it's a pretty good guess that the loop won't terminate, but the only way to prove that is to step through it.

This is where you have to be careful; if you use the Next Line command, the debugger will just execute the code that is in the other thread—that's the current code line being executed. Instead, a breakpoint is needed in the original code and the program must be run until it gets to it.

Put the breakpoint on the line where the if statement is and then press Continue (CTRL+F7). When the program reaches that breakpoint you're on the correct thread and the Next Line command can be used to step through and look at what is going on.

What you should see is that you keep getting if (i=2) and then returning to the beginning of the loop. So, what's happening? Go to the locals window and look at the value of i. On the loop code line, i is two. Once the loop code has been executed, i is 3. And when the if statement line has been executed, it goes back to 2.

It looks very much like the if statement may be setting the value of i to 2. Can you spot why? It's a common error: one equal sign has been used instead of two.

You might also be asking yourself why the program never gets to the continue line; why does it always keep jumping back from the if statement to the loop? This is down to the debugger—sometimes it isn't easy to match machine code (the code that actually gets processed) to a specific line in the code. In this case, the debugger is struggling to distinguish if(x=2) from the continue statement. This will happen every now and again with the debugger and, as time goes by, you will begin to pick up on it more easily.

Modifying Variables

When you're debugging, there may be occasions when you want the value of a variable modified. For example, you may want to ensure that a variable has been set to a specific value so that the code really does work. To do this, open the Watch window and right-click on any variable; to change it, choose Change Value and then set the variable value to what you want it to be.

Be careful that you don't do this just before the value is initialized; if you do, the value will be overwritten.

In summary, Code::Blocks debugger lets you understand what's happening in your program and helps to pinpoint problems, providing plenty of tools to help you sort things out.

Next, we will move on to more advanced programming concepts.

Chapter 4: Advanced Guide

Writing Larger Programs

Before we start, if you have gotten to this stage and do NOT have a proper understanding of everything you have read so far, do not go any further. Go back, read again and come back here when you think you're ready. This last section of the book is more advanced and contains some of the most important concepts and information in C++ programming.

So far, much of what we have talked about has given you a new way of doing things. Now we need to go bigger. Up until now, we have only written small programs and, as we have increased the programs in size a little, it might have sunk in how much harder the bigger programs are to work on. Some have problems if a program has a couple of hundred lines. Others have trouble with thousands.

Eventually, a program will become too big to understand properly. What if you want to build a game, software or an operating system? What you need are techniques that make large programs much easier to structure and to understand. Over the years, many programmers have come up against this and have developed techniques that can help you to build these larger programs. In this section we will discuss techniques and tools to build more sophisticated and larger programs and make designing smaller problems much easier too.

We'll start off with concepts that we will return to as we get into designing and building larger programs. The first thing is the actual code. We'll talk about laying your program out on disk in such a way that it isn't just one big cpp file. Then we'll move on to logical design, ways of writing programs without the need to remember every little detail of the way it all works all the time.

Breaking Your Program Down

As your program grows in size, you won't want to keep it all in one source file. It will get too hard to make changes and there's a good chance that you will just get lost and won't be able to find what you want. When your program reaches two thousand lines, start thinking about splitting it across several source files.

Doing it this way makes it easier to find what you want; the files are smaller and you can split them into specific sections of code. And program design will become much easier as each header contains the right interface for the source code and no other files can use the data structures or functions not defined in those headers. You might think this is limiting, but it isn't. Each subsystem implementation can be separated from the functionality that it gives another subsystem.

The C++ Build Process

Before you start splitting up your code, you must have a better understanding of the way that compilation in C++ works. To be fair, compilation isn't really the right word here— it doesn't in any way mean "to create an executable file."

That involves a process of several stages, the three most important being:

- Preprocessing

- Compilation

- Linking

The best way to refer to the process of starting with source code files and ending with an executable file is "build and compilation." You will, however, see people refer to the entire process as compiling. Let's go through each stage to see how it works.

Preprocessing

The very first step in the process is the compiler running the C preprocessor. The purpose of this is to enact changes in a textual format to a file before the compilation step is reached. The preprocessor will understand the directives—commands written into the source but only intended for the preprocessor, not the compiler.

Every preprocessor directive will be prefixed with a # symbol that stops the compiler from even seeing them. Take the following statement as an example:

#include <iostream>

This statement lets the preprocessor know that it should put the text from the iostream header into the file. Whenever a header is included, it gets pasted into the file before the compiler sees. The #include, which is the directive, is removed.

The preprocessor will also expand macros. Macros are strings of text that tend to get replaced by other more complicated strings of text. You can use a macro to put your constants into one place for easier management.

For example, you could write something like this:

#define MY_NAME "Billy"

Now, instead of writing "Billy" through the source file, you can just use MY_NAME.

You write

cout << "Hello " << MY_NAME << '\n';

and what the compiler sees is

cout << "Hello " << "Billy" << '\n';

If you want to use a different name, all you have to do is change the line in the code with the #define directive; you won't have to do a global search and replace across your entire code. A macro can place pieces of information in a central place so they can easily be changed. Let's say that you want to provide your program with a version number and refer to that number through the code. A macro could be used:

#define VERSION 3

// ...

cout << "The version is " << VERSION

And because the preprocessor does its work before the code is compiled, you can also use it for removing code. You might, on occasion, only want certain code compiled in a build specifically for debugging; all you do is tell the preprocessor that you want source code included ONLY if a certain macro is defined. Then, when that code is required, the macro is defined and, when the code isn't needed, you just remove the macro.

Let's say, for example, that you have debugging code that will print variable values but only want them printed at certain times. In this case, the debugging code could be included in the build conditionally:

#include <iostream>

#define DEBUG

using namespace std;

int main ()

```
{

    int x;

    int y;

    cout << "Enter value for x: ";

    cin >> x;

    cout << "Enter value for y: ";

    cin >> y;

    x *= y;
#ifdef DEBUG

    cout << "Variable x: " << x << '\n' << "Variable y: " << y;

#endif

    // further use of x and y

}
```

If you want the variable display turned off, just comment the #define DEBUG out:

```
// #define DEBUG
```

The preprocessor also has support for checking if a macro has NOT been defined. You could, for example, have code execute on the condition that DEBUG has NOT been set and you would use #ifndef for this—if not defined. We'll discuss this more when we get to multiple header files.

Compilation

Compilation is nothing more than transforming source code files that have the .cpp file extension into object files with the .o or .obj extension. Object files are where your program is written in a way that the computer processor understands it, i.e., in machine language, for every function that is the source file. Each file is compiled separately, which means that the object file will only have the machine language for the compiled source file.

For example, if you compile three files but don't link them, the output will be three separate object files and each will have a translation of the relevant source code into the machine language. You won't be able to run them though; first they must be transformed into executable files. That's where linking comes in.

Linking

Linking refers to the creation of an executable file, a .DLL or .EXE for example, from multiple libraries and object files. The linker will create one file in the correct executable format and put the contents from each of the relevant object files into it. It will also concern itself with any object file where functions that are outside of the original source file are referenced. An example would be referencing functions that are in the C++ standard library. Let's say you make a call of

cout << "Hi"

into the standard library. You're using a function that you haven't defined. It has been defined as the equivalent of an object file, just not one of yours.

When the compiler steps in, it will know that you used a valid function call because the iostream header file was included, but because the function isn't a part of your cpp file, the compiler will leave a marker at the call point. The liner will go through the file and, for each of the markers, will locate the right address from another linked object file.

This is often known as a "fixup" and, when your program is broken down into several source files, you can use this ability to fix up all the functions that are calling into another source file. If the linker can't locate a function definition, it will throw an undefined function error; the compiler may allow the code through, but that doesn't mean it's right. The linker is the first part of the process that will immediately look at the entire program in order to detect the issue.

Why is Compiling and Linking Separate?

Simply because not all functions have to be defined in the same object file; this makes it possible to compile your source files one at a time and link them back together later on. Let's say that you change a file called FrequentlyUpdated.cpp but don't change one called InfrequentlyUpdated.cpp; the InfrequentlyUpdated.cpp object file will not need recompiling. When you can omit compiling that isn't necessary, you save yourself a whole heap of time.

Splitting a Program Over Multiple Files

So, what is the best structuring code to take advantage of this? Let's say that we have a program that contains shared code. The program is called Orig.cpp and you want to use it in a different program. I'm going to separate out each step so you can understand it but, in practice, many of these steps will be done together.

1. **Splitting declarations and definitions**

If you haven't already started splitting your code into several files, you won't have a decent separation of the declarations and definitions for your functions. The very first step is to ensure that every function has a declaration and then move them all to the top of the file.

2. **Shared functions**

Once the definitions and declarations are separated, go through and work out which are specific to the file and which need to be in the common file

3. **Move your functions**

Now all the shared (common) function declarations can go into a new file called Shared.h and the shared implementations can be placed into a file called Shared.cpp. At the same time, you also need to include Shared.h from the Orig.cpp file. The shared functions can still be called because all their declarations are together in one place.

When Orig.cpp is built, it needs to be set up to link to the file called Shared.obj, but we'll talk about that shortly.

First, an example. This is a small program that contains generic code for a linked list. The code is written in Orig.cpp. We will take the code and split it into two—a header and a source file—that are reusable:

```cpp
#include <iostream>

using namespace std;

struct Node

{

        Node *p_next;

        int value;

};

Node* addNode (Node* p_list, int value)
```

```cpp
{
        Node *p_new_node = new Node;

        p_new_node->value = value;

        p_new_node->p_next = p_list;

        return p_new_node;
}
void printList (const Node* p_list)
{
        const Node* p_cur_node = p_list;

        while ( p_cur_node != NULL )
        {
                cout << p_cur_node->value << endl;

                p_cur_node = p_cur_node->p_next;
        }
}
int main ()
{
        Node *p_list = NULL;

        for ( int i = 0; i < 10; ++i )
```

```
        {

                int value;

                cout << "Enter value for list node: ";

                cin >> value;

                p_list = addNode( p_list, value );

        }

        printList( p_list );

}
```

First, the declarations need to be split from the definitions. I'm only going to show you the declarations—the remainder of the file doesn't need to be changed:

```
struct Node

{

        Node *p_next;

        int value;

};

Node* addNode (Node* p_list, int value);

void printList (const Node* p_list);
```

Because we don't have any declarations that are file-specific, there is nothing required to separate them. Immediately we can place all the declarations into a new file called linkedlist.h (a header file). Here are the files in their entirety:

Linkedlist.h

```
struct Node

{

        Node *p_next;

        int value;

};

Node* addNode (Node* p_list, int value);

void printList (const Node* p_list);
```

linkedlist.cpp

```
#include  <iostream>

#include "linkedlist.h"

using namespace std;

Node* addNode (Node* p_list, int value)

{

        Node *p_new_node = new Node;

        p_new_node->value = value;

        p_new_node->p_next = p_list;
```

```cpp
        return p_new_node;

}

void printList (const Node* p_list)

{

        const Node* p_cur_node = p_list;

        while ( p_cur_node != NULL )

        {

                cout << p_cur_node->value << endl;

                p_cur_node = p_cur_node->p_next;

        }

}
```

orig.cpp

```cpp
#include  <iostream>

#include "linkedlist.h"

using namespace std;

int main ()

{

        Node *p_list = NULL;

        for ( int i = 0; i < 10; ++i )
```

```
        {

                int value;

                cout << "Enter value for list node: ";

                cin >> value;

                p_list = addNode( p_list, value );

        }

        printList( p_list );

}
```

There should not be any function definitions in the header file. If you add one and the header file is included in two or more of your source files, the definition will appear multiple times when it comes to linking. This just confuses things.

Make sure that declarations don't show up more than once in any one source file. The Orig.cpp file may end up including a few more header files and one of those may have linkedlist.h:

newheader.h

#include "linkedlist.h"

// other code

orig.cpp

#include "linkedlist.h"

#include "newheader.h"

/* rest of code from orig.cpp */

Now Orig.cpp has included two instances of linkedlist.h: a direct and indirect inclusion though newheader.h.

To fix this, you need an include guard; this will use the preprocessor for controlling whether a file should be included or not. It should say:

if <this file has not been added >

    <mark that we added it in the file>

    <add it>

This can be used safely because there should never be a need to add a header file more than once.

Implementation of an include guard requires a preprocessor command of #ifndef—we mentioned it earlier. This command is saying "if not defined," the code block up to the next #endif statement should be included:

#ifndef ORIG_H

// header contents

#endif

What we're saying here is, if _ORIG_H has not been defined, include all the code up to the #endif. The trick here is that now we are able to define ORIG_H:

#ifndef ORIG_H

#define ORIG_H

// contents of the header contents

#endif

Just think about what will happen if this file is added in twice. On the first inclusion, ORIG_H hasn't been defined, and #ifndef will include the rest of the file. That includes the part responsible for defining ORIG_H. On the second inclusion, the #ifndef will not be true and none of the code will be added in.

It's important that you name your include guards with unique names. Best practice is to use the header file name and the _H. This will ensure that each guard is unique and won't conflict with any other include guards or #define values.

One last thing: do not directly include .cpp files. This just causes an issue because the compiler compiles the individual function definitions into each of the object files. The liner will then pick up on several definitions for one function, which is a big programming no-no.

Handling Multiple Source Files

To set up the correct linking for multiple source files, you need to have your environment set up correctly. We'll go through each environment set up:

Code::Blocks

1. Adding new source files to a current project requires you to click on File -> New -> Empty Source File

2. Click Yes on the message asking if you want the file added to your current project

3. Next, choose your file name

4. Code::Blocks will ask you which build configurations you want for the file. As far as source files go, this is the step that will include the file in the linking step. Enable all available options. Although header files are never linked, you can choose the Release and Debug options because Code::Blocks is clever enough not to include them in the linking options.

Using the new files will require a header and source file and the code changes that we discussed earlier.

G++

If you're using g++, you don't really need to do anything other than create and name the files using the command line. Let's say that you have the two source files from before— orig.cpp and shared.cpp—along with a header file called shared.h. One simple command will compile both source files:

g++ orig.cpp shared.cpp

No need to include the header file on the command line; this gets added by the .cpp files that need it. This recompiles all the given files on the command line. But if you want to reap the benefits of the separate compilation, then each file can be separately compiled using the -c flag of:

g++ -c orig.cpp

g++ -c shared.cpp

and then use the following command to link them:

g++ orig.o shared.o

Or, if there are no false object files in the current directory, you can just do the following:

```
g++ *.o
```

It's tedious doing separate compilations and an easier method is to use a makefile. Your program would process definitions and be used for encoding the source files; that way, if one source file is changed, makefile will know that any other source file depending on that file needs to be recompiled.

We won't go into any further detail about makefile because it's beyond the scope of this guide.

XCode

1. Adding a source file in XCode is as simple as clicking File -> New File

2. From the file options, choose C and C++ on the left pane and the C++ on the right. If you're only adding a header file, select Header. If you're adding a header and cpp implementation, choose C++ and press Next.

3. Select a file name and either choose the default location or one that you want.

4. If you opted for C++, now you can create the header file.

XCode sets the build process up automatically so the new cpp file you're creating is compiled and linked with other source files.

Take the quiz. Then, in the next section, we will look at program design.

Quiz 18

Which of these is not a part of the build process in C++?

A. Linking

B. Compiling

C. Preprocessing

D. Postprocessing

When would an error that is related to an undefined function happen?

A. The link phase

B. The compilation phase

C. When the program starts up

D. When the function is called

What might happen if you include a header file more than once?

A. Errors relating to multiple declarations

B. Nothing will happen because the header files only get loaded once

C. It will depend on the way that the header file is implemented

D. You can only include a header file in one source file at a time so this will not be an issue

Is there any advantage to having separate steps for compiling and linking?

A. No; it's far too confusing and will slow things down because you have several programs running.

B. Yes; you can diagnose the errors much more easily because you will know if the problems are arising in the compiler or the linker.

C. Yes; it means that you can recompile just the file that was changed, saving time in both linking and compilation.

Introduction to Program Design

We've looked at a way of storing code physically on disk to make editing easier as your code gets larger, so now we can move on to the next level: organizing your code in a logical manner so that it can be edited and worked with more easily. We'll start by going through some common problems that arise as your code gets larger.

Redundant Code

We talked very briefly about the problem of repetitive code when functions are introduced so let's go a bit deeper now. When your programs expand, you will find that certain ideas start to be repeated. Take a video game for example; it's going to require code that draws different graphical elements on the screen such as a bullet, spaceship, etc.

Before a spaceship can be drawn, you need to be able to draw a pixel. A pixel is one point of color on a screen and its location is found using two-dimensional coordinates. Most of the time a graphics library can be used for this.

You are also going to need code that will use pixels or other graphical elements provided by a graphics library, such as circles and lines, so that the game elements can be drawn.

If you're building games, this drawing is going to be common in your code. In our game, every single time a bullet or a spaceship moves, that drawing needs to be redrawn. If you insert all the code responsible for drawing the bullet each and every time, you will end up with a great deal of redundant code. All this does is add complexity to your program that really isn't necessary and make your program that much harder to read.

What you want is a standardized way of drawing things like bullets and spaceships so your code isn't having to repeat the process over and again. Why? Let's assume that you want to make a change—perhaps a new color for a bullet. If your program has code that displays the bullet in a dozen different places, you'll need to change every single piece of that code for each change you wanted to make.

That means, whenever you want a bullet displayed, you need to work the code out over and again or find a piece of the code and copy/paste it, perhaps changing a variable name here or there so conflicts don't arise. Whichever way you do it, you need to focus on how the bullet is being displayed and not just on being able to draw the bullet. And, when you go back over your code, you now have the onerous task of trying to figure out what everything does.

If you see this in your code

circle(10, 10, 5);

fillCircle(10, 10, RED);

it will be tougher to work out that it means a bullet should be drawn than if you see this:

displayBullet(10, 10);

Functions are used for providing useful names to code so that when you do read back over things, you can understand what is going on. You likely haven't come across it yet. However, as you start to build bigger programs, you will find yourself spending no small amount of time reading over your code, more so than you do writing it. For that reason, it's important that you use good functions and good names.

Assumptions About Data Storage

Code redundancy is a disease and algorithms aren't the only thing affected. Let's look at another code example where the redundancy is hidden. Let's say that we want a chess program using an array to represent the current position on the board. Every time the board is accessed, you can just access the array.

If you initialize rank two so it contains white pawns only, you can write:

```
enum ChessPiece { WHITE_PAWN, WHITE_ROOK /* and others */ };
```

```
// ... plenty of code
```

```
for ( int i = 0; i < 8; i++ )

{

        board[ i ][ 1 ] = WHITE_PAWN;

}
```

And later, if you want to see what chess pieces is on a specific square, you just read it from the array:

```
// ... plenty of code
```

```
if ( board[ 0 ][ 0 ] == WHITE_ROOK )

{
```

/ do something here */*

}

As your program gets larger, you will find that there is a lot of code that all uses the chessboard and is scattered everywhere. What harm is there in that? I mean, it's not like you're repeating yourself whenever you read the array; it's only one line of code. Yet, that is exactly what you are doing—repeating yourself, using the same data structure over and over. And by doing that, your code is making a special assumption about the way your chessboard is being represented. You may not be repeating the actual algorithm, but you're repeating the data representation assumption. Look at it like this: It may take just one code line to access the chessboard, but that doesn't mean that will always be the case. If your board is implemented in a different way, you might need to use a technique that's more complex to access it.

The more sophisticated of the chess programs will use different representations other than arrays. What they use is a multiple-bit board and these will always need more than just a single code line. If you want to write a chess program, start with an array; that way, you can focus on the algorithms needed before you need to think about optimizing the code for speed. And to make changing the board representation easier, you can hide the array. But how do you do this?

When we needed to hide the details of painting bullets, we used a function that could be called instead of writing lots of code that painted directly to the screen. We can do that in this case too, by using a function that hides the representation details. Instead of directly using the array, the code will call on a function that can access it. For example, you can write a function called getPiece, like this:

int getPiece (int x, int y)

```
{

    return board[ x ][ y ];

}
```

Our function takes two arguments and a value is returned in the same way it would be if we accessed the array. It doesn't mean any less typing because the same input data from before is still needed—an x and y coordinate. Where it differs is that we have hidden the means we need to access the board inside a function. From here on, the program should use this function for accessing the array and, if you later decide the representation needs to be changed, you can do it one function, not in 10 or 20 separate pieces of code.

This is all known as functional abstraction and applying it means that if you have any operation that needs to be repeated, you place it into a function. The functions will specify all of the inputs and outputs to the caller but won't tell the caller how the function is implemented. That is how the algorithm or the data structure is in use. The function lets callers use the "promise" that the function is making regarding the interface, but no details about implementation.

There are a few advantages to hiding algorithms and data in functions:

1. It makes life so much easier down the line. Instead of having to keep remembering how an algorithm is implemented, you just call on the function. So long as that function works properly for every valid input, the output can be trusted without the need to remember how everything works.

2. When you can trust your function to work, you can start looking at problem-solving by writing code that will reuse those functions over and again. There's no need to worry about details like accessing the board, leaving you free to focus on solving new problems.

3. If you do happen to find any mistakes in the logic, all you need to do is change a single function, not lots of code.

4. When you write a function to hide a data structure, you're also "writing in" flexibility about storage and representation of data. You'll start off with representations that are inefficient but easy to write and replace them later with implementations that are faster and only need require a couple of functions to be changed.

Design And Comments

When you create functions that are well-designed, it's important that those functions are documented. That isn't as simple as you might think. Using good comments will answer the questions that anyone reading your code might have.

So far, you have seen comments like this in this guide:

// declare the variable i and initialize it to 3

int i = 3;

Really, those are not the comments you will be writing because they're intended purely to answer the questions beginners may have. In the real world, the people reading your comments will already be up to speed with C++.

And, as time goes by, your comments will become outdated, so anyone reading them will be wasting their time and may also end up misunderstanding everything going on.

You need to write comments that answer questions such as "that's an odd approach— why did they do it like that?" Or "what values would the function take and what do the values mean?"

Below is an example of the type of documentation you should be writing for each of your functions:

```
/*

* computes the value of Fibonacci for the specified positive integer, n. If the

value of n is less than 1, the function

* will return 1

*/

int fibonacci (int n);
```

This description tells you exactly what the function is doing, the valid arguments and what will happen should an invalid input be provided. Documentation like this means that the function user doesn't need to go looking for how the function is implemented, which is great.

Writing good comments doesn't necessarily mean that you should write long comments and you don't have to comment every code line. Get into the habit of using comments on functions that are going to be used outside of one file and whenever you have a piece of code that is unusual or potentially tricky.

One bad habit to avoid: although you should keep your comments to a minimum, don't leave them until the development cycle is at the end. When the code has been written, you can't go back and write meaningful comments; you're doing nothing more than adding information that can be worked out by reading the code and run the risk of not understanding your own code. Best practice? Write your comments as you go along.

Take the quiz below, brush up on anything you don't understand and then we'll move on to how to hide structured data representations.

Quiz 19

Is there an advantage to using functions rather than accessing the data directly?

A. Yes, the compiler can optimize the function to ensure faster access

B. Yes, the function implementation can be hidden by the function from all callers, ensuring that the function caller can be changed

C. Yes, a function is the only way that the same data can be shared across several source files

D. No, there is no advantage

When should code be put into a common function?

A. Whenever you have a need to call it

B. Whenever the same code is called from more than one or two places

C. Whenever the compiler doesn't like the functions being too large to compile

D. B and C

What reason would you have for hiding the representation of the data structure?

A. It makes the data structure easier to replace

B. It makes the code that uses that structure a lot easier to understand

C. It makes it easier to use the data structure in other parts of the code

D. All of the above

Hiding the Representation of Structured Data

Up to now, we have looked at hiding data that is stored in an array or in a global variable. But data hiding isn't limited to that. One of the most common hiding places is a data structure. You might think this is strange; the layout of a structure is quite specific as is the set of values that can be stored in it. When you look at structures as a group of fields, they don't have any way to hide details of the implementation, such as the fields they are storing and the format they're in. In fact, you could be forgiven for thinking that the entire point of any structure is to provide specific data.

So why would you need to hide the data representation? Well, as it turns out, we can think of structures in another way, in a world where you want to hide the representation.

Most of the time, when you have lots of related data, the most important thing is not how the data is stored; it's what can be done with it. This is incredibly important and it can change the way you think. For that reason, I will say that again: it is NOT important how the data is stored but it IS important how the data is used.

Let's see this in context, using a simple example of a string.

Unless you're implementing the string class, it isn't important how you store the string. For any program code working with strings, the important things are how you get the string length, how you access each individual string character and how the string is displayed. It may be that the string implementation makes use of a character array and another variable for storing the string length, or it could even be that a linked list is used, even a C++ feature that you have never heard of.

For those who use the string, it doesn't matter how it has been implemented—all that matters is what can be done with it. The C++ string only has around 35 things that can be done with it, and most of the time you won't need them.

What you want is to be able to create a new data type without the need for exposing raw data. For example, when you create a new string, you won't have to worry about the buffer that's holding the characters. This is the way that the STL maps and vectors work: no need to worry about implementation to make use of them.

Hiding Structure Layouts Using Functions

Functions can be used for hiding the exact structure fields by creating a function that is associated with a particular structure. For example, take a small chessboard that is used to represent the board and whether it is white or black's turn to move. The player to move and the pieces will both be stored in enums:

enum ChessPiece { EMPTY_SQUARE, WHITE_PAWN / and the others */ };*

enum PlayerColor { PC_WHITE, PC_BLACK };

struct ChessBoard

{

ChessPiece board[8][8];

PlayerColor whose_move;

};

Functions can be created to operate on this board with the board as a function parameter:

*ChessPiece getPiece (const ChessBoard *p_board, int x, int y)*

```
{

        return p_board->board[ x ][ y ];

}

PlayerColor getMove (const ChessBoard *p_board)

{

        return p_board->whose_move;

}

void makeMove (ChessBoard* p_board, int from_x, int from_y, int to_x, int
to_y)

{

        // usually we would need code to validate the move first

        p_board->board[ to_x ][ to_y ] =
p_board->board[ from_x ][ from_y ];

        p_board->board[ from_x ][ from_y ] = EMPTY_SQUARE;

}
```

And you will use this the same way as any other function:

```
ChessBoard b;
// first we need code that will initialize the board
// and then we can use it like this
```

getMove(& b);

makeMove(& b, 0, 0, 1, 0); // move a piece from 0, 0 to 1, 0

There is nothing wrong with this approach and it has been used time and time again by C++ programmers. However, these functions are associated only with the structure for ChessBoard because the functions take that structure as an argument. There is nothing that says explicitly that the function should be thought of as a core part of this structure.

It would be nice if we could say that the structure contains the data AND all the ways that the data can be manipulated by it.

Well, you can, and C++ has built this right into the language. To do it, we use something called methods. These are functions that have been declared part of a structure and, unlike the functions that don't have an association to a structure, a method can easily be used to perform operations on the structure data. When the method is written, it is declared as part of the structure and this ties the method directly to that structure. By doing this, the method caller doesn't need the structure passed as a separate argument.

However, that requires special syntax.

Method Declaration and Call Syntax

The code below demonstrates what our functions would look like if we turned them into methods:

enum ChessPiece { EMPTY_SQUARE, WHITE_PAWN /* and others */ };

enum PlayerColor { PC_WHITE, PC_BLACK };

struct ChessBoard

{

```
ChessPiece board[ 8 ][ 8 ];

PlayerColor whose_move;

ChessPiece getPiece (int x, int y)

{

        return board[ x ][ y ];

}

PlayerColor getMove ()

{

        return whose_move;

}

void  makeMove (int from_x, int from_y, int to_x, int to_y)

{

        // usually we would need code to validate the move first

        board[ to_x ][ to_y ] = board[ from_x ][ from_y ];

        board[ from_x ][ from_y ] = EMPTY_SQUARE;

}

};
```

First off, as you can see, we have declared the methods in the structure. This tells the code that the methods are to be treated as an integral part of the structure. Plus, the method declarations do not need separate arguments for ChessBoard; the structure fields are available directly in the method.

When you write boar[x][y], you can directly access the board for the structure the method was called on. But how does our code know which structure instance it should work on? You might have more than one ChessBoard, for example.

A method call looks like this:

ChessBoard b;

// code that initializes board

b.getMove();

The code needed to call a function associated with a particular structure is very similar to the code needed to access a structure field.

The compiler handles all the details internally to let a method access the data held in the structure it was called on. In concept terms, .y is the syntax shorthand for "passing to," which should explain why we used it in the section on the Standard Template Library— the functions worked much the same as these methods do.

Removing a Function Definition from a Structure

It can start to get cumbersome if you include all function bodies in the structure and you will soon find your card is too hard to read. There is a way of splitting methods into two—a declaration that shows up in the structure and a definition that is outside of it. Take a look at this example:

enum ChessPiece { EMPTY_SQUARE, WHITE_PAWN /* and others */ };

enum PlayerColor { PC_WHITE, PC_BLACK };

```
struct ChessBoard

{

        ChessPiece board[ 8 ][ 8 ];

        PlayerColor whose_move;

        // method declarations are inside the structure

        ChessPiece getPiece (int x, int y);

        PlayerColor getMove ();

        void makeMove (int from_x, int from_y, int to_x, int to_y);

};
```

The method declaration may be in the structure but, otherwise, this looks like nothing more than a function prototype. The definitions need a way of tying them to the structure. We do that using "scoping" syntax; this will indicate that the method belongs in the structure. All the syntax does is write the method name as ::; but the rest of the code is the same:

```
ChessPiece ChessBoard::getPiece (int x, int y)

{

        return board[ x ][ y ];

}

PlayerColor ChessBoard::getMove ()

{

        return whose_move;
```

```
}

void  ChessBoard::makeMove (int from_x, int from_y, int to_x, int to_y)

{

        // usually we would need code to validate the move first

        board[ to_x ][ to_y ] = board[ from_x ][ from_y ];


        board[ from_x ][ from_y ] = EMPTY_SQUARE;

}
```

From now on, I will be splitting the declarations and definitions of any methods that go over more than a few lines. There are those who will tell you never to define methods in structures because it causes more information than you really need to know about implementation to be exposed. The more that happens, the more likely it becomes that code will be written to depend on the exact implementation details, rather than the method interface. For the rest of the guide, I will still occasionally place method declarations with the class, just to save some space.

As always, run through the quiz, and then continue with the guide. Next, we will discuss Bjarne Stroustrup's classes.

Quiz 20

Why would a method be better than directly using the field of structure?

A. The method is easier to read

B. The method is faster

C. It wouldn't be; it's always better to directly use the field

D. So that the data representation can be changed

Which of these is used to define the method that is associated with the structure struct MyStruct { int func(); }; ?

A. int func() { return 1; }

B. MyStruct::int func() { return 1; }

C. int MyStruct::func() { return 1; }

D. int MyStruct func () { return 1; }

What reason would there be for including a method definition in line with the class?

A. So that the class users can see how it works

B. Because it will make the code that much faster

C. There is no reason. Doing this would result in implementation details being leaked

D. No reason. It would just make the program really slow

The Class

When C++ was created by Bjarne Stroustrup, he wanted to bring home the idea of creating data structures defined by their functions rather than the data used for implementation. In theory, everything he wanted to do could have been done simply by extending the structure concept that already existed. Instead, he opted to go down a different route: a brand-new concept called the class.

Classes are very much like structures, but they provide something extra: the ability to define the data and methods that are internal to the class implementation and which methods are for the class users. When a class is defined, you create a new category of something. It no longer sounds as if it should be structured data; instead, methods are used to define a class and those methods are provided as part of the method interface. And classes are smart enough that they can stop you from using implementation details by accident.

That's right. With C++ we can stop methods from using internal class data if they don't belong to the class. In fact, when a class is declared it's set to the default that the only thing available to anyone is the methods that belong to the class. If you want anything to be accessible publicly, you will need to explicitly declare it.

By making it so that data can't be accessed from outside the class, the compiler can make sure that programmers aren't using any data that they shouldn't be. This is fantastic from the viewpoint of maintaining the code—basic class stuff can be changed, such as how the chessboard is stored, and there's no need to worry about any of the code outside the class breaking.

You may be the only programmer working on your project, but it's still reassuring to know that nobody can look beneath the method. And this is another great reason why methods are so useful: they're the only ones that can have access to internal data.

From now on, when I want to hide how data is being stored, I'll use classes. And I'll use structures when there's no good reason to hide it. You might actually be surprised at how little structures get used—being able to hide data is really very valuable in programming. To be honest, the only time I use a normal helper structure is when a class is being implemented and I need a structure that can hold some of the data. And because the helper structure is specific to the class, it won't be publicly exposed and there won't be any reason to turn it into a full class.

Hiding the Way Data is Stored

Let's look at the syntax needed to hide data using classes. With a class, you can classify each of the methods and fields, otherwise known as class members, as private or public. Public allows anyone to use the data while private is limited to class member access only.

Below is an example of methods declared as public and data declared as private:

```
enum ChessPiece { EMPTY_SQUARE, WHITE_PAWN /* and others */ };

enum PlayerColor { PC_WHITE, PC_BLACK };

class ChessBoard

{

public:

        ChessPiece getPiece (int x, int y);
```

```
        PlayerColor getMove ();

        void makeMove (int from_x, int from_y, int to_x, int to_y);
private:

        ChessPiece _board[ 8 ][ 8 ];

        PlayerColor _whose_move;
};
// The method definitions are the same
ChessPiece ChessBoard::getPiece (int x, int y)
{

        return _board[ x ][ y ];

}
PlayerColor ChessBoard::getMove ()
{

        return _whose_move;

}
void  ChessBoard::makeMove (int from_x, int from_y, int to_x, int to_y)
{

        // usually we would need code to validate the move first

        _board[ to_x ][ to_y ] = _board[ from_x ][ from_y ];
```

_board[from_x][from_y] = EMPTY_SQUARE;

}

This class declaration looks a little like the structure definition we saw earlier but has one main difference—the use of keywords "public" and "private." Anything declared after the public keyword can be used on the object by anyone; in our case, by the methods called makeMove, getMove and getPiece. Anything in the private section can only be accessed by methods that belong to the class called ChessBoard: _whose_move and _board.

You can switch from public to private and vice versa all you want. The next example demonstrates how to make the same things public:

class ChessBoard

{

public:

      ChessPiece getPiece (int x, int y);

private:

      ChessPiece _board[8][8];

      PlayerColor _whose_move;

public:

      int getMove ();

      void makeMove (int from_x, int from_y, to_x, to_y);

};

Note

I have used an underscore before the private class elements just to indicate what is private. This is not a C++ requirement and might look out of place, but it does make reading code easier. If you choose to do this, do NOT use a capital letter after it because some compilers take issue with it. If you use the underscore, use a lowercase letter and everything will work.

Personally, I always begin with a public section and then the private section. This serves to make it clear that the public part is meant for class users, i.e., other programmers, because it's the first thing they see.

Declaring Class Instances

Declaring a class instance is no more difficult than declaring a structure instance:

ChessBoard b;

And calling a method on a class isn't any different either:

b.getMove();

The difference lies in terminology. When a new variable is declared of a specific class, it's generally known as an object. That word, "object," should bring to mind real-world objects. Take the steering wheel in a car, for example; it's a small thing, but beneath it is a lot of complexity. Turning right requires you to do nothing more than turning the wheel right; you don't have to worry about how it all works, you just do it. The same thing applies in C++; all the details about the implementation of an object are hidden behind a curtain of function calls, all public, and these functions are what create the user interface. Once the interface is defined, the class can implement it in any way it sees fit; what's up to you is the data representation and method implementation.

Class Responsibilities

When a class is created, you can think of it as a new variable kind, a new type of data. This type is like a char or an int but has far more power. You've seen this before: C++ strings are classes and the string class is one of those new data types. It makes perfect sense to use public and private when you're creating new data types; you need to be able to provide functionality that is quite specific, along with a specific interface. An example of that would be a string that has the ability to work with a substring, display itself, work with individual characters and get the attributes, such as string length.

How the string is implemented isn't important.

If you consider class creation as the definition of new data types, it makes perfect sense to work out what should be public, i.e., what your class will do. Any programmer who uses that class can then use anything that is public—it's treated as an interface in the same way that functions have interfaces containing one or more arguments and return values. This must be considered carefully because, once the interface is in use, changing it will require all interface users to be changed. Because it's a public method, there may be a lot of callers and there's no easy way of limiting the needed change. Going back to the car; you can't develop a completely new way of driving because everybody would need to learn it, but you can design a new type of engine, such as an electric one. This won't require the interface to be changed, just the implementation.

Once you have the public interface, you need to start considering how the public methods the interface consists of are being implemented. If you have fields or methods being used for implementing the interface and you don't want them to be public, they must be made private.

Contrary to public interfaces, private data and methods can be changed quite easily. Because they're only available to class methods, public and private ones, they can be changed at a later date if you decide that you want the class functionality re-implemented— and there's a good chance you will!

Bear this in mind: data fields should never, ever, be made public, and all methods should be private by default. Move them to the public only once you're certain that they belong there. Changing from private to public is simple; it's not so easy to do it the other way around. If access is needed to a particular field, write getter and setter methods— getters are for reading and setters are for writing.

It might seem a bit over the top, never making data fields public. Surely you're going to have to write an awful lot of getters and setters, and many functions that only return private data fields?

Yes, on occasion, but that's a small price to pay. If you don't, you could find yourself in trouble when you discover that the trivial getter you wrote needs to be changed so it adds functionality. You could, for example, be storing data inside a variable and then decide that you want the value computed from other variables. If you don't have the getter and allow everyone access as a public field, you could have a problem on your hands.

If you think about it, you can probably come up with a few examples of fields that could be public. Seriously though—don't bother trying. You might save a bit of time typing, but you're potentially creating a large headache for yourself later on, and one consequence of wrong guesses is bad program design. As you know by now, that can't be easily changed.

So, what does private mean?

Just because you declare something private, it doesn't automatically guarantee any kind of security. All private fields of any class are stored in memory, just as the public fields are, and they're usually stored side by side. Any good programmer can write code that contains pointer tricks for reading the data. There are no guarantees made by the language or operating system that private data is protected from hackers. All the private marker does is ensure that the compiler can prevent private data from being accidentally used. Although there are no guarantees in terms of security, this is still useful.

There's a term we use to describe a public method that hides private data: encapsulation. This just means that your implementation is hidden or encapsulated so that class users can only work with specific methods that make up the class interface.

The class is an incredibly powerful C++ feature and is a fundamental building block. Using classes means you can create larger-scale programs that are easier to work with and understand. You've learned how to hide data. In the next few sections, we'll see a lot more class features, starting with the class life cycle. But first, take the quiz and see how you do!

Quiz 21

What reason is there for using private data?

A. To keep your data safe from a hacker

B. To stop other programmers from touching it

C. To clearly show what data is only intended to be used for the class implementation

D. Private data should never be used as it makes programming harder

Explain the difference between a class and a structure

A. There is no difference

B. Classes default to everything being public

C. Classes default to everything being private

D. Classes let you indicate which fields are private or public whereas a structure won't

What should you do with your class data fields?

A. They should all be made public by default

B. They should all be made private by default

C. They should never be made public

D. Classes don't have data!

Why would you make a method public?

A. You should never make methods public

B. You should always make methods public

C. They should only be made public if they're required for using the class's main features; otherwise, make them private

D. They should be made public if there's a chance that the method might be used by someone else

The Life Cycle of a Class

When creating classes, you want them to be as easy as possible to use. There are a couple of basic operations that any class will likely need to provide support for:

1. It needs to initialize itself

2. It needs to clean up memory and/or other resources

3. It needs to copy itself

All of these are very important for the creation of good data types. We'll use the string to demonstrate this. Strings must be able to initialize themselves, even if they're empty. They should need to rely on external code for that. Once the string is declared, it's immediately available for use. When you're finished with the string, it must be able to clean up because all strings allocate memory. When the string class is used, there is no need for another method to be called for that; the string does it automatically.

Lastly, it must be able to copy from one variable to another, the same way that integers can be copied between variables. Put together, all of this functionality should be made a part of all classes so that they can easily be used.

We'll take these three features, one at a time, and look at how easy C++ makes all of this.

Object Construction

You might have spotted that we didn't have any code for initializing the board in our ChessBoard interface, which was the public section of the code. We can fix that now.

When a class variable is declared, the variable needs to be able to be initialized:

ChessBoard board;

When an object is declared, the code that runs it is called the constructor and this should set the object up so that it needs no more initialization. Constructors can take arguments too—you saw this with the vector declaration of a particular size:

vector<int> v(10);

The vector constructor is called with the value of 10; the new vector is initialized by the constructor so that it can hold 10 integers immediately.

Creating a constructor is nothing more than declaring a function with the same name as the class, with no arguments and no return value. You don't even give it a void value; no type is provided for the return value:

enum ChessPiece { EMPTY_SQUARE, WHITE_PAWN / and others */ };*

enum PlayerColor { PC_WHITE, PC_BLACK };

class ChessBoard

{

public:

      ChessBoard (); // <-- no return value at all!

```cpp
        PlayerColor getMove ();

        ChessPiece getPiece (int x, int y);

        void makeMove (int from_x, int from_y, int to_x, int to_y);
private:

        ChessPiece _board[ 8 ][ 8 ];

        PlayerColor _whose_move;

};

ChessBoard::ChessBoard () // <-- no return value

{

        _whose_move = PC_WHITE;

        // empty the entire board to start with and then add in the pieces

        for ( int i = 0; i < 8; i++ )

        {

                for (int j = 0; j < 8; j++ )

                {

                _board[ i ][ j ] = EMPTY_SQUARE;

                }

        }

        // other code needed for board initialization
```

}

I won't keep showing you the method declarations, but I will continue to show you the class declaration, just so you can see how it all fits together.

Now, note that the constructor above is in the public part of the class. If we didn't make the ChessBoard constructor public, we couldn't create any object instances. Why not? Because, whenever an object is created, the constructor has to be called; if we make it private, it can't be called from outside the class. Objects can only be initialized by calling the constructor and, if you make it private, you won't be able to declare the object.

The constructor gets called on the same line the object is created on:

ChessBoard board; // calls ChessBoard constructor

Or when memory is allocated:

ChessBoard *board = new board; // this calls the ChessBoard constructor as part of the memory allocation

When multiple objects are declared:

ChessBoard a;

ChessBoard b;

Constructors are always run in the order of object declaration—a and then b. As with a normal function, constructors can take one or more arguments and several constructors can be overloaded by the type of argument if there is a different way of initializing the object. For example, a second constructor could be created for ChessBoard to take the board size:

Class ChessBoard

```
{
```

ChessBoard ();

ChessBoard (int board_size);

```
};
```

The function definition is the same as any class method:

ChessBoard::ChessBoard (int size)

```
{
```

// ... code

```
}
```

The argument is passed to the constructor like this:

ChessBoard board(8); // 8 is an argument to the ChessBoard constructor

When you use the new keyword, passing an argument looks like you're calling the constructor directly:

ChessBoard *p_board = new ChessBoard(8);

A note on the syntax: although parentheses are used for passing arguments, you can't use them to declare objects that have no-argument constructors.

You can't do this:

ChessBoard board();

The correct form is:

ChessBoard board;

However, you can use parentheses when the new keyword is used:

ChessBoard *board = new board();

This is one of the unfortunate little foibles of C++ parsing because the details are kept very obscure. Just don't use parentheses when you declare objects with a no-argument constructor.

So, what happens if a constructor isn't declared?

If a constructor isn't declared, C++ creates one. It won't take arguments or initialize ints, chars or any other primitive type, but it will initialize every class field by calling the default constructor for each one.

Generally, you should create constructors just to make sure everything gets properly initialized. As soon as call constructor is declared, C++ won't generate the default for you. The compiler makes the assumption that you know exactly what you're doing and that you're going to create the constructor you need. In particular, if you create constructors that take arguments, the code no longer has the default constructor unless you declare one specifically.

This can have unexpected consequences. If the automatically generated constructor is used and then you add a non-default one that takes arguments, the code that depends on the automatic constructor won't compile. It's up to you to provide a default constructor because the compiler won't do it for you.

Initializing Class Members

Each class member must be initialized within the constructor. Let's imagine that a string is a ChessBoard class member:

```
class ChessBoard

{

public:

        ChessBoard ();

        string getMove ();

        ChessPiece getPiece (int x, int y);

        void makeMove (int from_x, int from_y, int to_x, int to_y);

private:

        PlayerColor _board[ 8 ][ 8 ];

        string _whose_move;

};
```

You could, quite simply, assign the variable called _whose_move:

ChessBoard::ChessBoard ()

{

        _whose_move = "white";

}

You might be surprised at what code is actually being executed here. Right at the start of the constructor for ChessBoard, the _whose_move constructor is called. This is good news because it means that your class fields can be used in the constructor safely. If the class member constructors aren't called, there's no way to use them. At the end of the day, the whole premise of a constructor is that the object can be used.

If you prefer, arguments can be passed to a class member constructor instead of the default constructor being run. That requires unusual syntax:

ChessBoard::ChessBoard ()

> *// follow the colon with the variables list, with the argument*
>
> *// to the constructor*
>
> *: _whose_move("white")*

{

> *// now the _whose_move constructor has been called and it*
>
> *// has the value of "white"*

}

This is called an initialization list and you will see them a few times, using this syntax for initializing class members. Initialization list members are separated with commas. For example, if a new member were added to ChessBoard to count the number of moves made, the initialization list could be used to initialize it:

class ChessBoard

{

public:

> *ChessBoard ();*

```
        string getMove ();

        ChessPiece getPiece (int x, int y);

        void makeMove (int from_x, int from_y, int to_x, int to_y);
private:

        PlayerColor _board[ 8 ][ 8 ];

        string _whose_move;

        int _move_count;
};

ChessBoard::ChessBoard ()

        // follow the colon with the variables list, with the argument

        // to the constructor

        : _whose_move( "white" )

        , _move_count( 0 )

{

}
```

Initialization List and Const Fields

If the class fields are declared as consts, the file has to be initialized in the list:

```
class ConstHolder
```

```
{

public:

    ConstHolder (int val);

private:

    const int _val;

};

ConstHolder::ConstHolder ()

    : _val( val )

{}
```

Const fields can't be initialized by assigning to them because the fields are set and can't be changed. The only place where the class has not been formed fully is in the initialization list, so immutable objects can safely be set. For the same reason, if a field is a reference, it has to be initialized in the list.

When we get to the subject of inheritance, we will see more use of this list.

Object Destruction

In the same way that objects are initialized by a constructor, there will be times when you want code that cleans up objects that aren't needed anymore. For example, if the constructor allocates memory or another resource, eventually, these must be returned back to the operating system when the object isn't being used anymore. We call this "destroying" an object and a special method is needed: the destructor. These get called when objects aren't required any longer, such as when delete is called on an object pointer.

In the example below, we have a class representing a linked list. Implementation might include a field storing the list's current head:

```
struct LinkedListNode
{
    int val;
    LinkedListNode *p_next;
};
class LinkedList
{
public:
    LinkedList (); // constructor
    void insert (int val); // adds a node
private:
    LinkedListNode *_p_head;
};
```

As we've seen before, like all other elements, the head node in the linked list points to memory that was allocated using the new keyword. At some point, this means that, when the LinkedList object is no longer required, it must be cleaned up. That's why we use a destructor.

Let's take a look at adding a destructor to the type. Like the constructor, the destructor has a special name—the class name prefixed by a tilde (~).

Also like the constructor, there is no return value. However, unlike the constructor, the destructor will never take any arguments.

```cpp
class LinkedList
{
public:
        LinkedList (); // constructor
        ~LinkedList (); // destructor, notice the tilde (~)
        void insert (int val); // adds a node
private:
        LinkedListNode *_p_head;
};
LinkedList::~LinkedList ()
{
        LinkedListNode *p_itr = _p_head;
        while ( p_itr != NULL )
        {
                LinkedListNode *p_tmp = p_itr->p_next;
                delete p_itr;
                p_itr = p_tmp;
```

}

}

This is very much like what we saw earlier when we looked at deleting items in linked lists. There is a difference though; the class here has a special method that is intended purely for the cleanup. Isn't it more sensible if each node is responsible for cleaning up its own data? Isn't that what the point of a destructor is?

What if we do this:

class LinkedListNode

{

public:

       ~LinkedListNode ();

       int val;

       LinkedListNode *p_next;

};

LinkedListNode::~LinkedListNode ()

{

       delete p_next;

}

What this code does is initiate a whole load of recursive function calls. The call to delete has invoked the destructor for the object that p_next points to or, if p_next is NULL, it doesn't do anything In turn, the destructor will call delete and the next destructor is invoked. What's the base case though? Where does the chain stop? At some point, p_next will be NULL and the call to delete won't do anything. So, the base case is there, it's just hidden away inside the call to delete. As soon as we have the LinkedListNode destructor, the LinkedList destructor will need to invoke it:

LinkedList::~LinkedList ()

{

      delete _p_head;

}

The recursive chain is started by the call to delete and doesn't stop until it gets to the end of the list.

You could be wondering why a destructor is required. Surely we could just create a method and call it as needed? Yes, you could, but using a destructor offers one major advantage: it's automatically called when the object isn't needed anymore.

"When an object isn't needed anymore" can mean one of these three things:

1. When a pointer to an object isn't required any longer

2. When the object goes out of scope

3. When the object belongs to the class whose destructor it is being called.

Destruction On Delete

When you call delete, you're explicitly stating that the destructor is needed, as you saw earlier:

LinkedList *p_list = new LinkedList;

delete p_list; // ~LinkedList (the destructor) is called on p_list

Destruction When Out Of Scope

In the second case, when an object goes out of scope it's an implicit operation. Whenever you declare an object inside brackets, it will go out of scope at the end of the brackets:

if (1)

{

   LinkedList list;

} // list's destructor gets called here

It gets more complicated when objects are declared inside functions. If there's a return statement for the function, the destructor will be called as a part of coming out of the function. A destructor declared for an object in a code block will be executed at the end bracket, or at the closing one when the block is exited. That could be when the last statement is finished or if a break or return statement causes the block to exit:

void foo ()

{

   LinkedList list;

   // some code...

```
if ( /* some condition */ )

{

return;

}

} // list's destructor gets called here
```

In this case, although the return statement is in the if statement, the destructor can be thought of as running when the function gets to the closing curly bracket. The most important thing that you should take away from this is that the destructor only runs when the object is not in scope anymore, which means it can't be referenced without a compiler error being thrown.

If you have several objects that have destructors that are required to run when a code block ends, they will be run in the opposite order to which the objects got constructed. For example:

```
{

        LinkedList a;

        LinkedList b;

}
```

In this, destructor b runs first, followed by a.

Destruction because of Another Destructor

Lastly, with objects contained in another class, the object destructor is called once the class destructor has been run. For example, in a simple class:

```
class NameAndEmail

{

/* usually, we would have methods here */

private:

        string _name;

        string _email;

};
```

The destructor for both the _name and the _email fields is called when the NameAndEmail destructor has run. This is quite convenient because it means that, to get your class objects cleaned up, all you need to do is clean the pointers by calling delete on them.

If you don't add a class destructor, the compiler will still run destructor for the objects that belong to the class.

Initializing classes using a constructor and cleaning up using a destructor is commonly known as RAII, or Resource Allocation Is Initialization. Basically, in C++ it means that classes should be created for resource handling and the constructor will take care of initialization, while the destructor takes care of the cleanup. This will often result in a class like the one above; two strings that both clean up after they have finished so there is no need to write a destructor for the class.

Copying Classes

The next discussion revolves around copying class instances. It's common in C++ to create new classes that you can copy; for example:

```
 LinkedList list_one;
```

LinkedList list_two;

list_two = list_one;

LinkedList list_three = list_two;

You can make use of two functions in C++ that can be defined to ensure that copy operations work as they should. One function is called the assignment operator and the other is the copy constructor. We'll start with the assignment operator and then deal with the copy constructor.

You might wonder why you actually need functions; it should just work, shouldn't it? Yes, sometimes it will. C++ gives you defaults of both the assignment and the copy constructor. However, you won't always be able to rely on those defaults. On occasion, the compiler simply won't know what you want.

For example, the defaults of both functions will create something called shallow copies of pointers. A shallow copy is when a second pointer is assigned to point to the same memory that the first pointer is pointing to. Because the point-to-memory isn't copied, only the pointer itself is called shallow. This might work, but there will be times when it becomes a problem.

Let's use our LinkedList class as an example and write code like this one:

LinkedList list_one;

LinkedList list_two;

list_one = list_two;

The trouble with this is that the following code is generated by the default assignment operator:

list_one._p_head = list_two._p_head;

What we have now is two objects that both have the same pointer value and the destructor for each of the objects will attempt to free the associated memory.

When the list_two destructor runs, list_two._p_head gets deleted. Then the list_one destructor runs (remember, it will run in the opposite order to the constructors) and that will result in list_one._p_head being deleted. Because list_two._p_head was already deleted, you are now trying to delete a pointer twice and that will cause your program to crash.

Clearly, as soon as one destructor has run, the other list is no good. Using the assignment operator is the best way of dealing with this so let's see what things should actually look like.

The Assignment Operator

We call the assignment operator when an object is assigned to a preexisting object, like this:

list_two = list_one;

Implementing the assignment operator needs a little bit of new syntax so the operator can be defined:

LinkedList& operator= (LinkedList& lhs, const LinkedList& rhs);

This is very much like a declaration of a standard function; it takes two arguments, one of a non-const reference and one of a const reference. The only strange thing is the function name—operator=. What this means is that, instead of having to define an entirely new function, we define what the = sign means when used with the LinkedList class.

The first operator is on the left of the = sign and this is the thing that it's being assigned to and which makes it non-const. The second argument is to the right and this is the value that is being assigned, making it const.

lhs = rhs;

The reason the reference is returned to LinkedList is so that assignments can be chained together:

linked_list = lhs = rhs;

Mostly, rather than a standalone function being declared for operator=, classes will generally turn operator= into a member function so that it can work with the private fields in the class, rather than declaring it a free-floating function as we did earlier. This looks like this:

class LinkedList

{

public:

> *LinkedList (); // constructor*
>
> *~LinkedList (); // destructor, notice the tilde*
>
> *LinkedList& operator= (const LinkedList& other);*
>
> *void insert (int val); // adds a node*

private:

> *LinkedListNode *_p_head;*

};

Did you spot that an argument is missing? The reason for that is that all the member functions for a class implicitly take the class as an argument. In our case, the operator= method gets used when the class is to the left of an assignment. What we're saying is that, in this code:

lhs = rhs;

the operator= function gets called on the lhs variable. It's almost as though you had written this instead:

lhs.operator=(rhs);

And once the function has finished, lhs and rhs will both have the same value. So, how does the operator= function get written for the LinkedList class?

LinkedList& LinkedList::operator= (const LinkedList& other)

{

　　// what should go here?

}

If you paid attention, you will know that it isn't enough to copy the pointer address. Instead, we need the entire structure copied. Logically, we'll first need to free up the existing list because we no longer need it and then copy each individual list node to give us two separate lists. Lastly, because a value is to be returned, we need to return a copy of the current class. To do this last part, we need more new syntax, a way of referring to the current object.

In C++, we do this by using a special kind of variable which is known as the pointer. This is a pointer that is used to point to the class instance. For example, if you were to write:

list_one.insertElement(2);

the this keyword could be used inside insertElement to point to list_one. The this pointer can also be used for giving the method a bit of safety.

```cpp
LinkedList& LinkedList::operator= (const LinkedList& other)
{
        // ensure that we are not assigning to ourselves – we can ignore
        // that if it does happen. Note that use of 'this' to make sure
        // the other values doesn't have the same address as the object
        if ( this == & other )
        {
                // this object is returned to ensure the chain of assignments
        stays alive

                return *this;
        }
        // before the new values are copied, the old memory needs to be
freed
        // because it isn't being used anymore
        delete _p_head;
        _p_head = NULL;
        LinkedListNode *p_itr = other._p_head;
        while ( p_itr != NULL )
        {
                insert( p_itr->val );
```

```
        }

        return *this;

}
```

A few things need to be said about this; first, we are running a check for self-assignment. You don't expect this kind of thing to happen normally, but don't automatically assume it is safe. If you write:

a = a;

it should be safe and therefore require no changes.

Next, the memory associated with the old list needs to be freed because we have finished with it. The entire list can be deleted by deleting p_head, just as we did with the destructor.

Lastly, the list needs to be repopulated with the new values by looping over the list and inserting the individual elements from it into our list. That gives us a class that we can copy.

Thankfully, you won't need to do all this with all classes. If you don't have pointers as class members, you most likely won't need to use an assignment operator. That's because C++ provides you with a default assignment operator that will copy the elements. If it's a class object, it will run the assignment operator, and if it's a pointer or some other value, the bits will be copied. So, if there are no pointers in the class, the default can be relied on to a certain extent.

There is a rule of thumb that you should work by: if there is a need to write a destructor, there is likely also a need to write an assignment operator. Why? If you have a destructor, you are probably using it to clean up and free memory. If the memory is freed, you need to ensure that each copy of the class is given its own copy of the memory.

The Copy Constructor

One last thing to think about. What would you do if you wanted one object constructed to like another one?

LinkedList list_one;

LinkedList list_two(list_one);

This is nothing more than a special case of a constructor that will take an object that is the same type as the one that is being constructed. This is called a copy constructor and the new object should be created as a direct copy of the original one. In the example above, we should initialize list_two so that it looks like list_one.

This is much like using the assignment operator. However, rather than an existing class, we start with one that has not been initialized. This is good because there is no need to waste precious CPU time on class construction only to find that the values have to be overwritten. It's easy to implement the copy constructor and it looks like the assignment operator:

This is what it would like when used on LinkedList:

class LinkedList

{

public:

    LinkedList (); // constructor

    ~LinkedList (); // destructor, notice the tilde

```
        LinkedList& operator= (const LinkedList& other);

        LinkedList (const LinkedList& other);

        void insert (int val); // adds a node
private:

        LinkedListNode *_p_head;

};

LinkedList::LinkedList (const LinkedList& other)

        : _p_head( NULL ) // begin with NULL just in case the other list
is empty

{

        // this is very similar to the code used for operator=

        // Creating a helper method to do this in a real program

        // makes good sense

        LinkedListNode *p_itr = other._p_head;

        while ( p_itr != NULL )

        {

                insert( p_itr->val );

        }

}
```

If you don't write a copy constructor, the compiler provides you with a default one that behaves much like the default assignment operator. The copy constructor for each class object is run and a regular copy is made for values such as pointers and integers.

Most of the time, if an assignment operator is needed, a copy constructor will also be needed.

One thing about the copy constructor often comes as a surprise to beginners.

If you write this:

LinkedList list_one;

LinkedList list_two = list_one;

what do you think will happen? Will the assignment operator be called? No, it won't. Why? Because the compiler can see that the initialization of list_two has been based on list_one and the copy constructor will be called for you. That saves you from having to do unnecessary object initialization

Compiler Generated Methods

Now you have seen all the methods that the compiler generates automatically for you:

1. The default constructor

2. The default destructor

3. The assignment operator

4. The copy constructor

For each class created, you need to consider whether the default method implementation is acceptable. Most of the time it will be, but there will be times, particularly when you're working with pointers, that you will need to write your own and declare them. As a rule of thumb, if you need to write one, you need to write all of them.

Preventing Copying

There will be times when it's unnecessary to copy objects and all you want to do is say, "no, do not let the object be copied." If you can do this, you won't need to implement either the assignment or copy constructors and the compiler won't be at risk of generating versions of these methods that could be dangerous.

There will be times when an object simply shouldn't be copiable. For example, take a game with a class that represents the spaceship for the current user. You don't need that spaceship to be copied; all you need is one spaceship with all the data about that current user.

Copying can be prevented easily. Simply declare the assignment and copy constructors but do NOT implement them. Once the method is declared, it won't be automatically generated by the compiler. If you were to attempt using it, an error would happen at link time because you tried using an undefined function.

This could be confusing; the linker isn't going to tell you which code line the problem is on. The way to get better error messages is to make your methods private. That way, the error usually happens at compile time and will be much easier to read.

This is how we do that:

class Player

{

public:

    Player ();

    ~Player ();

private:

    // prohibited, when you declare the method but don't define them,

    // the compiler doesn't auto-generate them for us.

    operator= (const Player& other);

    Player (const Player& other);

    PlayerInformation *_p_player_info;

};

// The assignment and the copy constructors have not been implemented

As a summary, most of the time you should choose one of these options:

1. Use the default assignment operator and the copy constructor

2. Create your own assignment operator and copy constructor

3. Make the assignment operator and copy constructor private and don't implement them

If you don't do anything, the compiler will make sure you get the first option. Often, it will be easier to begin with the third option and add the copy constructor and assignment operator later, as required.

After you take the quiz, we will move on to discussing inheritance and polymorphism.

Quiz 22

At what point do you need to write a constructor for a class?

A. Constructors should always be created immediately. Otherwise you, can't use the class

B. When the class needs to be initialized with non-default values

C. Never write a constructor, the compiler does it for you

D. Only when there is a need for a destructor as well

Explain the relationship between the assignment operator and destructor

A. There is no relationship

B. The class destructor gets called before the assignment operator is run

C. The assignment operator must specify the memory that the destructor will delete

D. The assignment operator has to ensure that it's safe to run the destructors of both the new class and the copied class

When would you need to use an initialization list?

A. When you need your constructors to be highly efficient and don't want empty objects constructed

B. When a constant value is being initialized

C. When you want the non-default constructor of a class field run

D. All of the above

What function is the function being run on line 2 of the code?

string str1;

string str2 = str1;

A. The constructor for str2, and the assignment operator for str1

B. The constructor for str2, and assignment operator for str2

C. The copy constructor for str2. str2 has not yet been initialized so the copy constructor runs, rather than the assignment operator

Name the functions being called in the code and what order they are called in:

{

       string str1;

       string str2;

}

A. The constructor for str1, the constructor for str2

B. The destructor for str1, the constructor for str2

C. The constructor for str1, the constructor for str2, the destructor for str1, the destructor for str2

D. The constructor for str1, the constructor for str2, the destructor for str2, the destructor for str1

Assume that your class has a non-default copy constructor; which of the following statements about the assignment operator is true?

A. The class must have a default assignment operator

B. The class must have a non-default assignment operator

C. The class must have an assignment operator that has been declared but not implemented

D. B or C are valid

Inheritance and Polymorphism

So far, we have discussed using public interfaces and providing support for creating, copying and cleaning objects to create fully usable types out of our classes. I want to go a bit further with the interfaces.

Let's say that you have an old, rusty car. Sadly, in this scenario you live in a time where every car manufacturer has come up with a different steering mechanism. Some use the standard steering wheel, some use a mouse, others use joysticks (you can see where I'm going with this). Some of them even use gas pedals while others require a scroll bar to be dragged. How awful is that! Whenever you want to drive a car, you need to learn the steering mechanism. Whenever you rent or buy a new car, you have to learn to drive again.

Luckily, in the real world, all cars follow a set of specific standards. Whenever you get in a car, whatever the make, it has a standard interface with the only real difference being that some cars are manual transmission, while others are automatic. Those are the two auto interfaces: manual and automatic.

If you have learned to drive an automatic transmission, you can drive any car that has one and the same goes for manual. What's under the hood doesn't matter; the important thing is, no matter which car you drive, it has the same methods for braking, steering and accelerating.

What does all this have to do with C++? Well, it's entirely possible that you can write code that expects an interface that is well-defined and specific. In the car analogy, you are the C++ code and the interface is the steering mechanism. How the interface is implemented isn't important—the code can use any implementation of the interface so long as it understands that interface.

Now, think about when you would write some code that has similar properties. You must have seen this coming: a video game. You could have several objects that can be drawn to the screen, such as enemies, spaceships, bullets, etc. In the main game loop, each individual object has to be redrawn for each frame so all objects are in the right position. What you want is code in this format:

Clear the screen

Loop through a list of the drawable objects

> For each of the drawable objects, draw it

Ideally, that list of drawable objects would have every type of object that could possibly be displayed on the screen. Each would need to implement a common type of interface that allows for them to be drawn to the screen. But, the bullet, the spaceship and the enemy all need to be different classes; each has its own internal data. The ship will need hit points, the bullet will need to store how much damage it can do and the enemy requires AI to move.

All of that really isn't relevant to the loop drawing the objects; what's important is that each different class has support for an interface that allows drawing. You will need several classes that all have the same interface but will each have their own implementation of the interface.

To do this, the first step is to define what "being drawn" means:

class Drawable

{

public:

> *void draw ();*

```
};
```

This is a simple class called Drawable and it only defines one method called draw(). This will draw the current object, but how cool would it be if we could create a vector and then anything that implemented the draw method could be stored in it?

If that were the case, we could come up with some code that would allow everything to be drawn to screen using a loop to iterate everything in the vector and then by calling the draw() method. You can actually do this because C++ allows it through a feature called inheritance. Let's see how it all works

Inheritance

All inheritance means is that a class can get its traits from a different class. In our case, the class will be inheriting the Drawable class interface and, in particular, the draw() method. When a class inherits from another it's called a subclass while the class that is inherited from is called the superclass.

The superclass will often be used to define interface methods that each subclass can implement in a different way. In the example we are using, the superclass is Drawable and each class inherits the property of the draw() method. This means that any code that gets Drawable will also know that it can call on the draw() method. Each individual class implements its own version of draw()—this is set in stone; it must do this so that all Drawable subclasses contain a draw() method that is valid.

Next, we'll look at the syntax:

class Ship : public Drawable

{

};

The first line is indicating that the class called Ship will inherit from the class called Drawable. This code ensures that Ship will inherit the public data and public methods from Drawable, which is the superclass. As of now, the draw() method has been inherited and, if you were to write the entire method, it would look like this:

Ship s;

s.draw();

Calling the draw() method ensures that the method implementation in Drawable is invoked, but that isn't what we want; the Ship class needs its own way to draw itself instead of what comes with Drawable. For this to happen, there must be an indication in Drawable that the subclasses can override the draw() method. To do this the method is made into a virtual method—part of a superclass, but which may be overridden by one or more subclasses.

class Drawable

{

public:

      virtual void draw ();

};

There will be many times where no implementation needs to be provided by the superclass; instead, the subclass will be forced to have its own method implementation because, for example, there may not be a decent default for drawing an object. We do this by turning the function into a pure virtual that looks like this (note the use of = 0):

```
class Drawable

{

public:

        virtual void draw () = 0;

};
```

Yes, it does look a little strange, but it has some logic to it. When you set a method to 0, you're indicating that it doesn't actually exist. When a class has a pure virtual method, the method must be implemented by the subclasses. To do this, the method must be declared again by the subclass, this time omitting the = 0. This indicates that a real method implementation will be provided by the class:

```
class Ship : public Drawable

{

public:

        virtual draw ();

};
```

Now we can define the method the same way as any standard method:

```
Ship::draw ()

{

        /* code that does the drawing */

}
```

So, why do we need these superclasses? What purpose does Drawable serve if we are only making a draw() method that has no implementation? The superclass is required so that the interface all subclasses must implement can be defined. That way, code can be written that will expect the interface without needing to know the exact class type in use.

Some languages will let you pass any object to any function and, so long as the methods used by the function are implemented by the object, everything will work just fine. With C++, we need a function to be explicit about the argument interfaces. If the Drawable interface didn't exist, there would be no way of placing the classes within the same vector—there would nothing common between them that could be used to identify what goes in the vector.

Below is the code to show how the vector is used to draw all objects:

```
vector<Drawable*> drawables;

// create a new Ship pointer so Ship is stored in the vector

drawables.push_back( new Ship() );

for ( vector<int>::iterator itr = drawables.begin(), end =
drawables.end();

        itr != end; ++itr )

{

        // Don't forget, the - > syntax is required to call methods when

        // we've got a pointer to an object

        (*itr)->draw(); // calls Ship::Draw

}
```

All sorts of Drawable objects can be added to the vector. For the next example, we'll assume that we have a class called Enemy that will also inherit from Drawable:

drawables.push_back(new Ship());

drawables.push_back(new Enemy());

Everything works just fine. The Ship::draw method is called for the ships and the Enemy::draw method is called for the enemies.

As an aside, it's worth noting that it's important that we used a vector<Drawable*> and not a vector<Drawable>. The pointer makes a huge difference; without it, the code would not work. To understand why, just imagine that the code was written to hold the object without having that pointer:

vector <Drawable> drawables;

We will now have memory that has all different Drawable objects but all of the same size:

[Drawable 1][Drawable 2][Drawable 3]

If a pointer isn't used, the whole object must be stored by the vector but the objects can't all be the same size. For a start, Enemy and Ship may have different fields and it's perfectly possible that both are smaller than a standard Drawable— so it wouldn't work.

On the other hand, pointers are always the same size. We could say:

[Pointer to Drawable][Pointer to Drawable][Pointer to Drawable]

And a [Pointer to Ship] will take the exact same amount of memory as a [Pointer to Drawable]. This is why we had:

Vector <Drawable> drawables;*

Now, any pointer can be placed into the vector, so long as it points to a class that will inherit from Drawable. In the loop, each object is drawn using the draw method for the subclass.

All you need to remember is that, when you want a class to inherit a superclass interface, a pointer must be used to pass the class around.

So, what exactly did we do here?

1. We first defined the Drawable interface that the subclasses will inherit.

2. Drawable can be taken by any function or code that works with the interface. The code can call the draw method implemented by the specific object being pointed to.

3. This means that the existing code can make use of new object types but only those that will implement Drawable. New items can be added to the game, for example, powerup icons, extra lives, background pictures, whatever you want, and the code that will process them only needs to know they're Drawable.

This is about reusing existing code that works with new classes. We can write these classes so that they work with this code, such as the game loop responsible for drawing the game elements. Although the new class objects have to be added to the Drawable object vector, the loop will not change.

This is called polymorphism. Literally translated, it means "many forms." In other words, any class that implements a specified interface is a single form and, because the code is written to use only the interface that can handle several classes, the code supports several interface forms.

More Uses (and Misuses) of Inheritance

While polymorphism is dependent on inheritance, inheritance has more uses than just inheriting interfaces. It can also be used for picking up the implementation of functions. For example, if there were another non-virtual method for the Drawable interface, every single object that could implement Drawable would also inherit that method. This avoids the need to write that method for every subclass. It's quite limited in terms of reuse, though.

You could realize a certain amount of savings if you inherited entire method implementations, but that leads to the huge challenge of how to ensure that a method implementation is right for every subclass. This requires some very careful consideration about the validity of things in all cases.

Why is this so hard? Let's assume that we have two objects named Player and Ship; both methods implement Drawable and both classes have a method called getName. You could add the getName method into Drawable; that way, both classes could have the exact same implementation:

class Drawable

{

public:

      string getName ();

      virtual void draw () = 0;

};

Because getName is not a virtual method, all of the subclasses inherit the implementation. What would happen if you added another class, such as Bullet, that you wanted to draw? Does each individual bullet require a name? No, absolutely not! While it might not seem much of a problem to have a getName method that is quite useless for Bullet, if you continue to do this, over and again, your class hierarchies will end up being complicated and very confusing and the interface purpose won't be that clear.

Object Construction and Destruction

When a superclass is inherited from, the constructor for the subclass will call the superclass constructor, the same way as the constructor for every single class field would be invoked.

Take the following code:

```
#include <iostream>

using namespace std;

class Foo // Foo is the most common placeholder name in computer
programming

{

public:

        Foo () { cout << "Foo's constructor" << endl; }

};

class Bar : public Foo

{
```

```cpp
public:

        Bar () { cout << "Bar's constructor" << endl; }

};

int main ()

{

        // a lovely giraffe ;)

        Bar bar;

}
```

When we initialize bar, the Foo constructor will run first, followed by the Bar constructor, and the code output will be:

Foo's constructor

Bar's constructor

When the superclass constructor runs first, it can initialize all the superclass fields before the constructor for the subclass might use them. Doing it this way ensures that the superclass fields can be used by the subclass, having already been initialized.

The compiler does all this for you. There is nothing special that you need to do to ensure the superclass constructor is called. In the same way, once the subclass destructor has run, the superclass destructor is called automatically.

Here's what that looks like in code:

```cpp
#include <iostream>
```

```cpp
using namespace std;

class Foo // Foo is the most common placeholder name in computer
programming
{
public:
        Foo () { cout << "Foo's constructor" << endl; }

        ~Foo () { cout << "Foo's destructor" << endl; }
};

class Bar : public Foo
{
public:
        Bar () { cout << "Bar's constructor" << endl; }

        ~Bar () { cout << "Bar's destructor" << endl; }
};

int main ()
{
        // a lovely giraffe ;)
        Bar bar;
}
```

And the output from this will be:

Foo's constructor

Bar's constructor

Bar's destructor

Foo's destructor

Did you spot that the constructor and the destructor are both called on the opposite order? This is to make sure that the constructor for Bar can use the methods inherited from Foo safely because the data that the methods operate on remains valid and usable.

There may be times when you want a non-default constructor called in the superclass; we can do this by providing the superclass name in the initialization list:

class FooSuperclass

{

public:

    FooSuperclass (const string& val);

};

class Foo : public FooSuperclass

{

public:

```
    Foo ()

            : FooSuperclass( "arg" ) // sample initialization list

    {}

};
```

The call to the superclass constructor should appear before the fields of the class in the initialization list.

Object Destruction and Polymorphism

Object destruction is tricky, especially when it comes to the object being destroyed through an interface. You could have code like this, for example:

```
class Drawable

{

public:

        virtual void draw () = 0;

};

class  MyDrawable : public Drawable

{

public:

        virtual void draw ();

        MyDrawable ();
```

```cpp
        ~MyDrawable ();
private:
        int *_my_data;
};
MyDrawable::MyDrawable ()
{
        _my_data = new int;
}
MyDrawable::~MyDrawable ()
{
        delete _my_data;
}
void deleteDrawable (Drawable *drawable)
{
        delete drawable;
}
int main ()
{
        deleteDrawable( new MyDrawable() );
```

}

What's going on inside deleteDrawable? Remember, when delete gets used, the destructor is called, so the line that reads

delete drawable;

makes a function call on the object. But how does the compiler know where the MyDrawable destructor is? The compiler doesn't know what the exact type of the drawable variable is, but it does know that it's a Drawable, something that has a draw() method. All it really knows is how the destructor associated Drawable can be found by the MyDrawable destructor itself. As MyDrawable allocates memory in its own constructor, in order to free the memory the MyDrawable destructor must run.

Okay, so you could be thinking that this is what virtual functions are designed to fix. That's correct. What we should be doing is declaring the destructor virtual in Drawable; that way the compiler will know that it has to look for a destructor that has been overridden when delete has been called on a pointer to a Drawable:

class Drawable

{

public:

    virtual void draw ();

    virtual ~Drawable ();

};

class MyDrawable : public Drawable

{

```
    public:

    virtual void draw ();

    MyDrawable ();

    virtual ~MyDrawable ();

private:

    int *_my_data;

};
```

When we make the structure in the superclass virtual, and when delete frees up a Drawable interface, the overridden destructor gets called.

As a rule, when you make any superclass method virtual, the superclass destructor should be made virtual as well. Once one method has been made virtual, you are basically saying that the class can be passed around to methods that will take an interface. The methods can then do whatever they want and that includes deleting the object, so making the destructor virtual makes sure that the object is cleaned up properly.

The Slicing Problem

This is an issue that you really must be aware of when you work with inheritance. Object slicing occurs when you have code much like this:

```
class Superclass

{};

class Subclass : public Superclass

{
```

```
        int val;

};

int main()

{

        Subclass sub;

        Superclass super = sub;

}
```

The val field, from Subclass, will not be copied with the assignment to super and this is likely not what you want, even though it's allowed in C++. This is because the object is only partially there. This type of slicing can work sometimes but, more often than not, all it will do is cause your program to crash.

There is a way of getting the compiler to let you know when this kind of problem occurs; all you do is declare the Superclass copy constructor Private and then don't implement it:

```
class Superclass

{

public:

        // because we are declaring the copy constructor, we must now

        // provide the default constructor

        Superclass () {}

private:

        // prohibited, this method will not be defined
```

```
        Superclass (const Superclass& other);
};
class Subclass : public Superclass
{
        int val;
};
int main ()
{
        Subclass sub;

        Superclass super = sub; // this code line will now cause a
        compilation error
}
```

What if you want a copy constructor? There is another way to avoid the issue; make any superclass that you create contain one or more pure virtual functions and this will make sure that, should you ever write:

Superclass super;

The code won't ever compile because an object can't be created with a pure virtual function. However, you could still write:

Superclass *super = & sub;

So you will benefit from polymorphism without having to face the slicing problem.

Code-Sharing with Subclasses

We've talked about using private and public protection. A public method is available outside the class while private methods and private data are only accessible by class methods. But what if we want a superclass to give us methods that the subclasses can call but external classes can't? First, think about it. Are you ever likely to want this? You might. It's not uncommon for implementation code to be shared by subclasses.

For example, let's say that we have a method that can let an object draw itself by clearing a part of the screen. This method will be called clearRegion:

class Drawable

{

public:

> *virtual void draw ();*

> *virtual ~Drawable ();*

> *void clearRegion (int x1, int y1, int x2, int y2);*

};

We use inheritance here, not for the purpose of inheriting the interface; instead, we use it to let common implementation code be accessed by subclasses. This is a valid and good use of inheritance because all subclasses either need or might need to use the method. Because it isn't actually part of the class's public interface it's nothing more than a class hierarchy implementation detail being created.

How do we stop this method from being part of the class interface? When we make it public, as we have in the example, it allows the method to be called by anyone although it isn't actually designed for that purpose.

However, the method can't be made private because subclasses don't have access to private methods or fields; if subclass access were blocked, the whole point would be missed.

Protected Data

The answer lies in using the protected access modifier. Any method that is in the protected part of a class can, unlike a private method, be accessed by a subclass. However, unlike a public method it cannot be accessed from outside the class. The syntax used for the protected modifier is similar to that of the private and protected ones:

class Drawable

{

public:

    virtual void draw ();

    virtual ~Drawable ();

protected:

    void clearRegion (int x1, int y1, int x2, int y2);

};

Now, the only subclasses that can access clearRegion are those from Drawable.

While protected methods are useful on many occasions, protected data shouldn't ever be used unless it's absolutely vital. There really isn't a need for data access to be exposed to the whole class hierarchy for the same reason that data doesn't need to be exposed anywhere else. After all, you might need to change it sometime in the future. Instead, protected methods should be used for allowing access to the data in the subclasses.

Class-Wide Data

All we have done so far with classes is store data for individual object instances. Most of the time this will be more than enough. However, there will be times when you want data stored that is specific to the class as a whole and not to any one specific object. An example of that would be if we created a class that needed a unique serial number for each object. How would you track the next number you want assigned? You would need somewhere to store that next number and this needs to be done at class level; this way, whenever we construct a new object, we know what value it should be given.

Why would you want to do something like this? When you use a serial number for each object, identifying objects in log statements is made so much easier. You can trace the object over any number of lines in the log file by using the serial number.

Class-wide data is created with a static class member. Static data, unlike standard class data, is not a part of any object. Instead, all class objects can access it and, if it's made public, anyone else can access it too. Static variables are much like global variables; the exception is that accessing a static variable from outside the class requires the class name to be prefixed by the variable name.

To see what it looks like, here we have a class declaring the static variable:

class Node

{

public:

      static int serial_number;

};

// not in the class declaration--so Node:: must be used as

// a prefix

static int Node::serial_number = 0;

As well as static variables, you can also use static methods; these are part of the class but can also be used without object instances. In the next example, we look at how to use a private static method named _getNextSerialNumber to create a serial number for each individual node:

class Node

{

public:

    Node ();

    private:

    static int _getNextSerialNumber ();

    // static, one copy for the entire class

    static int _next_serial_number;

    // non-static, available to every object, but not to the static methods

    int _serial_number;

};

// not inside the class declaration-- so Node:: must be used as

// a prefix

```
static int Node::serial_number = 0;

Node::Node ()

        : _serial_number( _getNextSerialNumber() )

{ }

int Node::_getNextSerialNumber ()

{

        // use the postfix version of ++ to return the value that was

        // in the variable  before

        return _next_serial_number++;

}
```

Remember: when a static method is used, that method becomes part of the class but doesn't have any access to the fields that are object-specific. It can only have access to static data and doesn't have a this pointer being passed to it.

Implementing Polymorphism

I will not be going into this subject fully as it is a more advanced topic. Instead, I will give you just enough information that you understand it. Learning how this is done isn't so important when you first start getting to know polymorphism. So, if you want some idea of how it is implemented, keep reading; if you don't, move on to the next section— you can always come back later.

The key to polymorphism is that, rather than a concrete subclass, a function that operates on an interface doesn't need details on what function should be called to a specified machine code line. For example, in this code:

```
Vector <Drawable*> drawables;

void drawEverything ()

{

        for ( int i = 0; i < drawables.size(); i++ )

        {

                drawables[ i ]->draw();

        }

}
```

When we call

drawables[i]- >draw()

because the draw method is virtual, it will not compile into a specific function call. Depending on the object that inherits from Drawable, any number of methods could be called—the spaceship for a specific user, drawing a bullet, a power-up, an enemy spaceship and so on.

Not only that, but drawEverything calls code that it has absolutely no knowledge about. The code calling the draw method only needs to see the Drawable interface; it doesn't need any knowledge about who is implementing Drawable. But how does this work if it calls a method on a Drawable subclass?

The object will carry a list of virtual methods as a hidden field; in our case, we have one entry—the draw method address. Each of the methods on a specific interface will be assigned a number and, when a virtual method is called, the number that has been associated with the method gets used as the index into the virtual method list for the object. Calling a virtual method will compile into a method lookup in the virtual method list and then a call to that looked-up method. In our above example, draw call becomes a lookup to method 0 in the methods table and then a call to the address. The virtual method list is also known as vtable.

The object carries its own method table and that means that the compiler is able to change the address in that table when different classes are compiled to provide a certain implementation of a virtual method. You don't need to do any of this because the compiler does it for you. The code that makes use of the table only needs to know what index it needs to use for the individual virtual methods so that it can locate it in the table.

Virtual methods only contain those methods that have been declared virtual. The mechanism is not required by non-virtual methods. If a class is written without any virtual methods, the class won't have a virtual table.

When you call a virtual method, the code accesses the vtable and uses the index to find the method.

When you write:

drawables[i]->draw();

the compiler treats it as if you said:

1. Retrieve the pointer that is stored in drawables[i]

2. Using the pointer, locate the virtual table address for the method group that is associated with type Drawable interface—in our case, we have only one method

3. Find the function that has the specified name, (in our case, draw), in the function table. The table is a set of addresses that stores the memory location for each individual function

4. The function is called along with the associated arguments

Normally, the second step will not be accomplished by using the function name; instead, the compiler will turn each of the function names into indexes in the table. This way, at runtime, a virtual function call is very fast and there's very little difference between it and a standard function call.

Although the following syntax is made up, you could think of the code generated by the compiler as looking like this:

call drawables[i]->vtable[o];

There is, however, a drawback to virtual functions. The object has to carry at least one vtable for each of the inherited interfaces. What this means is that each of the virtual interfaces will increase the object size by a few bytes. In practice, this will only be of concern to code that has many objects that don't have many member variables.

Take the quiz and then we'll proceed to the next topic.

Quiz 23

When is the destructor for a superclass run?

A. When the object has been destroyed through a call to delete on a pointer to the superclass

B. Before the subclass destructor is called

C. After the subclass destructor has been called

D. At the time the subclass destructor is being called

Look at the class hierarchy below; what is required in the constructor for Dog?

class Mammal {

public:

*   Mammal (const string& species_name);*

};

class Dog : public Mammal

{

public:

*   Dog();*

};

A. Nothing special is required

B. The initializer should be used to call the constructor for Mammal with an argument of "dog"

C. The constructor for Mammal should be called from inside the Dog constructor with an argument of "dog"

D. The Dog constructor should be removed and the default constructor used instead.

What is wrong with this class definition?

class Nameable

{

      virtual string getName();

};

A. The getName method is not made public

B. There is no have a virtual destructor

C. There is no implementation of getName, but it also doesn't declare getName to be pure virtual

D. All of the above

When a virtual method is declared in the interface class, what must the function have the ability to do in order to use that method to call a subclass method?

A. Take the interface as a pointer or a reference

B. Nothing. It can copy the object

C. It must know what the subclass name is for the method to be called on

D. What's a virtual method?

How does reuse improve by using inheritance?

A. Because it allows code to inherit a method from its superclass

B. Because a superclass can implement a virtual method for a subclass

C. Because it lets us write code that expects an interface and not concrete classes; this allows new classes to implement that interface and reuse the code

D. Because it allows inheritance of concrete class traits by new classes, allowing use with a virtual method

Which of these statements about class access levels is correct?

A. Subclasses may only inherit public classes and their data from the parent class

B. Subclasses can have access to the parent class private methods and data

C. Subclasses may only access the protected methods and data from the parent class

D. Subclasses can have access to both the public and protected methods and their data from the parent class

Namespaces

As you begin to pick up steam on your coding and create even more classes, you might start to wonder if anyone else has written code that does the same thing that you want to do. And if they have, can you use it? Sometimes, the answer to both those questions will be yes. Quite a few data structures and core algorithms, such as binary trees and linked lists, have already been created and implemented in ways that they can be reused. The one thing you need to be careful of, when you use code created by someone else, is that you don't get into trouble with name conflicts.

Let's say, for example, that you write a class named LinkedList for storing your linked list implementation. It's perfectly possible that you're using some code that already has a class called LinkedList but has a different implementation of it than yours. It is NOT possible to use two classes that have the same name.

You can avoid this type of conflict by creating namespaces that extend to the type's basic name. As an example, you could place your linked list class into a namespace that is called com::cprogramming. This will ensure that the type's fully qualified name is com::cprogramming::LinkedList. When you use a namespace, you significantly reduce the risk of conflicts between names. The :: operator is the one we use for accessing the static members in a class or to declare methods. However, rather than accessing class elements, we use it to access namespace elements.

So, if these namespaces are so good, why aren't they used by the standard library? As it turns out, if you have been paying attention, you've already seen these namespaces. At the top of each program we write, we had

using namespace std;

We use this so we don't need to use fully qualified names when we refer to the objects like cout and cin. If this statement wasn't used, we would need to write std::cout or std::cin whenever those objects were needed. This will only work for as long as the namespaces are not actually needed to avoid conflicts in the file; this gives us a convenient little shortcut to use when you know that there won't be any issues. When there will be conflict issues, just leave the namespace using declaration out of the code and make sure that each type is fully qualified in the file.

We can see how that works with our earlier code example. If we had two classes named LinkedList, most of our files would need the declaration of

using namespace com::cprogramming::LinkedList

If a file had name conflicts, that file would need to be changed so that your LinkedList class was referred to as com::cprogramming::LinkedList. Rather than needing all the code changed all over the place, we only need the files changed that need to use both LinkedList types. In those files, the fully qualified name would be used and the namespace com::cprogramming statement would be removed.

Take a look at the example below, showing you how some code is declared part of a namespace. In this case, it's a single variable:

namespace cprogramming

{

    int x;

} // <-- note that we don't need to use the semicolon

Now, x must be referred to as cprogramming::x. Or you could say

using namespace cprogramming;

And then all you have to do is write x into the file with the code line reading

using namespace cprogramming

Namespaces can also be nested inside one another. Let's say you were working in a large organization that had multiple units and each one needed to do its own development. For this kind of scenario, you could use the organization name as the outer namespace and then place each individual unit in an inner namespace.

The next example shows how a nested namespace for com::cprogramming would be declared:

namespace com {

namespace cprogramming

{

        int x;

}}

x now has a full name of com::cprogramming::x. Note that I have not used the indent for each namespace. If you had several namespaces and indented each of them, you would have a problem with the tabs.

You could write:

using namespace com::cprogramming;

as a way of accessing the namespace elements.

A namespace is classed as being open, which means that code can be placed into one namespace in several files. If, for example, a header file was created to contain a class, and that class was placed into a namespace:

```
namespace com {

namespace cprogramming

{

class MyClass

{

public:

        MyClass ();

};

} }
```

In the source file that corresponds to this, you could write:

```
#include "MyClass.h"

namespace com {

namespace cprogramming

{

        MyClass::MyClass ()

{}

} }
```

Both of these files can add code in the namespace, just as you want them to.

When to use the "using namespace" Declaration

Generally, using declarations should only be placed in cpp files, not into header files. The main problem is that all files that make use of the header are going to be subject to name conflicts. Every cpp file should have control of the namespace it uses. As a rule of thumb, only use fully qualified names in header files and use the using declarations in your cpp files.

However, as with everything, there are a few exceptions to the rule. The first one is that the standard library violates said rule, for a good reason. If you were to write:

#include <iostream.h>

And not

#include <iostream>

there would no longer be a need to add the using declaration for std. As it turns out, what's inside iostream.h is:

#include <iostream>

using namespace std;

The reason for this is backward compatibility with the programs created before C++ began using namespaces. If you have something like this:

#include <iostream.h>

int main ()

```
{

        cout << "Hello world";

}
```

It can still be compiled with namespaces added into the standard library.

For writing new code, use the new header file that doesn't have the .h so that you don't have to worry about this. It will take little time to write

using namespace std

to each file and ensures that you're using the most up-to-date version of C++.

When to Create a Namespace?

If the program you're working on has just a few files, it probably won't be necessary to create namespaces. These are really only used with you start creating programs that have many files in many directories because this scenario is where you're likely to see the name conflicts.

As a recommendation, place code into namespaces when you think that you will want to reuse it at another time or when your program grows to a size where you need to start breaking it down into separate directories. If your code has reached that level of complexity, you need to be using every tool at your disposal to keep it as organized as possible.

Namespaces are not the most exciting feature in C++ but you will soon begin to see that they are handy when you have large code bases to work on. If you can understand what they are and why you see them in other code, you will find it easy to learn when to integrate code written by others into yours.

After the usual quiz, we will move on to File I/O.

Quiz 24

When should a using namespace directive be used?

A. After the include statement in every header file

B. They should never be used. They are dangerous!

C. At the beginning of any cpp file where there is no conflict with namespaces

D. Just before a variable from the namespace is used

What is the purpose of namespaces?

A. They give the compiler writers something interesting to get their teeth into!

B. They provide more code encapsulation

C. On a large code base they prevent name conflicts

D. They are used to clarify the purpose of a class

When should code be put in a namespace?

A. Always

B. When you are developing a large program that has more than a couple dozen files

C. When you're developing a library that is to be shared with other people

D. B and C

Why shouldn't a using namespace declaration go in a header file?

A. Because it's illegal

B. There isn't any reason not to, because a using declaration will only be valid in the header file

C. Because it will force the using declaration onto whoever uses the header file, regardless of whether it causes conflict or not

D. If several header files have the using declarations, it can cause conflicts

File I/O

If there is one thing that a computer needs, it's files. Without them, no matter what your computer does, it will only last until you reboot it or the application you're using terminates. It kind of goes without saying that C++ can read files and write to them and we call this business of working with files 'File I/O'—input/output.

File reading and writing looks very similar to when we use cin and cout. However, where cin and cout are global variables, with I/O you need to declare the objects you want to be read or written to. To do this, you have to know what the types are.

The data types are ifstream, which stands for input file stream, and ofstream, which stands for output file stream. Streams are nothing more than data that you can read or write to. These types take files and transform them into long data streams that we can access, just as though we were interacting with a user. Both types need an fstream header file to work.

Reading from Files

We'll start by talking about reading from files. To do this, the ifstream type is required. An ifstream instance can be initialized using the name of the specific file to be read from:

#include <fstream>

using namespace std;

int main ()

{

```
        ifstream file_reader( "myfile.txt" );

}
```

This is only a small program but it tries to open the file named myfile.txt. To do that, it needs to find the file and will look for it in the directory where the program execution happens—the working directory. You could supply a full path if you wanted, something like c:\myfile.txt.

Note that I said the program tries to open the file: if the file doesn't exist, it can't. To see what the result would be of creating an ifstream if the file were opened, you can call the method of is_open. This will indicate if the file was successfully opened by the ifstream object:

```
#include  <fstream>

#include  <iostream>

using namespace std;

int main ()

{

        ifstream file_reader( "myfile.txt" );

        if ( ! file_reader.is_open() )

        {

        cout << "The file could not be opened!" << '\n';

        }

}
```

When you're working with files, there really is no choice: you have to write code that can handle potential failures. A file might not exist. It may be corrupted or in use by another system process. Some operations on the file will fail. And failure is something you always have to be prepared for when you work with files—loss of power, corrupted files, disk failure, bad sectors on the hard drive. Every one of these will cause an operation to fail.

As soon as the file has been opened, an ifstream can be used in the same way that we use cin. The code below will read a number for a specified text file:

```cpp
#include <fstream>

#include <iostream>

using namespace std;

int main ()

{

        ifstream file_reader( "myfile.txt" );

        if ( ! file_reader.is_open() )

        {

                cout << "The file could not be opened!" << '\n';

        }

        int number;

        file_reader >> number;
```

```
}
```

In the same way as if you were reading from user input, the line reads the digits in the file until it gets to a space or some other type of separator. If the following text were in the file, for example:

12 a b c

When the program was run, 12 would be the number stored.

Because these are files we are working with, it's important to know if any errors occur. With C++, there is a way to check what the result is from the function that carried out the read operation.

It's done like this:

```
#include  <fstream>

#include  <iostream>

using namespace std;

int main ()

{

        ifstream file_reader( "myfile.txt" );

        if ( ! file_reader.is_open() )

        {

                cout << "The file could not be opened!" << '\n';

        }

        int number;
```

```
        // we need to check if the operation to read an integer in was
successful or not

        if ( file_reader >> number )

        {

                cout << "The value is: " << number;

        }

}
```

When we check the result from the call to file_reader>> number, we can see if there were any issues that arose from reading the disk media or any problems with the data format.

Can you remember, right back at the start of this guide, when we talked about how a letter can be used to represent a number? This is the way that you guard against this happening. The return value from the input routine can be checked. If true, all is good and the data can be trusted. If false, something is wrong and you must treat it as an error.

File Formats

When you request a user for input, you can tell them exactly what you want and, if bad input is received, you can give the user some guidance on how to correct the problem. When reading from files, you can't do that.

Why? Because the file is written already, most likely before you even thought about creating the program. In order for the data to be read back in, you have to know what format the file is. The format is the file layout, but it doesn't have to be complex. For example, we could have a list of high scores you want saved between each program run. You could have a very simple format, perhaps 10 lines, each with one number.

An example of a list like that could look like:

1000

987

864

766

744

500

453

321

201

98

5

And to read in this list you could write a program like this:

```cpp
#include  <fstream>

#include  <iostream>

#include  <vector>

using namespace std;

int main ()

{
```

```
ifstream file_reader( "highscores.txt" );

if ( ! file_reader.is_open() )

{

        cout << "The file could not be opened!" << '\n';

}

vector<int> scores;

for ( int i = 0; i < 10; i++ )

{

        int score;

        file_reader >> score;

        scores.push_back( score );

}

}
```

This is really quite simple code—all it does is open the file and then read in the scores one at a time. It isn't even reliant on newline characters separating the scores; it works equally well with spaces. That is an accidental feature of the implementation, not a file format feature. If you have other programs working with the file format, they might not be so kind in what is expected to be read in.

There is a principle called Postel's Law that you should run with when you work with file formats: "be liberal in what you accept and conservative in what you send." In other words, any code that produces files should follow the specification carefully, whereas code that reads the format should be robust enough to withstand smaller errors made by programs that aren't quite so well written. In the example above, we've been liberal by accepting the space separator alongside the newline.

End of File

The code has been written so that it conforms to a specific format and will not attempt to handle errors. For example, if we have less than 10 entries, the code will continue to read from the file even when it gets to the end. Our game might only have been played three times, so we wouldn't yet have those 10 scores. EOF tends to be used to indicate the state is at the "end of file."

We can create robust code by writing in handling for when there are fewer than 10 items in the list. We do this by checking, once again, to see the result of the method used for reading the input:

```cpp
#include <fstream>

#include <iostream>

#include <vector>


using namespace std;

int main ()

{

    ifstream file_reader( "myfile.txt" );

    if ( ! file_reader.is_open() )
```

```
        {

                cout << "The file could not be opened!" << '\n';

        }

        vector<int> scores;

        for ( int i = 0; i < 10; i++ )

        {

                int score;

                if ( ! file_reader >> score )

                {

                        break;

                }

                scores.push_back( score );

        }

}
```

When this code is run on a file that has less than 10 entries, as soon as it gets to the end, it stops reading. Using vectors makes it far easier to handle the shorter files than if you were using a fixed-size array. The vector holds the exact input that was read in—nothing more, nothing less. If we use an array to do this, we need to track the number of entries stored. We shouldn't assume that the entire array has been filled.

On occasion, you will want to read in all the data in a given file, right up to the very end of that file. For this you need to be able to tell the difference between read failures because you reached the end and read failures because there is an error within the file. The EOF method indicates whether you are at the end of the file or not. A loop can be written to read in as much data as is possible, checking the read result each time, until a failure happens. At that point you can check to see whether EOF has returned true—if it has, you have reached the end of the file; if it hasn't, an error has occurred.

The fail() method can also be called to look for other failures. This method will return true if an input was bad or if a problem occurred while reading from a device. Once you reach the end of the file, the clear() method must be called for further file operations to be carried out. When we get to the section where we write a new score into our high score list, you will see an example where we use all of these methods.

One more important difference between reading from a file and user interaction needs to be highlighted. What might happen if our high score list was changed so that the player name was added with the score? We would need to read in two pieces of information—the name and the score. And that would mean changes to the code so it could handle this. However, any older versions of the program would not be able to read the new format and this can cause serious headaches if you have many users and want your file format updated. You can use a number of different techniques to future-proof the format by adding in some extra, optional fields or providing the older versions with the ability to just ignore the new format elements. We won't be discussing these techniques as they are outside the scope of this guide; for now, you just need to understand that file format definitions are in many ways far more of a commitment than basic interface definitions.

Writing Files

We need to use the ofstream type for writing files. It's almost the same as the ifstream type except we use it like cout instead of cin. Below is a simple program that will write the values from 0 to 9 into a highscores.txt file. Very soon we will be making this code produce something that looks a lot more like a list of high scores:

```
#include <fstream>

#include <iostream>

#include <vector>

using namespace std;

int main ()

{

        ofstream file_writer( "highscores.txt" );

        if ( ! file_writer.is_open() )

        {

                cout << "The file could not be opened!" << '\n';

                return 0;

        }

        // because we don't yet have real scores, the numbers from 10 to 1
will be output instead
```

```
for ( int i = 0; i < 10; i++ )

{

file_writer << 10 – i << '\n';

}

}
```

We don't have to worry about getting to the end of the file here. When the file is written to and you get to the end of it, ofstream extends it for you. This is known as appending to the file.

Creating New Files

When ofstream is used for writing to files, it will create the file if it doesn't already exist or, if it does, it will overwrite it. This is ofstream's default behavior. Depending on what you're saving, this may save you a great deal of time. For example, if you're saving a list of high scores, overwriting it each time is not a problem because you're going to be writing back the data anyway. However, if you're keeping something like a running log to track the time and date whenever your program is launched, the last thing you need is for it to be overwritten every time.

Luckily, the constructor for ofstream will take another argument that is used to specify the way the file should be handled:

ios::app   Append to the file, and after each write, set the position to the end

ios::ate   Set the current position to the end

ios::trunc   Truncate the file, i.e., delete everything in it

ios::out   Allow for output to the file

| ios::binary | Allow for binary operations on the stream. Should also be available when reading from the file |

ofstream a_file("test.txt", ios::app | ios::binary);

Using this code, the file can be opened without destroying any of the current content. That allows for binary data to be written at the end of it.

File Position

When a program reads or writes to a file, the I/O code has to know where that read or write is going to happen. Think of this as being much like your mouse cursor; where it is on the screen indicates where the next character is going to be typed.

For a simple operation, the position really doesn't matter; the code can be written so it reads whatever comes next in the file or writes to wherever is next to be written to. However, the position in the file can also be changed without needing to do a read. This is likely to be necessary when the files you're working with store complicated or complex data, such as a PDF or a ZIP file, or if you're working with a very large file where it would be too slow, if not impossible, to read in each and every byte, such as if a database is being implemented.

A file has two different positions—one that indicates where the program reads next and one that indicates where the program will next write. The current position can be acquired by using two methods called tellg and tellp. The tellg method (g is for get) provides the current reading position and tellp (the p is for put) provides the current writing position.

There are two methods to use for setting the file position, moving from the current position: seekp and seekg. Moving around the file is called seeking and when you seek through a file, the read or write position is set to a new location. Both methods take two parameters—the distance for seeking and the seek operation source.

Bytes are used for measuring the distance. The source is the start or end of the file or the current position. Once seeking is done, you can read or write from the new file position. And if you change a position by seek, it will not impact the other position. There are three position flags in the file:

ios_base::beg	Seek from the start of the file
ios_base::cur	Seek from the current position
ios_base::end	Seek from the end of the file

If, for example, you want to move to the beginning of the file before you start writing, you would say something like:

file_writer.seekp(0, ios_base::beg);

The value that tellp and tellg return is a special type of variable called streampos and is defined by the C++ standard library. This variable allows us to convert to and from an integer. However, when you use streampos, you can be far more explicit about the type. Integers can be used just about anywhere, but the streampos has a specific purpose: storing positions in a file and seeking to those specified positions. It's important to use the correct variable type in code so the variable's purpose is very clear.

streampos pos = file_reader.tellg();

There are cases where you won't need to use seek because reading or writing from start to finish will be sufficient. However, there are quite a few file formats that have been optimized for the purpose of adding new data into a file. When new data is added, it's easier and faster to add at the end of the file than to try and insert in the middle.

Insertion into the middle comes with a problem: everything in the file after the point of insertion has to be moved, much like when elements are inserted into arrays.

Let's go back to the high scores program we started earlier and modify it so a new score is added. And, just to make it more interesting, the value will be inserted to the right position.

Doing this requires that we read AND write to the file, so we need to use the fstream class. fstream is a combination of both ifstream and ofstream, allowing reading and writing.

First, a new high score is read in from the user and then each line of the file will be read in until we get to a score that is lower than the input score. That's where the new score is to be inserted. The position will be saved, all the remaining lines read into a vector and then returned to the new position. The new score is written out and then the rest of the scores are written back out to replace the lines already there.

Because we're using fstream, we can read and write. But now the constructor needs to be explicitly told that file is to be opened for both reading and writing. To do that, we use two flags—ios::in and ios::out—so it's clear what needs to be done. Before you start, this isn't going to create an empty file, so you need to make a high score file. Then you can add this code:

```
#include <fstream>

#include <iostream>

#include <vector>

using namespace std;

int main ()

{

        fstream file ( "highscores.txt", ios::in | ios::out );
```

```
if ( ! file.is_open() )

{

        cout << "The file could not be opened!" << '\n';

        return 0;

}

int new_high_score;

cout << "Input a new high score: ";

cin >> new_high_score;

// the while loop we use below will search the fil until it gets to a value

// that is lower  than the current high score; at this point, we now know that the

// high score should be inserted just before that value. To ensure

// that we know what the correct position is, we must track the position up to the

// position before the current score; the pre_score_pos

streampos pre_score_pos = file.tellg();

int cur_score;

while ( file >> cur_score )

{
```

```
            if ( cur_score < new_high_score )

    {

            break;

    }

    pre_score_pos = file.tellg();

}

// if fail evaluates true, and we know we are not at eof, we know that
there is some bad input

if ( file.fail() && ! file.eof() )

{

        cout << "Bad score/read--exiting";

        return 0;

}

        // if we don't call clear, we can't write to the file if we hit eof

        file.clear();

        // return to the point just before the last score that was read, for
        reading

        // so that all the scores lower than the high score can be read in

        // and moved one position on in the file

        file.seekg( pre_score_pos );
```

```cpp
    // now we read all the scores in beginning with the one we
    // read in previously
    vector<int> scores;
    while ( file >> cur_score )
    {
        scores.push_back( cur_score );
    }
    // we are expecting, through this read loop, to get to the end of the
file because
    // we want all the scores in the file read in.
    if ( ! file.eof() )
    {
        cout << "Bad score/read--exiting";
        return 0;
    }
    // because we reached eof, the file needs to be cleared once again
    so that
    // we can write to the file again.
    file.clear();
    // look back to the position we want to do our insert done
```

```cpp
file.seekp( pre_score_pos );
// if we are not writing to the start of the file, we need must
// add a newline. This is so that, when a number gets read in, it will
// stop at the first whitespace so that the position we are at
// before writing is not at the beginning of the next line;
// it is at the end of the number
if ( pre_score_pos != 0 )
{
        file << endl;
}
// write out the new high score
file << new_high_score << endl;
// loop through the remaining scores, and output all of them
for ( vector<int>::iterator itr = scores.begin(); itr != scores.end();
++itr )
{
        file << *itr << endl;
}
```

}

Accepting Command Line Arguments

When you write a program that can interact with a file, more often than not you will want your users to provide the name of the file as a command line argument. Very often, this is much easier to use and it's far easier to write a script that will call your program. Let's put reading and writing files aside for a moment and use this feature to give our programs a bit of a boost.

A command line argument is provided after the program name. It's passed from the operating system into the program:

C:\my_program\my_program.exe arg1 arg2

These arguments get passed straight into the main function and, to make use of command line arguments, you need to give the entire declaration of that main function. Before now, we have only seen main functions with argument lists that are empty. The main function does, in fact, take two parameters—one indicates how many command line arguments there are and the other lists all command line arguments.

The full main function declaration looks like this:

int main (int argc, char *argv[])

The integer called argc is the argument count, indicating how many arguments are passed from the command line to the program, and it includes the program name. So, why did we not do all this right from the start? Why aren't these arguments included with all our programs? The answer to that is simple: if you don't put the arguments in, the fact that they have been passed into the function will be ignored by the compiler.

Next we have an array of character pointers that lists every one of the arguments. The program name is argv[0] or, if there is no name, an empty string is used. Following from that, each of the element numbers that is less than argc will be a command line argument. Each of the argv elements can be used like a string and argv[argc] is a NULL pointer.

Below we have an example program that will take a command line argument. In our case, this will be a program taking a file name and outputting all the text from the file to the screen:

```cpp
#include <fstream>

#include <iostream>

using namespace std;

int main (int argc, char *argv[])

{

        // for execution to be correct, argc should be 2, the program name

        // and the filename

        if ( argc != 2 )

        {

                // when the usage instructions are printed, argv[0] can be used

                // as the file name

                cout << "usage: " << argv[ 0 ] << " " << endl;

        }
```

else

{

    // We make the assumption that argv[1] is a name of the file to be opened

    ifstream the_file(argv[1]);

    // you should always check that the opening was successful

    if (! the_file.is_open())

    {

        cout << "The file could not be opened " << argv[1] << endl;

        return 1;

    }

    char x;

    // the_file.get(x) will read the next character from the file

    // into x, and will return false if we hit the end of the file

    // or if an error occurs some kind of error happens

    while (the_file.get(x))

    {

        cout << x;

    }

} // the destructor implicitly closes the_file is implicitly here by its destructor

}

The full main function declaration is used to access the parameters on the command line. First, the program will check that a file name was provided by the user. Next, it will try to open the file to see if it's valid or not. If it is, the file is opened. If it isn't, an error gets reported. If the file opening succeeds, the program will print each of the file characters onto the screen.

Numeric Command Line Arguments

If you wanted to use a command line parameter as a number you could do it by reading the parameter in as a string and then calling a function called atoi—this stands for ASCII to integer. This function will take a char* and will return the integer that the string represents. To use it, the cstdlib header must be used.

For example, the program below will read the command line argument, convert it so it becomes a number and then print out the square of the conversion:

#include <cstdlib>

#include <iostream>

using namespace std;

*int main (int argc, char *argv[])*

{

if (argc != 2)

{

```
        // when the usage instructions are printed, argv[0] can be
used

        // as the file name

        cout << "usage: " << argv[ 0 ] << " " << endl;

    }

    else

    {

        int val = atoi( argv[ 1 ] );

        cout << val * val;

    }

    return 0;

}
```

Binary File I/O

Up to now, we have looked at working with files that have contained data in textual form. Now we should turn to looking at binary files. To work with binary files we need to use programming techniques that are a little bit different. Don't get confused here! Every one of the files on your system is already stored in binary. However, much of the time, the file has been written in a user-friendly way, which means the user can read it.

C++ source files, as an example, are entirely made up of characters that can be read by a basic computer text editor. Files like this, where each byte in the file is a character or a part of one can be read, are text files.

However, not every file will have only text. Some files have bytes that are not characters that can be printed. Instead, they're nothing more than raw binary data that comes from one or more data structures written straight to disk.

As an example, let's assume that we have a data structure representing a player:

struct player

{

    int age;

    int high_score;

    string name;

};

You have two options for writing this data structure into a file.. First, the age, name and the high_score could be recorded as text fields; that way, the entire file could be opened in a text editor. That could look something like this:

18

150000

Harry

The high score is represented by six characters and, as we learned before, one byte is required to store each character. Six bytes are required for storing the high score. However, we have an integer for the high score and integers, on 32-bit systems, are only four bytes. So, why do we need six? We don't we only need four? If the number were written using four bytes we wouldn't be able to use a text editor to open it and see the number. Why not?

When 150000 is written into the file as a character string, it gets encoded; each of the characters uses one byte for storing the digits as characters. When a number is placed directly into the file, the bytes do not get encoded into characters. So, you now have the four bytes needed for the integer that is written to the file. If the file gets read by a text editor, the four bytes will be treated as four characters. But, when the characters are printed, they will bear no relation to the number that we show. Because the file has been encoded differently, the result will have no meaning.

A binary format will take up less space. We saw in our earlier example that it takes 50 percent more space to store 150000 in characters than it does to use the binary representation. If you had a small hard drive, a slow hard drive or were using the network to send data, that could make a world of difference. However, binary files are not so easy to understand; you can't open one up in a text editor to see what's in it. Designers of file formats find themselves facing a trade-off: creating formats that can be read and modified by any human or creating formats that are efficient. Often, XML and other text-based markup languages are used for creating file formats that can easily be read by humans and understood but that take up quite a bit more space.

When space becomes a problem, if your processor is fast enough, file compression technology, such as ZIP, can be used for reducing how much space is needed while maintaining the file as text-based when it has been unzipped. Because unzipping a file is very easy, humans can still work with these files although they're much smaller than the uncompressed version would be.

However, binary files are still common and there are many file formats that are binary. If a file format stores video, images or audio, it can't be properly represented by a text-based format. And when you need to save space, or need top performance, binary files win hands down. They're here to stay and whenever you need to come up with a file format it's up to you to decide whether you want better implementation (text) or size and performance (binary).

Next we'll look at how to work with these binary files.

How to Work with Binary Files

The first step to working with binary files is opening a file in binary mode:

ofstream a_file("test.bin", ios::binary);

When the file has been opened, the input and output functions that we saw and used earlier cannot be used. Instead, we need specific functions that can work with binary data. The bytes need to be written from a memory block straight into the file. We will use a method called write() and this will take one pointer to a memory block and the memory size to be written into the file. We use a char* as the pointer type, but the data does not necessarily have to be characters. So, if that's the case, why do we need to use a char? Because, with C++, working with individual bytes is best done using a single byte variable, which would be the char or a pointer, to a sequence of bytes which, in our case, is char*.

If you wanted a literal sequence of bytes written to a file, a char* would be needed so that the individual bytes could be written to the file. Writing an integer to file would require that it be treated as a char* and the pointer passed to a method used for writing the bytes to file from memory. In order for that to be done, the write() method is used to write out each of the characters and bytes individually and sequentially. Let's say, for example, that you have a number of 255. This would be represented in memory by the byte of 0xFF, which is 255 in hex. If an integer stored the 0xFF byte, in memory it would be like this:

0x000000FF

Or, in terms of byte for byte:

00 00 00 FF

For writing an integer to a file we need to be able to directly refer to this byte set. And that is why char* is used—not because it can represent ASCII characters but because it can work with bytes.

We also need to be able to let the compiler know that the data needs to be treated as if it were a character array.

Converting to Char*

So, how do we do tell the compiler that a variable should be treated as a pointer to a char and not as a pointer to the true type of the variable? This is a process known as typecasting. The typecast convinces the compiler that it really does know what it is doing and, yes, that variable really should be used in such a manner. We want the variable to be treated as a sequence of bytes, so a cast is needed to get the compiler to allow access to each of the bytes individually.

There are two basic typecasts that we use: static_cast and reinterpret_cast. The first, static_cast, is used when we have related types that we want to cast between. For example, we could tell the compiler that we want a double treated as an integer so it can be truncated, i.e., static_cast(3.4). We provide the type to cast to inside a set of brackets following the cast name.

However, in this case, the type system is to be ignored completely; we want the compiler to take a series of bytes and reinterpret it as being of a different type. For example, if we wanted an array of integers treated as an array of characters, we would write:

x[10];

reinterpret_cast(x);

As a note, when you work with binary data, it is one of the very few places where it is a good idea to use a reinterpret_cast. Whenever you see one, you should be just a little bit suspicious. It is one of the most powerful ways of forcing a compiler to do something it wouldn't do normally and a result of this is that the compiler doesn't run checks on the code that is using cast in the same careful way it would check the other code.

In our case, we want to get memory that is nothing more than a byte sequence so we really do need it. If, on the other hand, that is not what you intended, don't use reinterpret_cast.

At long last we can look at binary input and output. The code example below will fill an array and then get it written to a file. The write() method is used; it takes a char* as the source data and takes the data size to be written from the source. In this code, the source is the array and the array size is the array length in bytes:

int nums[10];

for (int i = 0; i < 10; i++)

{

        nums[i] = i;

}

a_file.write(reinterpret_cast(nums), sizeof(nums));

As a starting point, we have an array of integers; when it is cast to a char*, it will be treated as nothing more than a byte array written straight to disk. When those bytes are read in again later, it goes back to memory as the exact set of bytes and the memory can be cast back to an integer so we get the exact same value.

Note that we use the sizeof operator for providing the size to write. This command is one of the most useful for getting a given variable's size and, in our case, it will return the total byte number of the array nums.

However, you do need to be careful when you use the sizeof command on a pointer; the return will be the pointer size and not the memory the pointer points to. The code example above will work because we declared nums as an array and not a pointer and the sizeof command knows what size the array is. If you had a pointer variable of

*int *p_num*

the variable size would normally be four bytes because it only needs that to hold the variable address. If you wanted to get the size of whatever was being pointed to, you would write

*sizeof(*p_num)*

The result would be exactly the same as sizeof(int). If the pointer is pointing to an array, such as if you wrote:

*int *p_num = new int[length]*

You would get the total size like this:

*sizeof(* p_num) * length*

The write method can also be used for writing structures directly to file. As an example, let's assume that we have a structure of:

struct PlayerRecord

{

      int age;

      int score;

};

All you would need to do is create a PlayerRecord instance and write that to the file:

rec.age = 10;

rec.score = 890;

a_file.write(reinterpret_cast(& rec), sizeof(rec));

Note that the address of rec was taken so that a pointer to the structure could be passed in.

Storing Classes in Files

What happens if we want a non-basic type added to our structure? What if, for example, we add a string to the structure above?

struct PlayerRecord

{

      int age;

int score;

string name;

};

All we have done here is add the player name to the structure as a string, But now, if that has been written to the file, what's going to happen when we reach the string? What will happen is that the information stored in the string will be written, but not the string content itself.

We implement the string type as a pointer to a string and might even add in some other data, like the string length. When the struct is written out in binary data, it writes what the string stores. In our case, this is the pointer and the string length. But the problem is that this pointer will only be valid while the program runs. The actual value of the pointer, or the memory address, is no longer useful when the program has ended because there won't be anything stored at the address. The next time the structure is read in, a pointer will be used that points to memory that hasn't been allocated properly or it will point to data that has nothing at all to do with this string.

What we need is a fixed format that is well-defined for representing the binary data on disk and not just writing the structure out to disk. The format we will use is string characters written along with the string size. Very soon you will understand why we need the string size but, for now, examine what it looks like:

PlayerRecord rec;

rec.age = 11;

rec.score = 200;

rec.name = "James";

```
fstream a_file( "records.bin", ios::trunc | ios::binary | ios::in | ios::out
);
a_file.write( reinterpret_cast( & rec.age ), sizeof( rec.age ) );
a_file.write( reinterpret_cast( & rec.score ), sizeof( rec.score ) );
int len = rec.name.length();
a_file.write( reinterpret_cast( & len ), sizeof( len ) );
a_file.write( rec.name.c_str(), len + 1 ); // + 1 for the null terminator
```

First, it is worth pointing out that, to get a pointer to the string in memory, we used the c_str method and not the string object—that does not have a guaranteed layout in memory. If your string reads "abc," calling c_str will provide the address of a character sequence that contains the letters "abc." The string ends with a character that has a value of 0; this is known as the null terminator and is used to indicate that the string is at its end.

There is nothing wrong with the fact that we are writing character data to a binary file; it is still classed as binary data even though it is characters—it's just binary data in a format that humans can read.

It's also okay not to write the exact structure that we began with; the most important thing is that the format of the file on disk can be converted into an object in memory, not that the bytes from memory are directly written to the disk. Both file formats and structures store the exact same data, but the structure in memory doesn't have to have the same format as the data in the file.

Reading From a File

Reading back from a binary file requires the use of the read() method and its arguments are almost the same as the arguments for the write()

method: somewhere for the data to go and how much data is being read. For example, if we wanted an integer read back from a file, we could put

int x = 3;

a_file.read(reinterpret_cast(& x), sizeof(x));

When working with files, you always need to have ways of both reading and writing every data structure type that you want stored in the file. Using our PlayerRecord program, let's see how to read it back. We'll do the easy bit first. The file position is rest and then the fields of score and age, both written to disk with no change in format, are read back:

a_file.seekg(0, ios::beg);

PlayerRecord in_rec;

if (! a_file.read(reinterpret_cast(& in_rec.age), sizeof(

in_rec.age)))

{

    // handle error

}

if (! a_file.read(reinterpret_cast(& in_rec.score), sizeof(

in_rec.score)))

{

    // handle error

}

But what about the string? Can we read that in? We can't read the char* that is in the file at the top of the string because the format stored in memory isn't the same as the format on the disk. What we need to do instead is read the char* in and then a new string will need to be created.

Now it should be clear why the string length was needed—we need to know the space required to be allocated for holding that char*. The string length will be read in and the memory will be allocated before we read the string into memory:

```
int str_len;

if ( ! a_file.read( reinterpret_cast( & str_len ), sizeof( str_len ) )
)

{

        // handle error

}
// A sanity check is needed here to ensure that too much memory isn't
// allocated!
else if ( str_len > 0 && str_len < 10000 )
{

        char *p_str_buf = new char[ str_len ];
        if ( ! a_file.read( p_str_buf, str_len + 1 ) ) // + 1 for null
terminator
```

```
        {
                // handle error
        }
        // we need to validate the string to check it is null-terminated
        if ( p_str_buf[ str_len ] == 0 )
        {
                in_rec.name = string( p_str_buf );
        }
        delete p_str_buf;
}
cout << in_rec.age << " " <
```

Try it with this working program:

```
#include <fstream>
#include <string>
#include <iostream>
using namespace std;
struct PlayerRecord
{
        int age;
```

```cpp
        int score;

        string name;
};
int main ()
{
        PlayerRecord rec;

        rec.age = 11;

        rec.score = 200;

        rec.name = "James";

        fstream a_file( "records.bin", ios::trunc | ios::binary | ios::in |
ios::out );

a_file.write( reinterpret_cast<char*>( & rec.age ), sizeof( rec.age )
);

        a_file.write(reinterpret_cast<char*>( & rec.score ),
sizeof( rec.score
) );

        int len = rec.name.length();

        a_file.write(reinterpret_cast<char*>( & len ), sizeof( len ) );

        a_file.write( rec.name.c_str(), rec.name.length() + 1 );
```

```
PlayerRecord in_rec;

a_file.seekg( 0, ios::beg );

if ( ! a_file.read( reinterpret_cast<char*>( & in_rec.age ), sizeof(
in_rec.age ) ) )

    {

        cout << "Error reading from file" << endl;

        return 1;

    }

if ( ! a_file.read( reinterpret_cast<char*>(& in_rec.score ), sizeof(
in_rec.score ) ) )

    {

        cout << "Error reading from file" << endl;

        return 1;

    }

int str_len;

if ( ! a_file.read( reinterpret_cast<char*>( & str_len ), sizeof(
str_len ) ) )

    {

        cout << "Error reading from file" << endl;
```

```
                    return 1;

            }
// A sanity check is needed here to ensure that too much memory isn't
// allocated!
            if ( str_len > 0 && str_len < 10000 )

            {

                    char *p_str_buf = new char[ str_len ];
                    if ( ! a_file.read( p_str_buf, str_len + 1 ) ) // + 1 for null
terminator

                    {

                            delete p_str_buf;

                            cout << "Error reading from file" << endl;

                            return 1;

                    }
                    // we need to validate the string to check it is null-
            terminated
                    if ( p_str_buf[ str_len ] == 0 )

                    {

                            in_rec.name = string( p_str_buf );
```

```
        }

        delete p_str_buf;

    }

    cout << in_rec.age << " " <<in_rec.score << " " << in_rec.name
<< endl;

}
```

Run the program and then try opening it in a text editor such as Notepad. You should be able to read the name "James" because it has been stored as characters in a string. However, that is the only thing that will make any sense.

After the quiz, we will move on to our final C++ topic: Templates.

Quiz 25

Which of the following types may be used to read from a file?

A. ifstream

B. ofstream

C. fstream

D. A and C

Which of these is a true statement?

A. Text files don't take up as much space as binary files

B. It is easier to debug a binary file than a text file

C. Binary files use space more efficiently than text files

D. Text files are far too slow for use in real programs

When you write to a binary file, why can't a pointer be passed to a string object?

A. Because a char* always has to be passed into the write method

B. String objects cannot be held in memory

C. We don't know what the string object layout is; it could have pointers that would then be written to the file

D. Strings are far too big and need to be written bit by bit

Which of these statements about file format is correct?

A. You can change a file format as easily as you can any input

B. To change a file format requires some thought about what will happen if an older program version reads a file

C. To design a file format requires thought about what will happen if a new program version opens an old file version

D. B and C

Templates in C++

Well done! You have made it to the final chapter in this guide! I promise it won't be as long as the last one.

Up to now, everything you have done has required that you specify a type. If you wanted to declare a variable, it needed a type. And for a function, you needed the types from all the local variables, the return value and the parameters.

There will be times when all you want is a generic code. It won't matter what the type is because the logic will be identical for all types. We've seen examples of this—code that someone else writes—when we looked at the STL which, as you know, is a collection of algorithms and data structures. These work in a generic way, holding any type that a programmer asks for.

When an STL vector is used for storing items, you need to tell that vector what data type it's storing. You no longer have to work with only the possibilities that are predefined. By using a C++ feature known as "templates," the authors of the STL were able to write just one implementation of a vector that can store all data types.

These allow you to write templates of classes or functions without the need to write all the types in. Then, when you need support for a specific type, a version of the template can be created by the compiler and will have all the types filled in. When you write vector vec; that is exactly what is happening: the compiler fills the vector template in with the int type and provides you with a class you can use.

As you can see, templates are pretty straightforward to use and, in this last chapter, we will talk about how to create template classes and template functions of your own, starting with the template functions.

Template Functions

Templates are the answer to creating generic functions. Let's say that you want a helper function that will compute a triangle's area:

int triangleArea (int base, int height)

{

   *return base * height * .5;*

}

Now, what if we wanted the triangle's area with both a height and a base of .5? Well, both values get truncated to zero because both of the arguments are integers. That means the function is going to return 0 even though, clearly, it isn't.

You could write another method:

double triangleAreaDouble (double base, double height)

{

   *return base * height * .5;*

}

This looks identical to the first function, with one exception—the line where all the types were declared as doubles, rather than integers. If we wanted another type, such as a custom number class, we would need to write yet another implementation of that function.

This is just the kind of scenario that C++ templates are perfect for. Templates allow you to factor the types out. Rather than the function caller needing to list all the types to be used, instead a function is generated by the compiler for each type requested.

The syntax for declaring templates can look a little bit overwhelming so I'm going to break it all down for you so it makes more sense.

Here we have the function above written with the template syntax:

template <typename T>

T triangleArea (T base, T height)

{

      return base * height * .5;

}

First, we use the template keyword to declare the function as a template. After this, the parameters for the template are listed inside angled brackets. These are the values specified by the template user, such as the int that is in the expression vector. Template parameters are meant to be types, not values, so the typename keyword is used. Immediately after that is the parameter name of T. This all looks much like when an argument is declared to a function. When the function caller provides a parameter of the function type, any references to the T parameter will be treated as that type by the template. Again, it's much like when we use function arguments to pass a value into a function.

Let's say the function caller writes:

triangleArea<double>(.5, .5);

Everywhere that T is in the code is replaced with a double. It's as if the triangleAreaDouble function has been written. Quite literally, the code that we wrote is nothing more than a template used by the compiler to create the specialized and specific function for handling the double type.

To put it more in context, you could consider the entire line of

template <typename T>

as saying that that the class or the function ahead is a template and, in that template, the letter T is used as a type—maybe a char, a double, an int—or a specific class' name. When someone requires the template, T must be provided with a specific type. We do this by placing the type in the angled brackets before the function or class name.

Type Inference

Sometimes a template function caller won't need to explicitly provide the parameter for the template because the compiler may be able to infer the parameter values based on the function arguments. Let's say that you write:

triangleArea(.5, .5);

The compiler would work out that T is meant to be a double because the T parameter has been used for declaring the function arguments. Because the compiler knows what type the arguments are, it infers the type of T.

Type inference will work whenever a template parameter is used as a function argument type.

Duck Typing

Have you heard the saying, "If it looks like a duck, walks like a duck and quacks like a duck, it's probably a duck"? Well, this is used quite often when it comes to templates. When a template parameter is passed in, the compiler will need to make a decision on whether the parameter is valid for that template.

In our compute_equation template, for example, the types of values that get passed to the function have to support the addition and multiplication arithmetic operators:

*return x * y * 4 * z + y * z + x;*

However, there are types that can't be multiplied. An integer and a double can be, but a vector can't. The mere thought of trying to multiply a vector is nothing short of absurd, and there is no support for it in the vector class.

If you attempted to pass three vectors into compute_equation, the function call just wouldn't compile:

int main ()

{

    vector<int> a, b, c;

    compute_equation(a, b, c);

}

The compiler is incredibly precise and will tell you exactly which operations have no support from vector<int>:

template_compile.cc: In function 'T compute_equation(T, T, T) [with T =

std::vector<int, std::allocator<int> >]':

template_compile.cc:13: instantiated from here

template_compile.cc:5: error: no match for 'operator*' in 'y * z'

template_compile.cc:5: error: no match for 'operator*' in 'x * y'

This is a long error message but it can be broken down. Line one is telling you that compute_equation is the function with the problem. Line two is indicating the line number on which you attempted to use it and that's normally the line that you will need to look at. The third and fourth lines are telling you the reason for the compile failure. In our case, it's telling you that isn't a match for "operator*" in "x*y." All this means is that it couldn't work out how x and y should be multiplied because vectors don't have a * operator. Both of the variables are vectors, so you should be able to work out that vectors simply don't have support for multiplication.

In other words, the vector doesn't act like a number, doesn't look like one and certainly doesn't talk like one. When you use a template function, the compiler will work out if the provided type will work in the template. It isn't concerned about anything other than whether the type has support for the operations and methods called on it. It only needs to look like a type that will work.

Duck typing is nothing like polymorphic functions. The latter will take a pointer to an interface class and will only call methods that have been defined on the specified interface class. With the template, the parameters do not have to conform to any specific or predefined interface. So long as the template type and any variables of the same type may be used the way the function specifies, it will compile.

Template Classes

While template classes tend to be limited to library writers who want classes such as map and vector, everyday programmers can also benefit from being able to make their code more generic. You shouldn't use a template just because you can; instead, you should be looking for opportunities to get rid of classes that only differ by the type.

Yes, you are likely to find yourself writing more template methods than classes, but you still need to have some idea of how to use them, especially if you have a data structure of your own that you want to implement.

Declaring a template class isn't very different to a template function. Let's say that we want to build a small class that will wrap an array:

template <typename T> class ArrayWrapper

{

private:

   *T * _p_mem;*

};

As with the template function, we begin with the declaration that a template is being introduced. We use the template keyword, and then the template parameters are added. We only have one parameter here, T.

Type T can be used whenever we want the type that would be specified by a user, just like with the template functions. When a function is defined for a template class, the template syntax also has to be used. So let's add a constructor called ArrayWrapper to our class:

template <typename T> class ArrayWrapper

{

public:

   ArrayWrapper (int size);

private:

```
        T *_p_mem;

};

// so that the constructor can be defined outside the class, we start by

// indicating that the function is a template

template <typename T>

ArrayWrapper<T>::ArrayWrapper (int size)

        : _p_mem( new T[ size ] )

{ }
```

We start with the basic template introduction and redeclare the parameter for the template. The difference is, the class name now has the ArrayWrapper template in it, which tells everyone that this belongs to a template class and isn't a template function on a standard class called ArrayWrapper.

In this implementation, the template parameter can be used to stand in for the provided type, just as with the template functions. However, the function caller will never need to provide the parameter—it gets taken from the first template type declaration. For example, instead of writing

```
vec.size<int>()
```

or

```
vec<int>.size();
```

to get the size of a vector of integers, all you need to write is

```
vec.size().
```

Template Tips

Very often, you will find that it's much easier to write classes for types first and then use templates to rewrite them. For example, let's say that you declare a class of integers; from that class declaration you then design a generic template. You don't have to do this, especially if you're comfortable writing templates, but when you first start, it can be helpful to sort out problems between template syntax issues and the algorithm.

Let's see a simple example of a calculator class that will work only on integers. To start with:

class Calc

{

public:

      Calc ();

      int multiply (int x, int y);

      int add (int x, int y);

};

Calc::Calc ()

```
{}
```

```
int Calc::multiply (int x, int y)

{


        return x * y;

}
```

```
int Calc::add (int x, int y)

{


        return x + y;

}
```

This works incredibly well for the integer, so now we can turn the class into a template; this will let us build calculators that work with non-integer types:

```
template <typename Type>

class Calc

{

public:
```

```
        Calc ();

        Type multiply (Type x, Type y);

        Type add (Type x, Type y);

};

template <typename Type> Calc<Type>::Calc ()

{}

template <typename Type> Type Calc<Type>::multiply (Type x, Type y)

{

        return x * y;

}

template <typename Type> Type Calc<Type>::add (Type x, Type y)

{

        return x + y;

}

int main ()

{

        // demonstrate a declaration

        Calc<int> c;

}
```

We need a few modifications here:

First, we needed to declare a template type named Type:

template <typename Type>

Next, the template declaration had to be added before the class and before every function definition:

template <typename Type> class Calc

template <typename Type> int Calc::multiply (int x, int y)

Then, each function definition had to be modified to indicate that it belongs to a template class:

template <typename Type> int Calc<Type>::multiply (int x, int y)

Lastly, wherever int appeared in the code, it had to be replaced with Type:

template <typename Type> Type Calc<Type>::multiply (Type x, Type y)

When you get used to working with templates, you will find it easy to turn a class that has been defined for one type into a template class that can work for multiple types. Over the course of time, you will find that you are getting more comfortable with using the template syntax and will start writing your own template classes without needing to write any other code first.

Templates and Header Files

Up to now, the templates we have looked at have been directly written into .cpp files. What if we wanted to place our template declaration into the header file? Could we? The problem here is that code that makes use of template classes or template functions needs to be able to access the whole template definition for every single function call to the template as well as to every member function that is called on template classes.

This is not the same way that a standard function works; these only require the caller to know about the declaration. If, for example, you placed the Calc class inside its header file, you would also need to add the full constructor definition along with the add() method instead of putting them all into one .cpp file as you would normally. If you didn't do this, you would not be able to use Calc.

This is a rather unfortunate thing about templates and it's all about how templates have been compiled. Most of the time, when the compiler parses them the first time, it pretty much ignores templates. It's only when a template is used that has a concrete type attached that the code is generated by the compiler for that type. To do that, the template has to be available to the compiler so the code can be generated. A result of this is that all template code has to be included in all of the files that will use that template. And, when a file that has a template is compiled, you may not learn of any syntax errors in that template until the template is used for the first time.

The easiest thing to do, when creating template classes, is to place all template definitions into the header file. It's also helpful if you use an extension other than .h, just to clearly indicate that the file is a template—.hxx for example.

Analyzing Template Error Messages

If there is one major downside to using templates, it's that many compilers will throw out error messages that are not easy to understand when a template is misused, whether you write it or not. You could end up with pages of error messages just for one mistake.

Template error messages are not easy to read simply because the template parameters are expanded to their fullest, even those that you don't normally use, such as the default parameters.

Look at the vector declaration below:

vector<int, int> vec;

Looks okay, yes? No, look more carefully. There's a small problem: there should be only one parameter. Simple enough mistake, but compiling will throw up what looks like an Armageddon of error messages:

/usr/lib/gcc/x86_64-redhatlinux/

4.1.2/../../../../include/c++/4.1.2/bits/stl_vector.h: In instantiation

of 'std::_Vector_base<int, int>':

/usr/lib/gcc/x86_64-redhatlinux/

4.1.2/../../../../include/c++/4.1.2/bits/stl_vector.h:159:

instantiated from 'std::vector<int, int>'

template_err.cc:6: instantiated from here

/usr/lib/gcc/x86_64-redhatlinux/

4.1.2/../../../../include/c++/4.1.2/bits/stl_vector.h:78: error: 'int'

is not a class, struct, or union type

/usr/lib/gcc/x86_64-redhatlinux/

4.1.2/../../../../include/c++/4.1.2/bits/stl_vector.h:95: error: 'int'

is not a class, struct, or union type

/usr/lib/gcc/x86_64-redhatlinux/

4.1.2/../../../../include/c++/4.1.2/bits/stl_vector.h:99: error: 'int'

is not a class, struct, or union type

/usr/lib/gcc/x86_64-redhatlinux/

4.1.2/../../../../include/c++/4.1.2/bits/stl_vector.h: In instantiation

of 'std::_Vector_base<int, int>::_Vector_impl':

/usr/lib/gcc/x86_64-redhatlinux/

4.1.2/../../../../include/c++/4.1.2/bits/stl_vector.h:123:

instantiated from 'std::_Vector_base<int, int>'

/usr/lib/gcc/x86_64-redhatlinux/

4.1.2/../../../../include/c++/4.1.2/bits/stl_vector.h:159:

instantiated from 'std::vector<int, int>'

template_err.cc:6: instantiated from here

/usr/lib/gcc/x86_64-redhatlinux/

4.1.2/../../../../include/c++/4.1.2/bits/stl_vector.h:82: error: 'int'

is not a class, struct, or union type

/usr/lib/gcc/x86_64-redhatlinux/

4.1.2/../../../../include/c++/4.1.2/bits/stl_vector.h:86: error: 'int'

is not a class, struct, or union type

/usr/lib/gcc/x86_64-redhatlinux/

4.1.2/../../../../include/c++/4.1.2/bits/stl_vector.h: In instantiation

of 'std::vector<int, int>':

template_err.cc:6: instantiated from here

/usr/lib/gcc/x86_64-redhatlinux/

4.1.2/../../../../include/c++/4.1.2/bits/stl_vector.h:161: error: 'int'

is not a class, struct, or union type

/usr/lib/gcc/x86_64-redhatlinux/

4.1.2/../../../../include/c++/4.1.2/bits/stl_vector.h:193: error: no

members matching 'std::_Vector_base<int, int>::_M_get_Tp_allocator' in

'struct std::_Vector_base<int, int>'

/usr/lib/gcc/x86_64-redhatlinux/

4.1.2/../../../../include/c++/4.1.2/bits/stl_vector.h: In destructor

And, trust me, way more than that!

What's going on? Who is responsible for designing an error message like this? Here's the problem: vector has a second, default template parameter which the compiler would normally auto-supply. However, when the second int is filled in, the compiler will try to use it as the second default parameter, but that default can't be an int. You will find that the error message tells you this quite early on:

error: 'int' is not a class, struct, or union type

The template is attempting to use the parameter in ways that integers cannot be used. Let's say that you have a piece of code like this:

template <typename T>

class Foo

{

    Foo ()

      {

          T x;

          x.val = 1;

      }

};

T can't be an integer. That's because x, which is a T type, has to have a filed named val, and integers don't have fields, do they! They certainly don't have fields named val.

If we were to write

Foo<int> a;

the code simply wouldn't compile.

This is duck typing again. The template really isn't concerned about what type is provided so long as that type fits the code. In the above case, the x.val syntax isn't supported by the integer so it's rejected by the compiler.

There is a similar constraint on the second parameter for the vector template— this one requires a type that has support for more functionality than the humble basic integer gives us. The errors are all complaining about the multitude of ways that int just isn't a valid type for the parameter.

When you see a huge error message like this, try not to be too daunted by it. Start at the top and work through the errors one at a time. Below, I have pulled out the text only up to the point where the word "error" appears:

/usr/lib/gcc/x86_64-redhat-

linux/4.1.2/../../../../include/c++/4.1.2/bits/stl_vector.h: In instantiation of 'std::_Vector_base':

/usr/lib/gcc/x86_64-redhat-

linux/4.1.2/../../../../include/c++/4.1.2/bits/stl_vector.h:159:

instantiated from 'std::vector'

template_err.cc:6: instantiated from here

/usr/lib/gcc/x86_64-redhat-

linux/4.1.2/../../../../include/c++/4.1.2/bits/stl_vector.h:78: *error: 'int'*

is not a class, struct, or union type

That's a bit better isn't it? Not so many lines, much like what we saw in the section on duck typing—much easier to handle. Going through this error message, on the first line, where it says "In instantiation of std::_Vector_base," you'll see the error is telling you that the template can't be created with the provided parameters.

On the next line, it tells you that Vector_base template (a helper class for implementing vector) has not compiled because of the attempt at creating the template vector. The message tells you where it came from too: file template_err.cc, line 6. That is our code, so we now know where to go to fix the error.

Finding the code line where the error is will always be the first step to working out where it all went wrong. More often than not, and even more so as you gain experience and confidence, a simple look at your code will tell you what the error is. If it isn't that obvious, you just keep going through the instantiation list until the proper error message appears: "error: int is not a class, struct or union type." The compiler expected a structure or a class, not any of the built-in types such as int. A vector should hold any type, so the error lies in the parameter given to the vector.

You should make sure you know how a vector is declared and that it only needs one template parameter.

Now that the problem has been found, we can fix it and then compile the code again. Sometimes you will be able to work out and fix a few errors at the same time, but where templates are concerned, the first error is normally the root of the problem for all others. Fix things one at a time and you will find that any other errors fix themselves.

In our final example above, all those error messages resulted from one simple mistake: giving a second template parameter of an int.

That brings us to the end of this guide. I hope you enjoyed it as much as I enjoyed writing it. Take your final quiz and give yourself a big pat on the back.

Quiz 26

When should templates be used?

A. When you want to save a bit of time

B. When you want your code to run a bit faster

C. When you need to write the same code several times but with different types

D. When you need to be able to reuse your code later

When would you need to provide the type for a template parameter?

A. Always

B. Only when you declare a template class instance

C. Only if there is no way to infer the type

D. For template functions, only if there is no way to infer that type, and for template classes, always

How will the compiler know if a template parameter can be used with a specified template?

A. It will implement a specific interface

B. When you declare the template, you need to specify the constraints

C. It will try to use the parameter and, if the type will support all the required operations, it will accept it

D. Every valid template type must be listed when you declare the template

What is the difference between placing a template class and a regular class in a header?

A. There's no difference at all

B. You can't define any methods for the regular class in the header file

C. You must define all the methods for the template class in the header file

D. There is no need for a corresponding .cpp file for the template class, whereas there is a need for the regular class

When should a function become a template function?

A. Right from the start. You don't know when you might need the same logic for another type, so template methods should always be made

B. Only if there is no way of casting to the type required by the function

C. Whenever you write almost the same logic for a different type but with properties similar to those for the type used by the first function

D. Whenever you have two functions that do pretty much the same thing and a couple of Boolean parameters can help with tweaking the logic

At what point will you see most of the errors in your code?

A. At the time the template is compiled

B. At the time of linking

C. When the program is run

D. When the code that instantiates the template is first compiled

Conclusion

We've come to the end of this book but this is just the start of a long and fruitful journey for you, a life of programming. With the basics of C++ under your belt, it's time to start your real learning. Start writing those programs! Start implementing data structures and algorithms.

You can think of learning a programming language as being akin to learning a human language. Basic grammar is just the start. In the same way that you won't go from learning a language like English to being a best-selling novelist immediately, you won't go from this guide straight into building operating systems.

The most important thing now is that you have a foundation from which to work. So, where do you go next?

Read books about algorithm design and software engineering.

Start writing programs. If necessary, clone existing tools and learn what you need to do with them. At the end of the day, the more you write, the better you will be.

Look for online courses or college courses that can take you further.

Find other C++ programmers and work with them.

Enjoy your journey. If you don't have fun while you program, it isn't for you. Make it fun, make it exciting and make it the reason you want to get up in the mornings.

Good luck with your journey.

Quiz Answers

Quiz 1

Think about a program completing successfully. What would be the right value returned to the operating system?

Answer – C. 0

Name the single function that must be included in every C++ program:

Answer – C. main()

What type of punctuation is used for starting and ending a code block?

Answer – A. {}

What punctuation mark is used for ending most C++ code lines?

Answer – B. ;

Which of these is written correctly as a comment?

Answer – C. /* Comment */

Which of these is written correctly as a comment?

Answer – C. iostream

Quiz 2

To store a number like 3.1415, what variable type do you use?

Answer – C. double

To compare two variables, which of these is the right operator?

Answer – D. ==

How do you access the string data type?

Answer – C. include the string header file

Which of these isn't a variable type?

Answer – B. real

How do you read in a whole line from a user?

Answer – C. use getline

Take this expression: cout<<1234/2000. What would you expect to see as the output?

Answer – A. 0

If we already have integers, why is there a need for a char type in C++?

Answer – Because it is far easier to read in and print out characters than it is numbers, even though the char gets stored as a number.

Quiz 3

Which of these is true?

Answer – E. all of the above

Which of these is the Boolean 'and' operator?

Answer – B. &&

Take the expression !(true && ! (false || true)). What does it evaluate to?

Answer – A. True

Which of these is the right syntax for an if statement?

Answer – C. if (expression)

Quiz 4

If the code int x; for(x=0; x<10; x++){} was run, what would the value of x be?

Answer – A. 10 If you are confused by this, think about what would happen if you added a cout statement to the end of a for loop.

Take an expression of while(x<100); when would the code block after this execute?

Answer – A. When x is less than 100

Which of these isn't a loop structure?

Answer – D. repeat until

What is the guaranteed number of times a do-while loop will loop?

Answer – C. 1

Quiz 5

Which of these is not a proper prototype?

Answer – B. double funct(char x) Note that there is no semicolon.

Take the function with the prototype of int func(char x, double v, float t); what is the return type?

Answer – B.int

Assuming that the function exists, which of these would be a valid function call?

Answer – C. funct();

Which of these is a complete function?

Answer – B. int funct(int x) {return x=x+1;}

Quiz 6

Which of these should follow a case statement?

Answer – A. :

To avoid falling through from one case to another, what should be used?

Answer – B. break

What keyword is used for unhandled possibilities?

Answer – C. default

The output from the code snippet

Answer: D. ZeroHelloWorld

Quiz 7

If you did not call srand before you called rand, what would happen?

Answer – C. Whenever the program runs, rand returns the same number sequence

What would be the purpose of seeding srand with the current time?

Answer - A. To make sure that your program always runs the same way

What range of values does rand return?

Answer - C. 0 to RAND_MAX

What does the expression 11 % 3 return?

Answer - D. 2

When should srand be used?

Answer - C. Just once, at the beginning of your program

Quiz 8

Which of these is the correct way of declaring an array?

Answer - A. int anarray[10];

In an array of 29 elements, what is the index number of the last element?

Answer - B. 28

Which of the following is a two-dimensional array?

Answer - B. int anarray[20][20];

Which of these is the correct way to access the seventh element of an array called foo with 100 elements?

Answer - A. foo[6];

Which of these is the correct way of declaring a function that will take a two-dimensional array?

Answer - B. int func (int x[10][]);

Quiz 9

Which of these is used to access a variable in structure b?

Answer - A. b->var;

Which of these is a properly defined structure?

Answer - D. struct a_struct {int a;};

Which is the correct way of declaring a structure variable, type foo, called my_foo?

Answer - B. foo my_foo;

Final value from code:

Answer - A. 5

Quiz 10

Which of these isn't a good reason to use a pointer?

Answer - D. You want quicker access to variables

What is a pointer used for storing?

Answer – A memory address, but it may not be another variable

When your program is executing, where would you get more memory from?

Answer – C. The free store

What could go wrong when you are using pointers?

Answer - D. All of the above

When you declare a normal variable in a function, where does the memory come from?

Answer – B. The stack

Once memory has been allocated, what do you do with it?

Answer – B. When you've finished with it, you return it to the OS

Quiz 11

Which of these is the correct declaration of a pointer?

Answer - D. int *x;

Which of these will give the memory address of integer variable a?

Answer - C. &a;

Which of these will give the memory address of a variable pointed to by pointer p_a?

Answer - B. *p_a;

Which of these will give the value stored at the address pointed to by the pointer p_a?

Answer - C. *p_a;

Which of these is the correct way of declaring a reference?

Answer - D. int &my_ref = my_orig_val;

Which of these is not a great time for using a reference?

Answer - A. For storing addresses that have been allocated dynamically from the free store

Quiz 12

Which of these is the right keyword to use for allocating memory in C++?

Answer - A. new

Which of these is the right keyword to use for deallocating memory in C++?

Answer - B. delete

Which of these is a true statement?

Answer - C. You can treat a pointer like an array but they are not arrays

Final values in code:

Answer - C. x = 25, p_p_int = 27, p_int = 3

How can you indicate that a pointer has no valid value that it points to?

Answer - B. Set it as NULL

Quiz 13

What is the advantage of using a linked list over an array?

Answer - B. Linked lists can grow dynamically so they can hold individual new elements without needing to copy the existing elements

Which of these statements is true?

Answer – D. You can add an element to the middle of a linked list much faster than you can an array

When would a linked list normally be used?

Answer – C. When you need to dynamically add elements and remove them

Why is it okay to declare a linked list that has a reference to the list item type?

(struct Node {

Node* p_next; };)

Answer – C. Because the type is a pointer and you only need the space to add a single pointer. The memory for the next real node will be allocated at a later time

Why should you have a NULL at the end of the linked list?

Answer - A. Because it's the only way of indicating that the list has ended

In what ways are arrays and linked lists similar?

Answer - B. Both let you store and access data sequentially.

Quiz 14

What is tail recursion?

Answer – C. When a recursive function calls itself and it's the last thing it does before it returns

When would recursion be used?

Answer – B. When an algorithm is more naturally expressed in terms of a subproblem than a loop

What elements are required for a recursive algorithm?

Answer - D. All of the above

What might happen if you don't have a complete base case?

Answer - D. You could have a stack overflow

Quiz 15

Name the binary tree's primary virtue

Answer - C. It lets you do fast data lookups

When would a linked list be better than a binary tree?

Answer - C. When you need to have the ability to add to the front or end quickly without ever accessing the middle items.

Which of these is true?

Answer - A. You can change the structure of a tree by changing the order you add items

Which of the following is the right way of describing why a binary tree can find nodes so fast?

Answer - B. Each node has a pair of subtrees whose creation is based on whether the items in them are of lesser or greater value than the current node's value

Quiz 16

When is it appropriate to use a vector?

Answer - C. When you don't want to have to worry about the details involved in updating the data structure

How do you remove all the items from a map at once?

Answer - D. Call clear

When should you implement a data structure of your own?

Answer - C. When you have a need to take advantage of the data's raw structure, like when you build an expression tree

Which of these is the correct way of declaring an iterator that can be used with a vector?

Answer - C. vector<int>::iterator itr;

Which of these will access the element key that an iterator over a map is currently on?

Answer - B. itr->first

How can you tell if an iterator can be used?

Answer - B. You compare it to the result of calling end() on the container that is being iterated over

Quiz 17

Which of these is valid code?

Answer - C. const int x = 12; const int *p_int = & x;

Which of the function signatures will allow the code snippet to compile:

Answer - D. A and C

Which of these is the best way of telling if a string search failed?

Answer - C. Compare the result position to string::npos

How is an iterator for a const STL container created?

Answer - C. By using a const_iterator

Quiz 18

Which of these is not a part of the build process in C++?

Answer - D. Postprocessing

When would an error that is related to an undefined function happen?

Answer - A. The link phase

What might happen if you include a header file more than once?

Answer - A. Errors relating to multiple declarations

Is there any advantage to having separate steps for compiling and linking?

Answer - C. Yes; it means that you can recompile just the file that was changed, saving time in both linking and compilation

Quiz 19

Is there an advantage to using functions rather than accessing the data directly?

Answer - B. Yes, the function implementation can be hidden by the function from all callers, ensuring that the function caller can be changed

When should code be put into a common function?

Answer - B. Whenever the same code is called from more than one or two places

What reason would you have for hiding the representation of a data structure?

Answer - D. All of the above

Quiz 20

Why would a method be better than directly using the field of structure?

Answer - D. So that the data representation can be changed

Which of these is used to define the method that is associated with the structure struct MyStruct { int func(); };

Answer - C. int MyStruct::func() { return 1; }

What reason would there be for including a method definition in line with the class?

Answer - C. There is no reason. Doing this would result in implementation details being leaked

Quiz 21

What reason is there for using private data?

Answer - C. To clearly show what data is only to be used for the class implementation

Explain the difference between a class and a structure

Answer - C. Classes default to everything being private

What should you do with your class data fields?

Answer - C. They should never be made public

Why would you make a method public?

Answer - C. They should only be made public if they are required for using the class's main features; otherwise, make them private

Quiz 22

At what point do you need to write a constructor for a class?

Answer - B. When the class needs to be initialized with non-default values

Explain the relationship between the assignment operator and destructor

Answer - D. The assignment operator has to ensure that it's safe to run the destructors of both the new class and the copied class

When would you need to use an initialization list?

Answer - D. All of the above

What is the function being run on line 2 of the code?

Answer - C. The copy constructor for str2. str2 has not yet been initialized so the copy constructor runs, rather than the assignment operator

Name the functions being called in the code and what order they are called in

Answer - D. The constructor for str1, the constructor for str2, the destructor for str2, the destructor for str1

Assume that your class has a non-default copy constructor; which of the following statements about the assignment operator is true?

Answer - D. B or C are valid

Quiz 23

When is the destructor for a superclass run?

Answer - C. After the subclass destructor has been called

Look at the class hierarchy below; what is required in the constructor for Dog?

Answer - B. The initializer should be used to call the constructor for Mammal with an argument of "dog"

What is wrong with this class definition?

Answer - D. All of the above

When a virtual method is declared in the interface class, what must the function have the ability to do in order to use that method to call a subclass method?

Answer - A. Take the interface as a pointer or a reference

How does reuse improve by using inheritance?

Answer - C. Because it lets us write code that expects an interface and not concrete classes; this allows new classes to implement that interface and reuse the code

Which of these statements about class access levels is correct?

Answer - D. Subclasses can have access to both the public and protected methods and their data from the parent class

Quiz 24

When should a using namespace directive be used?

Answer - C. At the beginning of any cpp file where there is no conflict with namespaces

What is the purpose of namespaces?

Answer - C. On a large code base they prevent name conflicts

When should code be put in a namespace?

Answer - D. B and C

Why shouldn't a using namespace declaration go in a header file?

Answer - C. Because it will force the using declaration onto whoever uses the header file, regardless of whether it causes conflict or not

Quiz 25

Which of the following types may be used to read from a file?

Answer - D. A and C

Which of these is a true statement?

Answer - C. Binary files use space more efficiently than text files

When you write to a binary file, why can't a pointer be passed to a string object?

Answer - C. We don't know what the string object layout is; it could have pointers that would then be written to the file

Which of these statements about file format is correct?

Answer - D. B and C

Quiz 26

When should templates be used?

Answer - C. When you need to write the same code several times but with different types

When would you need to provide the type for a template parameter?

Answer - D. For template functions, only if there is no way to infer that type, and for template classes, always

How will the compiler know if a template parameter can be used with a specified template?

Answer - C. It will try to use the parameter and, if the type will support all the required operations, it will accept it

What is the difference between placing a template class and a regular class in a header?

Answer - C. You must define all the methods for the template class in the header file

When should a function become a template function?

Answer - C. Whenever you write almost the same logic for a different type but with properties similar to those for the type used by the first function

At what point will you see most of the errors in your code?

Answer - D. When the code that instantiates the template is first compiled

References

https://www.geeksforgeeks.org

https://beginnersbook.com

https://www.programiz.com

www.cplusplus.com

https://www.tutorialspoint.com

https://www.tutorialcup.com

https://en.cppreference.com

https://www.w3schools.in

https://www.learncpp.com

https://www.guru99.com

https://www.javatpoint.com

https://www.studytonight.com

www.infocodify.com

https://codescracker.com/

Made in the USA
San Bernardino, CA
14 September 2019